Judaism's Challenge
Election, Divine Love, and Human Enmity

Jewish Thought, Jewish History: New Studies

Series Editor: Gregg Stern

Judaism's Challenge
Election, Divine Love, and Human Enmity

•

Edited by
Alon Goshen-Gottstein

BOSTON
2020

Library of Congress Cataloging-in-Publication Data

Names: Goshen-Gottstein, Alon, editor.
Title: Judaism's challenge : election, divine love, and human enmity / Alon Goshen-Gottstein.
Description: Boston : Academic Studies Press, 2020. | Series: Jewish thought, Jewish history: new studies
Identifiers: LCCN 2019030426 (print) | LCCN 2019030427 (ebook) | ISBN 9781644691489 (hardback) | ISBN 9781644691496 (paperback) | ISBN 9781644691502 (adobe pdf)
Subjects: LCSH: Jews--Election, Doctrine of.
Classification: LCC BM613 .J83 2020 (print) | LCC BM613 (ebook) | DDC 296.3/1172--dc23
LC record available at https://lccn.loc.gov/2019030426
LC ebook record available at https://lccn.loc.gov/2019030427

Copyright © 2020 Academic Studies Press. All rights reserved.

ISBN 9781644691489 hardback
ISBN 9781644691496 paperback
ISBN 9781644691502 ebook PDF
ISBN 9781644693735 ePub

Book design Lapiz Digital Services.
Cover design by Ivan Grave.

Published by Academic Studies Press
1577 Beacon Street
Brookline, MA 02446, USA
press@academicstudiespress.com
www.academicstdiespress.com

For YOSSI and YOEL
Passionate partners in addressing Judaism's challenge
Who together with
SARAH and NOMI
Provide the foundations of friendship and community
For this common exploration

Contents

Preface

Israel and the Call of Love to Humanity   xi
Alon Goshen-Gottstein

The Election and Sanctity of Israel in the Hebrew Bible   1
Israel Knohl

A Kingdom of Priests and a Holy Nation   13
Alon Goshen-Gottstein

Israel as Blessing: Theological Horizons   50
Eugene Korn

Jewish Chosenness—A Contemporary Approach   71
Jerome Gellman

Aleinu—a Prayer Common to Jews and Gentile God-Fearers   83
Menachem Katz

Two Dimensions of Jewish Identity   98
Stanislaw Krajewski

Images of the Non-Jew in the *Kedushat Levi*:
A Textual and Theological Exploration   112
Or Rose

Israel's Election and the Suffering of the Holocaust   129
Gershon Greenberg

Israel's Election and the Moral Dilemma
of Amalek and the Seven Nations of Canaan   143
Reuven Kimelman

From Enmity to Unity—Recovering
the Ba'al Shem Tov's Teachings on Non-Jews   174
Menachem Kallus

Conclusion: Judaism's Challenge—Being Israel in
    Changing Circumstances   189
Alon Goshen-Gottstein

Notes on Contributors   201

Index   204

Preface

The present book is a chapter in a larger project of convening conversations among Jewish scholars and thinkers on concerns in the domain of Jewish theology of religions. The first book that set the stage for later projects was the 2012 *Jewish Theology and World Religions*, co-edited with Eugene Korn and published by the Littman Library. My introductory essay in that publication identified several key issues that a Jewish theology of religions must tackle. Subsequent volumes are each focused on one of those issues. Jewish scholars of different theological and philosophical orientations explore diverse aspects of the particular issue. Election (or more broadly stated: Jewish particularity) has been identified as an issue that is foundational to a Jewish view of other religions. Election and an understanding of Jewish particularity would seem to inform Jewish views of other religions, either invalidating them or somehow subordinating to the superior religious form that is Judaism. To the extent that a Jewish theology of religion seeks to do more than to simply affirm such a perspective, it must tackle the implications of claims of election for Jewish approaches to other religions. This is the goal of the present volume. The more specific focus this receives in the present volume will be presented in the introductory chapter.

Two more volumes are set to appear, complementing the present focus on election. Roughly at the same time as this publication will appear, Littman Library will publish *Religious Truth: Towards a Jewish Theology of Religions*. The relevance of truth to the concerns of theology of religions require no further elaboration. A final book in the series will appear with Academic Studies Press. This volume will be devoted to understanding idolatry, or in its native Jewish expression—Avodah Zarah. This is probably the most fundamental category that defines Jewish views of other religions and working out what a contemporary understanding of idolatry or Avodah Zarah might consist of is an urgent theological task.

I am grateful to Academic Studies Press for grasping the urgency of these conversations and facilitating publication of two volumes in this series. The initial impetus came from Gregg Stern, who attended a session I had organized around some of these theological concerns as part of the World Congress of Jewish Studies. Gregg recognized the potential for developing conversations further and I am grateful to him for suggesting Academic Studies Press as a home for these conversations. Alessandra Anzani, my editor at Academic Studies Press, was key in cementing the relationship in the friendliest way possible, especially as far as the formal parameters of the relationship were concerned. Kira Nemirovsky ably shepherded the project through its production and I am grateful to her for bringing it to its successful completion.

The present volume evolves from a project that the Elijah Interfaith Institute ran together with Yeshivat Chovevei Torah Rabbinical Seminary. The project, supported by a grant from the Henry Luce Foundation, sought to advance theological thinking and more particularly the concerns of theology of religions as part of the formation of rabbinical seminarians. Rabbi Dov Linzer, then dean and Rosh Yeshiva and now president of the school, was an invaluable partner in conceiving and implementing the project. The theme of election was developed through a series of textually oriented study units, that sought to present different aspects of the question, as these found expression in key texts. The materials were used in programs developed for YCT students as well as for other seminarians, Jewish and non-Jewish. We had envisioned an interactive website that would serve as a resource for Jewish theology of religions, and facilitate further conversations between theologians and educators on this subject. The technical side of the project met with difficulties and it was eventually realized that the idea of a Jewish theology of religions website, along the such lines, would be too complicated to maintain both technologically and financially. The commitment to share these materials more broadly remained and it eventually found expression in the present book.

I am grateful to the authors of the essays in this volume. They have shared the belief in the importance of the conversation and this faith has carried them patiently through the process of first developing the study units and then adapting them to the more classical format of essays. They are all part of a scholarly-intellectual community that cares deeply about the issues explored in this book. Their existence and dedication give me the encouragement and hope that through conversations such as these the field of Jewish theology of religions can grow and become a vital component of a contemporary Jewish theological and educational program.

Alon Goshen-Gottstein
Jerusalem, Erev Rosh Hashana 5781
A time of new reckoning for Israel's universal calling

Alon Goshen-Gottstein

Israel and the Call of Love to Humanity

The Particularity of the Present Project

The theme of the election of the Jewish people—"Israel," as it is classically known, is one that engages Jewish thought throughout the ages. Its foundations are biblical, its expansion is rabbinic, its elaboration is medieval and its further development and problematizing are modern and contemporary. One cannot think of Judaism without taking some stance relating to Israel's special status.

Not all periods witness the same intense interest in the subject. In a recent essay, Eliezer Schweid notes that the question of the election of the People of Israel lost its place in public Israeli discourse following the Yom Kippur war and only gained prominence as it served contemporary political needs.[1] Complementing ongoing reflection on Israel, its status and vocation, occasioned by the study of biblical and later materials, carried out as part of philosophical and theological teaching and reflection, engagement with the theme of Israel's election also serves contemporary needs and therefore takes different forms in different periods. In a just-published monograph on the idea of Israel's election in Jewish philosophy, Hanna Kasher proposes that particular stances taken on the subject reflect

---

1 Eliezer Schweid, *Raayon Ha'am Hanivchar Vehaliberaliyut Hahadasha* (Tel Aviv: Kibbutz Hemeuhad, 2017), 15–31.

a polemical reality, primarily in relation to Christianity and secondarily in relation to Islam.[2] While I am personally suspicious of the close association suggested by Kasher, it does bring to awareness that the question of Israel's election has two dimensions—one theoretical and timeless and one related to making sense of Israel's vocation in changing circumstances.

The subject of Israel's election has received ample historical and philosophical/theological attention in recent decades. We benefit from several collections of essays dedicated to the subject.[3] We also possess several monographs that contribute to a philosophical-theological analysis of election. Some are carried out as historical surveys.[4] Some seek to understand election conceptually.[5]

The particularity of the present collection owes to several features. Compared with the monographs and collections mentioned above, it does not seek to offer an account or to justify Israel's election.[6] This is why I prefer to not describe the thematic focus of the present volume simply as "election," reserving that term for theoretical discussions of special divine

---

2   Hanna Kasher, *Elyon Al Kol Hagoyim* (Tel-Aviv: Idra, 2018), 16.
3   Perspectives range from biblical to broad comparative collections. A worthwhile collection of biblical (both Jewish and Christian), as well as later materials in dialogue with biblical sources, is Gary Anderson and Joel Kaminsky, ed., *The Call of Abraham: Essays in the Election of Israel in Honor of Jon D. Levenson* (Notre Dame: University of Notre Dame Press, 2013). A broad comparative historical collection is *Raayon Habechira Beyisrael Uva'amim*, ed. Shmuel Almog and Michael Hed (Jerusalem: Zalman Shazar, 1991). I am not aware of a collection of essays that covers the full gamut of Jewish sources—biblical, rabbinic, philosophical, kabbalistic, hasidic, and modern. Every monograph or collection of essays tackles the subject through some limiting principle.
4   Hanna Kasher, focusing on the philosophical tradition.
5   Notably Michael Wyschogrod, *The Body of Faith: God in the People of Israel* (San Francisco: Harper and Row, 1989) and most recently Jerome Gellman, *God's Kindness Has Overwhelmed Us: A Contemporary Doctrine of the Jews as the Chosen People* (Boston: Academic Studies Press, 2012). David Novak's *The Election of Israel: The Idea of the Chosen People* (Cambridge: Cambridge University Press, 1995) is a cross between a historically oriented presentation and an attempt to work the topic philosophically.
6   With the exception of one important contribution by Jerome Gellman. This contribution antedates the publication of the main thesis in his *God's Kindness Has Overwhelmed Us*. Due to the importance of the piece and the conceptual opportunities it opens up in relation to other contributions, it has been kept in the collection. For justifications of election, see Hanna Kasher's work. See also the essays on election in Daniel Frank, ed., *A People Apart: Chosenness and Ritual in Jewish Philosophical Thought* (Albany: SUNY Press, 1993).

choices.⁷ Rather, it grapples with several dimensions that are related to Israel's being and vocation.

The first relates to the psychology and orientation that inform Israel's special position, in terms of its self-understanding. How can Israel's particular status and vocation be approached not in the abstract, but in terms of concrete orientations, concepts, and ideals? Awareness of being Israel is inseparable from attitudes to non-Jews. Every theory of Israel and every articulation of the issue of election is also a view of the other, the non-Jew. Rather than engage the more theoretical question of the status of the non-Jew, a focus on the mentalité of election will consider the flip side of election, in the attitude to the non-Jew. As complex as the issue of election is, so the view of the non-Jew is equally complex. It is driven both by the theoretical considerations of what might be the status of the unelected and the historical and psychological factors that relate to Jewish suffering at the hands of non-Jews. Accordingly, to consider what it means to be Israel by way of orientation involves us also in the view of the non-Jew. As far as I know, the mutual and interrelated exploration of these two dimensions has not been previously undertaken.

This leads to the next point that defines the particularity of the present collection: its overall orientation is educational and contemporary. As the above survey suggests, studies of "election" focus on the history of an idea or the philosophical and theological challenges it presents. Certainly, every philosophical articulation also has educational consequences. However, these are often implicit and were not at the forefront of the author's intention at the time of writing. The present project, however, grows out of a self-aware educational initiative. At its foundation is a series of contributions that were intended for educators to advance discussion, reflection, and creative thinking regarding Israel and its particularity. The project was originally conceived as study units, geared to serving religious and educational leadership. For reasons related to technology and the long-term viability of this as an online project, it was decided to make the materials available in the present format. In appreciating the particularity of the project it is important to recall its roots in a theological-educational setting, rather than in a more theoretical academic setting. This accounts for the choice of topics and for the overall concerns of the project.

---

7   I speak here as an editor. Some of the discussions do refer to "election." The distinction has become apparent to me during the final stages of the project, as I sought to articulate the particularity of our project, in relation to other studies and collections.

An educational and contemporary focus requires us to state what is the historical context within which the discourse takes place. More specifically, what is the problem against which we explore what it means to be Israel and how it relates to the other that is non-Israel? Educational challenges are framed by an understanding of the hour and its challenges.

We come then to the point of articulating the contemporary context and challenge against which the reflections gathered here were offered. The entire project has emerged out of the recognized need to advance a Jewish conversation in the field of theology of religions and the recognition that exploring Israel's vocation and its relations with other people and other religions is essential to the agenda of a contemporary Jewish theology of religions.[8] While Judaism, the religion, and Israel, the people, may in theory be distinguished, for most practical purposes they are identical. The election and special status of Israel is thus closely related to the positioning of Judaism in relation to other world religions. If earlier articulations of Israel's status and being were informed by the competitive and polemical situation that governed relations between religions in earlier times, the present volume has its birth in a more irenic moment in the relations between religions.

The relationship between "being Israel"—the question of "election"—and other religions is not a simple one on one equation. It is not as if some understanding of Israel will necessarily open up to other religions, while other understandings will not. The complexity of Israel's identity as people and as the carrier of a religion leads to various permutations of peoplehood and religion. Attitudes to other religions are informed by multiple factors: scriptural, theological, historical, and more. Still, the question of Israel's relations with other religions cannot be tackled without some reference to how "Israel" is approached, theoretically, existentially, and psychologically.

The concerns of a Jewish theology of religions continue to inform the present publication. However, in the process of editing for publication, I have recommended the focus be less exclusively placed on this historical challenge. Rather, the educational, psychological as well as philosophical challenges related to Israel, its vocation and positioning on the stage of history should be considered more broadly and in relation to other contemporary realities. At least two other such realities are relevant to the present

---

8   The theoretical articulation of this understanding is found in my introductory essay in *Jewish Theology and World Religions*, ed. Alon Goshen-Gottstein and Eugene Korn (Oxford Littman Library, 2012).

collection. The one is the existence of the State of Israel. While Israel the people and Israel the state should not be identified in a facile way in theological terms, there is a strong case for pondering the significance of the establishment of Israel, the state, in terms of the fulfillment of long-term aspirations relating to Israel, the people. Various ideologies and theologies have been attached to the establishment of the state that stand in continuity or dialogue with traditional understandings of Israel, the people, and its historical mission and vocation. It is therefore both an educational and theological challenge to consider Israel's vocation from the particular vantage point of the establishment of the state. The challenge is doubled when this very perspective is also associated with the view of other religions, considered from the vantage point of Israel's political independence.

While the point is not made explicitly in any of our contributions, it is also worth considering that the nexus of people, statehood and relations with other religions can play out in ways that can hamper advances in interreligious relations. The irenic and positive orientation imagines statehood as the framework for revisiting, restating, and enacting Israel's mission and consequently examines how this relates to Israel's views on other religions. However, this combination of factors also plays out a reverse dynamic. Politically motivated attacks on Israel are religiously colored, thereby heightening a sense of isolation and confrontation that is in continuity with centuries of antagonism. This can heighten religious exclusivism, undermining advances in relations between faiths. Sadly, this is increasingly the case in contemporary Israel.

A parallel historical context for exploring the broader mentality and approach associated with being Israel is the socially and theologically liberal reality that we find in the United States. While this reality does not in and of itself preclude continuing adherence to the idea of election, it does make some of the attitudes associated with it, in particular with reference to non-Jews, harder to accept as authoritative or having a commanding presence in the spiritual reality of the teacher and seeker. The problem of the flipside of election, the attitude to the non-elect, particularly the one marked as negative, rather than the neutral non-elect,[9] is therefore a pressing educational, moral and spiritual challenge for some authors. Several authors engage this dimension, as they grapple with biblical or hasidic sources.

---

9   The distinction between non-elect and anti-elect was elaborated in Joel Kaminsky, *Yet I Loved Jacob: Reclaiming the Biblical Concept of Election* (Nashville: Abingdon Press, 2007).

Having framed the volume in terms of its particularity, orientation, and goals, I would like to now tell its story. Putting it in this way suggests there is a story, a message that emerges from the volume in its entirety, that is told through its various components, and is greater than the sum of its individual parts. It is for me, as the editor, to tell the story. I only became aware of this broader message as I read the essays as an ensemble, seeking to identify the connections between them and how they contribute to a broader agenda. What follows is at one and the same time a presentation of the essays in terms of their specific and intended message and a recasting of the individual messages as a broader message that emerges from the ensemble of essays. It is I alone who bear "responsibility" for this broader message. If the way in which I draw together different insights and views into a composite picture is valid, then this larger picture is itself a meaningful contribution to the discourse of Israel, its particularity and its relations with the nations. The title of the present collection derives from my own reading of what can be heard from the ensemble of essays. Rather than another collection of essays on "election," I discover in the present offering a means of framing the challenge that faces Judaism, as it continues to uphold a sense of chosenness and as it seeks to engage the world beyond it—nations, as well as religions. The challenge is captured by the dual implication of election, placing Israel in the tension, dynamics, and complexities of divine love on the one hand and enmity with others on the other. Israel's election, mission, and vocation are played out within this tension of love, grounded in God and extending to humanity, and the opposite of love, as this finds expression in Israel's relations with others. Election involves Israel in both contradictory dimensions—love and hate. Israel has to work out the purpose of its election and its realization in history in the tension between these two extremes.

Exploring election through the lens of divine love, its challenges and its limitations opens us to a consideration of the different circumstances within which love, and its opposite, are affirmed. Such exploration is essential to taking stock of our beliefs and attitudes to others. It forces us to consider Israel's special relationship with God, its vocation, and its relations with others under changing circumstances, good and bad, painful and hopeful. Those changing circumstances also include the present-day opportunities created through advances in interfaith relations and how Israel's special calling might be considered within this particular circumstance. I will return to this issue in the book's conclusion. For the time being, I would like to relate to the different essays (though I will not attempt to summarize them), to point to various points of contact between them and to how the ensemble tells the story, how it contributes to the thesis I identify as the message of the present collection.

Weaving the Project Together

The collection begins with Israel Knohl's "The Election and Sanctity of Israel in the Hebrew Bible." We open with this essay because it presents us with biblical foundations and poses some of the questions that will be weaved throughout this collection. In terms of method, Knohl seeks to cultivate an appreciation for multiple voices, multiple theologoumena—theological units of thought, within the Bible. Recognizing multi-vocality is fundamental to a project of situating ourselves as readers and students of the Bible and of the entirety of Jewish tradition. Rather than a view of a monolithic tradition to which one submits, our collection assumes multiple voices throughout Jewish history. These are sources of inspiration, dialogue partners, and resources that challenge us to understand them in context, and to seek their meaning in the context of our lives.

I would like to single out three themes in Knohl's presentation. The first relates to the parallel between Abraham and Israel regarding election. The parallel is fundamental to the notion of election and to the sense of being Israel in relation to others and we encounter it in the majority of the volume's contributions. This parallel allows us to explore a second theme that is fundamental to our project—the question of continuity or discontinuity between Israel and the nations. It is a very different understanding of election when understood as continuous or as discontinuous with the rest of humanity. Is Israel building upon humanity, extending it forward, and bringing something to it, or is it viewed as distinct, potentially in conflict? This question serves as a meta-question for all discussions of election and for many of the papers in the present volume that explore the meaning of being Israel in relation to the nations. The third theme that emerges from Knohl's presentation is the grounding of election in divine love and the question of the relationship between divine love and purpose. This question too will serve as a leitmotif for our volume. For Knohl, love has no reason, is irrational, cannot be accounted for and has no purpose. At least, the biblical sources do not provide us with the reasoning that justifies divine love. Consequently, we cannot relate divine love to the question of Israel's relations with humanity. Knohl's contribution frames issues that will be worked out by other authors, even if many of the sources we shall encounter take the opposite stance to Knohl's.

One more issue comes up in Knohl's discussion—the boundaries of Israel. Knohl struggles with the question of multiple definitions or perspectives on what constitutes Israel and the possibility that there are partial definitions, based on race or on behavior that allow others to join the Jewish people, even if not fully. These definitions come to light as part of broadening the boundaries of Israel and inviting others within, the *ger*. Israel's election involves not only establishing boundaries for its definition but also establishing criteria and categories by means of which its boundaries can be expanded to incorporate others within. Problematizing the boundaries of what is Israel is also relevant for contemporary social challenges in the State of Israel. The question of partial membership also brings us back to the question of A possible continuity with the rest of humanity and a means of absorbing it into Israel's vision, story, or identity.

The next two essays explore biblical themes in their historical evolution.[10] Beginning with biblical foundations, they examine two notions that are not common in describing the people of Israel, recovering their potential for contemporary religious thought. By uncovering the history of interpretation of Israel's description as a Kingdom of Priests and the related notion of Israel being a blessing to others, they seek to introduce a language that is not often used and to explore dimensions of Israel's being that are not often treated. The study of the history of interpretation of these two notions provides a window onto multiple understandings of how Israel is conceptualized and how its role is envisioned in relation to others. Exposure to a diversity of understandings is an invitation to reflect, to choose, and to position oneself on a spectrum of understandings of what it means to be Israel. Both Alon Goshen-Gottstein's "A Kingdom of Priests and a Holy Nation" and Eugene Korn's "Israel as Blessing: Theological Horizons" touch upon the question of continuity and discontinuity. The biblical notion of Israel as a blessing to others and the related notion of a Kingdom of Priests readily suggest relationship, responsibility, mission, and caring for others. While some interpretations exist that minimize these ideals, including

---

10   The two essays are developments of study units created by Alon Goshen-Gottstein and Eugene Korn that had thematic resonance and overlap. Hence the similar work the two essays do, with each of the authors developing one of the jointly authored study units into an essay.

postponing them to a messianic future, there is a robust tradition that considers them as dimensions of Israel's ongoing responsibility towards the nations. Opinions differ, however, on how this is realized. Does fulfilling these two ideals require active intervention, or does Israel fulfill these dimensions of its vocation simply by being true to itself, by its very being. One notes a robust tradition that considers both these ideals as related to a teaching vocation. The alternative is for these ideals to be fulfilled through prayer or as the outcome of Israel's living its spiritual life to the full.

Returning to the question of continuity and discontinuity, it is impossible to consider these notions without assuming some form of continuity. Fulfillment in practice requires contact and fulfillment as a radiation of being assumes continuity. Moreover, such continuity is explicitly featured by some authors, notably Rabbi Yehuda Leib Ashlag, as an expression of love. Love is the chain of being that ties Israel to God, to each other and to the world at large, for which Israel serve as priests who disseminate divine love. While the notion of blessing and its application to the nations is not tied to love explicitly in the sources analyzed by Korn, the very act of blessing would seem to manifest an attitude of care and love.[11] That both concepts are tied, at various points in the history of their interpretation, to the figure of Abraham reinforces the relationship between Israel's election, status and being and that of Abraham. This also allows us to carry over the common association of the Patriarch and love to the context of Israel and its relations to the world at large.

The lessons of these two essays offer an important complement or corrective to Knohl's claim that love is irrational and has no purpose. In contrast, the close association of blessing and a priestly vocation to an outward facing mission, engaging and involving others, leads one to the suggestion that the purpose of divine love, made manifest in Israel, is to reach out to others and to expand the blessing of divine love. In other words, Israel received the divine blessing of love, with an eye to extending it to all of humanity. In this reading, it is not simply that Israel is to be perfect in itself, nor that it has a mission of teaching or otherwise blessing humanity. More powerfully, Israel is considered as a crucial link in a process of divine love reaching outward to all of humanity, through Israel. In terms of a theory of election, one could articulate a theory of instrumental election, with

---

11   This highly intuitive association finds expression in the ritual blessing preceding the priestly blessing. Israel are to be blessed with love.

those beyond Israel as its ultimate purpose and justification. In terms of the subjective and interior reality, what we call "being Israel," we find in these sources an internal orientation that is not only mindful of the world beyond Israel, but that positions Israel as a crucial link, stretching its awareness to the nations, and serving as a bridge of divine love to the world at large. God's elective love reaches beyond Israel in some form of invitation to share in the divine love, as Israel reaches out to the nations.

While the theme of blessing is related by some authorities to active outreach to the nations, as Korn shows, this association is even more predominant with regards to the notion of a Kingdom of Priests. The most dominant interpretation associates this notion with Israel's teaching mission for the nations. This in turn raises the question of the anticipated outcome of such activities. The texts that refer to the issue explicitly relate to the seven noachide commandments and to the status of *ger toshav*, a partial convert. However, the messianic fulfillment of the priestly function to the nations can also carry a heavier weight, leading to the ultimate identification of the future status of the nations with that of Israel. If so, there are dimensions where "being Israel" opens up to "becoming Israel," whether partially or fully.

This leads us to the fourth essay, that of Jerome Gellman, "Jewish Chosenness—A Contemporary Approach." Of all the contributions in this collection, Gellman's seeks to articulate a theory of Jewish election. The elements highlighted above all fit into a theory of election, suggested by Gellman. Consistent with the elements highlighted above, Gellman suggests two major points as constitutive of his novel view of Jewish chosenness—love and being a model for the nations. Election is a demonstration of divine love. This demonstration is meant to provide a model for others, an invitation, extending the proof of divine love from Israel to all of humanity. What distinguishes Israel from others is that whereas the optimal vision of love is one freely chosen, in the case of Israel it is an overpowering love, that comes at the expense of free choice. This is needed in order to ensure the existence of the precedent that is then emulated without the coercive element. Gellman's theory of election, in a word, is a vision of divine love, extending from God to all humanity, through the agency of Israel. These elements that were noted in the preceding essays come together to form a theory of Jewish chosenness.

Love and suffering are closely related. Suffering is a measure of the depths of faithfulness and of the mutual attachment of God and Israel.

Suffering, in this scheme, does not posit Jews against gentiles. Rather, the Jewish people are sacrificed by the very reality of a love that is forced upon them, for the sake of humanity.

Gellman's theology of chosenness is driven by the ever-present danger of Jews interpreting the doctrine of chosenness in ways that endorse ethnocentric supremacy, cultural isolation, and the defamation of other religions. Such a rendering of the doctrine in our times signifies not only an agonistic stance toward other peoples and other religions, but a serious spiritual shortcoming within Judaism itself. This statement of what motivates Gellman's theological restatement captures well the assumptions of the present project.

Accordingly, each of God's acts of love to the Israelites is also a promise for gentiles, whether it be the Exodus or the giving of the Torah, for Jewish history mirrors human history as a whole. It is not only that the Torah has in it a universal potential. More fundamentally, the very structure of Judaism and the underlying election of Israel are shaped with an eye to the expansion and hence to the fundamental potential for a common denominator with all of humanity.

This provides a segue to the contribution of Menahem Katz, "*Aleinu*—A Prayer Common to Jews and Gentile God-Fearers." Katz seeks to retrieve the historical context of the composition of the first part of the famous *Aleinu* prayer and to draw theological conclusions from it. According to Katz, the us vs. them that characterizes the affirmation of faith in the *Aleinu* does not relate to Jews vs. gentiles, or to a rejection of those who believe in Jesus. Rather, it reflects a Temple-based reality in which Jews and gentiles alike could affirm their belief in the one God, creator of heaven and earth, who is worshipped in the Temple. Recognition of the same God allows us to redraw the boundaries of "us" and "them" and to recognize fundamental commonalities. The category of God fearers, described by Katz, suggests one way of expanding the boundaries of Israel and its message that does not require full entry into Israel, yet allows for the establishment of a framework of unity that undercuts existing boundaries. This understanding of the *Aleinu* echoes rabbinic voices that recognize a common ground between Jews and believing non-Jews, that includes prayer, Torah and more. Katz' contribution allows us to consider who is the "us" that is fundamentally characteristic of being Israel and the sense of its particularity. Following Katz, we realize that this sense of "us" need not be defined exclusively by ethnic boundaries. Rather, it can also be constituted by faith boundaries and these provide a meeting point for Jews and gentiles, in the framework of the Jerusalem Temple and the faith it points to. In addition to expanding the sense of "us" that characterizes a prayer that is typically understood in oppositional terms, in relation to others, Katz also provides an illustration for Gellman's thesis and more broadly for the understanding that Israel's vocation points to a calling to the nations. Katz shows how this has come to expression in a specific institutional setting—the Temple and the *ma'madot* liturgy, and how it remains with us in the form of the oft-recited prayer, the *Aleinu Leshabeach*.

At this point our volume moves from the descriptions of the ideal to the challenges of the real. If election perforce engages us in relations with the other and these are ideally imagined as based on continuity, influence and ultimately the extension of love, in reality Israel's encounter with the other has been all too often oppositional. The conflict that characterizes Israel's relations with the nations for millennia is not only a historical fact. It shapes Israel's consciousness and ultimately informs the very sense of what it is to be Israel, shaping a mentalité that is oppositional, and all too often far removed from the ideals presented above. Exploring what it is to be Israel therefore requires of us to also engage negative attitudes to the other and the oppositional frame of mind that has come to dominate so much of what it means to be Jewish, membership in the Jewish people and more recently in the State of Israel.

Stanislaw Krajewski's "Two Dimensions of Jewish Identity" opens the exploration with a theoretical contribution on different means of establishing group identity—negative—in opposition to another, and positive—based on values and ideals. Krajewski's piece is a phenomenological/philosophical exploration of how election works in subjective consciousness, a crucial aspect of what it is and what it feels like to be Israel. His focus is on the notion of identity, and only by way of the example of Israel. The alternative poles are accordingly defining identity in terms of the other or in terms of Israel's mission, how it can serve and what it can bring to the other. It is perhaps worth noting that the tension between choice and lack thereof as this relates to the relationship with God, which Gellman proposed as the basic distinction between Israel and others, finds a different expression here. In Krajewski's treatment, Israel itself has the choice of defining and understanding itself in terms of choice or lack thereof. Choice is the higher reality, inasmuch as it allows Israel to freely follow its vocation and consequently to serve others. Based on his juxtaposition of two types of identity,

Krajewski associates the lachrymose view of history, a prism through which Jewish history is viewed, with negative identity construction.

One aspect of positive identity construction noted by Krajewski is Judaism's messianic vision and its hope for others. Biblical messianic promises affirm the continuity between Israel and the nations and the ultimate reception of Israel's message by the nations. A messianic future serves as the necessary counterpoint to the sufferings of the present. While messianic visions do not necessarily spell out an irenic relationship with the other, they do provide the outlet for the positivity that would characterize Israel's attitude to the nations, absent conflict and the pain of history. A messianic perspective also informs some applications of the views of Israel as blessing and the notion of a Kingdom of Priests, whose fulfillment is considered in a messianic framework.

The oppositional view is tackled head on in Or Rose's "Images of the Non-Jew in the Kedushat Levi: A Textual and Theological Exploration." Rose frames his exploration from the perspective of a teacher and theologian who seeks guidance and value in the teaching and in the works of one hasidic master, R. Levi Yitzhak (RLY) of Berdichev. Rose's presentation struggles openly with the flip side of the special status associated with Israel and the special love they receive—the negativity, even hatred, with which non-Jews are considered in his work. RLY is not alone. He is heir to a rich tradition that is oppositional in relation to non-Jews and that at times sees them in dualistic terms, viewing the distinction between Jew and non-Jew as related to the powers of good and evil. While RLY is in no way unique, his role in Rose's own spiritual life presents him with the challenge of how to position himself in relation to these materials. Historical circumstances obviously play a major role. Rose recognizes the conditions under which RLY and a long line of hasidic and kabbalistic masters operated as preventing them from developing the more open, equal and accepting attitude that he himself practices in his present-day American society and that makes it impossible for him to simply accept RLY's teachings in an uncritical manner. The matter cannot be reduced to a contrast between the insider's "authentic" perspective, contrasted with Rose's own perspective, influenced as it might be by American ideals. Rose cites various Jewish teachings relating to humanity at large that would be hard to reconcile with the oppositional perspective. One is forced to therefore deal with different voices within tradition and to establish means of choosing, sifting, contextualizing or otherwise coming to terms with them. Beyond historical contextualization, Rose suggests a strategy of recognizing light and darkness and the need to identify the shadows even in the teachings of great masters. One assumes his historical vantage point and the values he upholds equip him to apply this strategy. Part of choosing is also identifying alternative voices even within RLY's teachings. Not surprisingly, RLY can offer a messianic perspective that offsets some of the negativity found in other perspectives. The various strategies for upholding some ideas at the expense of others thus lead one to profile different teachings even within the works of an individual teacher or school and to making choices or accounting for the differences, described by Rose in terms of light and darkness.

Rose's essay demonstrates what is stake in the conversation on election, on being Israel, and on relating to others. For the teacher, and even more so for the student, there is great difficulty in accepting certain views of the other; and these views in turn reflect on the views of Israel and its special status. Both issues reflect on the reliability of masters of the tradition and strands of the tradition as sources of significance. If the risk is an inability to receive from these teachers due to these concerns, the challenge and the solution are an ongoing conversation, of which Rose's essay is a part.

That Rose's challenges are contextual in relation to how he is positioned in a particular context is highlighted by encountering some of the same themes in a strikingly different historical context. For me, it was illuminating to consider some of the same passages that Rose struggled with presented as part of Holocaust-related meaning-making. Gershon Greenberg's "Israel's Election and the Suffering of the Holocaust" studies how election was thematized by thinkers during and following the Holocaust, with reference to the events of the Holocaust. Greenberg presents a range of thinkers and responses. Despite their different ideologies and worldviews, they provide us with a lens on how election is thematized in the context of the Holocaust. Not only election but also divine love, suffering, and the hatred of others for Israel are frequent themes. Affirming election and its purposefulness is one major strategy that infuses suffering with higher meaning.

The example of Abraham that we encountered early on resurfaces with reference to the *Akedah*. Abraham can provide meaning for blessing the nations as well as to the utmost suffering delivered by others. The idea that Israel as chosen people is a sacrifice for God, suggested by Gellman, receives concrete and contextual articulation by authors reflecting on the Holocaust. The problem of the non-elect becomes the problem of the anti-elect, resorting to the most fundamental dualistic thinking and to Israel's symbolical arch-enemy—Amalek. The challenge of Israel's special vocation is understood not with reference to the generality of humanity, the other broadly construed, but with reference to manifestations of extreme evil, that turns against Israel itself. A sacrificial attitude and recognition of the value of suffering are all that can be offered in response. From a different perspective, also described by Greenberg, Messianism provides the lens for making sense of the Holocaust. Unlike earlier references to messianism, thinkers like Rav Harlap developed an apocalyptic view of history, within which the Shoah was interpreted. Election, suffering and messianism thus combine in light of the particular challenges of the time.

The following essay stands in an interesting relationship to its immediate predecessors. Reuven Kimelman's "Israel's Election and the Moral Dilemma of Amalek and the Seven Nations of Canaan" seeks to understand at one and the same time the essence of Israel's election and its flip side—attitudes to Israel's arch-enemy Amalek, as well the moral challenge presented by the biblical commandment to destroy the indigenous nations of the Land of Canaan/Israel. The challenges are not only theoretical but relate to ongoing educational challenges and discussions, especially in the State of Israel today. Seen in light of one another, these themes raise concern over an ethnic understanding of election that could in turn lead to a (mistaken) view of these biblical commandments as expressions of genocide. Kimelman's method is to highlight the multivocality of tradition and of texts within the same canon. Biblical witness is itself more complex and rabbinic and later tradition similarly move the discussion in ways that balance out first appearances of ethnically based criteria. Instead, moral criteria govern these themes and these are common to Jews and non-Jews, thereby reaffirming the fundamental continuity that most of the sources we study affirm.

The issue of election brings us back, once again, to Abraham. Justice and righteousness are key to God's choice of Abraham and later to God's election of and expectations of Israel. As such, they provide a moral basis and demand that is universal. They thereby provide continuity between Israel and the nations, in light of the same spiritual and moral ideals. Kimelman cites various biblical verses that juxtapose love and justice, either as virtues to be practiced or as God's own love of righteousness. This framing allows us to also consider the theme of divine love that we have been exploring in relation to the objectivity of moral behavior. Following this line of reasoning would suggest that walking a path of justice and righteousness is the means for extending love beyond Israel, by Israel as well as by God.

I would like to lift up one more notion out of Kimelman's rich tapestry of biblical and rabbinic texts. One of the ideas that has been raised in the history of interpretation to account for the non-implementation of the commandment to kill the Canaanites is that they converted. This strand brings the moral struggles described by Kimelman in line with a theme that has been echoed time and again in our studies. Conversion assumes the possibility of change and the beneficial impact of encounter with Israel. However it may be conceived, this notion can in theory also extend to Israel's arch-enemies. The continuity provided by common moral ground can be understood as or extended in line with the notion of conversion. In the case of Amalek, the point is explicit and Kimelman references conversion from Amalek in historical and legal sources. Kimelman's argument for common ground also considers repentance as a dimension of religious behavior that could counter the commandment to wipe out the Canaanites. Read in tandem with the notion of conversion, we may suggest a spectrum of transformation, that runs the gamut from moral to religious, perhaps from partial to full conversion. Engaging the other, even in what seems initially like the utmost oppositional manner, yields upon further scrutiny an invitation to identify the common moral and religious ground, culminating in different degrees of what may be considered conversion.

Kimelman provides us with a strategy for redeeming some of the difficult commandments. In so doing he shows us how applying the same spiritual principles within and without helps us to overcome the moral and educational challenges that these texts present us with. The same may be said of the essay that concludes the volume. Menachem Kallus' "From Enmity to Unity—Recovering the Ba'al Shem Tov's Teachings on Non-Jews" moves the discussion to the level of individual piety and practice. Kallus seeks to retrieve a line of kabbalistic teaching that is often unrecognized and that constitutes the alternative to the dualistic vision, championed by the Zohar and seen in the writings of R. Levi Yitzhak of Berdichev. Kallus recognizes an alternative kabbalistic strand that considers the nations of the world as part of the same fundamental structure as Israel, even if occupying a different rung in that structure. Continuity between Israel and others is, in this view, metaphysically grounded. Kallus suggests that such a worldview has continued into the hasidic tradition and can be identified in the teachings of the Ba'al Shem Tov and his immediate disciples. Once again, the practice of identifying multiple voices and theological options serves as a means for advancing a contemporary theological and educational agenda.

Kallus' presentation features various other strategies for affirming continuity. Common creation, common humanity and a sense of mutual responsibility (*arevut*) even for non-Jews are some of the ways in which this is achieved. We recall Katz' common space of worship for Jews and non-Jews based on the recognition of one common creator God. Recognition of divine unity is another strategy for affirming solidarity and transcending the dichotomy of good and evil.

Kallus brings us back to the theme of divine love. The universal God provides the basis for universal love. Perhaps because God is at the center of the texts brought by Kallus, we note a prominence of the theme of love, as it relates to both Jews and non-Jews. A way of being grounded in the unity of God and of all being and expressing itself in love can ultimately not draw boundaries between Jews and non-Jews. If for Kimelman morality provided the common ground between Jews and non-Jews, for the hasidic authors treated by Kallus this is achieved by means of a unitive vision of reality.

The command of love translates itself also to the very confrontation with the evil of the non-Jew. Kallus shares a catalogue of hasidic texts from the school of the Ba'al Shem Tov that apply a method of transformation of the enemy through the practice of positivity and love. Finding good in the enemy and even praying for him are the counterpart of the interiorization of external reality. In earlier essays we noted expressions of individualization and interiorization of themes such as being a priest. Such interiorization establishes the spiritual life within and can potentially offset the oppositional consequences of Israel's particularity, when these are marshalled ideologically. The texts brought by Kallus show how full interiority accompanies recognition of divinity and allows the practitioner to transcend the duality and negativity associated even with one's enemies, including the non-Jewish enemy. Going further than Kimelman, the wicked can be appreciated even in their wicked state, and not only when they eventually turn to the good. Significantly, prayer is part of the arsenal of spiritual tools by means of which this process is attained. We have not had recourse to prayer since the description of Israel as priests who pray for the welfare of humanity.

The messianic perspective is also important for affirming the deeper metaphysical foundations of commonality and the expected processes of transformation associated with it. The messianic perspective enables a projection of deeper connectivity and union to a future time when the oppositional reality of the present will be transcended and the higher reality realized.

Finally, I'd like to return to the question of conversion. The notion has appeared in many of the sources we have encountered along the way, as consequential to Israel's being and vocation. Kallus' discussion is not dedicated to Israel and the nations but rather to the practices of unity and transformation that the individual engages in, also in relation to his or her environment. Nevertheless, it seems that the entire thrust of the process described by his sources is upon transformation for the good. This certainly conforms with the overall pattern we have seen, even if its expressions are less formal in terms of conversion.

When we read the volume's contributions as a whole, a coherent vision emerges. Israel's special status, its election, is closely related to the world at large. Divine love ultimately reaches all and Israel have a crucial role to play in that extension. History, however, presents Israel with a reality that is anything but the manifestation of love. That leads to an oppositional view of others. It requires a deeper look, whether hermeneutical, historical, or spiritual, to recover the higher or deeper teaching of unity and love that brings God back to the center and reaffirms Israel's vocation. History, then, is an important dimension of Israel's story, of how its status comes to expression and how it has been variously understood. History allows for one vision of Israel and its relations to the nations to emerge at one point in time and then for another to resurface at another. We must therefore also pay attention to the particularity of the historical moment and how it informs the present exercise. How do present-day challenges and opportunities inform the present discussion? I shall return to this matter in the volume's concluding chapter.

Israel Knohl

The Election and Sanctity of Israel in the Hebrew Bible

Methodological Introduction

There are various approaches to the biblical text. As an introduction to the following collection of sources and in the interest of allowing them to speak to us and enabling our active interpolation of these texts for their meaning, some words are in order regarding the method I shall be using in the present study. Let us consider the image of a diamond. One may look at the diamond in its totality, admire its shape and how it reflects the light. One may also look more closely at how the diamond has been cut, each of its angles, the way the light is refracted here in one way and there in another. One may, similarly, study the diamond in terms of its mineral composition, age, or degree of perfection and imperfection. But what makes diamonds precious is the sense of beauty they inspire in us, the appreciation of their transparency and how they contribute to us—be it in beauty or in wealth.

I offer this analogy as a way of introducing my approach to the biblical text. In what follows, I share with the reader a series of texts that are related to the question of Israel's election and their relationship with God. Each of these texts is a facet of a diamond. Each facet shines a light on a subject, entices us, inspires us, calls us to engage in it, to query it, possibly to integrate its teaching.

This method of appreciating individual texts exposes tensions and differences between biblical texts. Whereas later tradition often reads one text in light of the other, harmonizing them, or ignores the testimony of one text on account of the other, the method followed below listens to each text fully. A deeper listening to texts in their individuality, without the immediate concern for harmonization or for affirming a truth known either from other biblical texts or from later traditions, opens the biblical texts to us with new insight. It is precisely the points of tension and conflict between the texts that invite us to revisit our faith in dialogue with the biblical sources.

In considering the question of Israel's election, a series of texts is shared with the reader. The texts either refer to the notion of election as such—thereby allowing to study both Abraham's election and that of Israel, or refer to Israel through categories other than election, by means of which other dimensions of its special relationship with God is expressed.

The sum total of the texts and reflections below is an invitation to dwell upon and contemplate different dimensions of Israel's special relationship with God. Such dwelling is an invitation to further reflection. This reflection may point to post-biblical sources and to the millennia-long attempt to make sense of this relationship or it may point directly to the student who is invited to relate to, struggle with, make sense and ultimately own some dimension of the enduring biblical testimony to Israel's special relationship with God.

Understanding Election

Election as a phenomenon finds diverse expression in biblical sources. I would like to enter into the domain of biblical texts by recognizing the parallels that exist between Israel's election and that of Abraham. The two are related in multiple ways. Abraham's election is already a part of Israel's election, and therefore holds a key to it. From another perspective, the two elections parallel each other, and therefore allow us to gain fundamental insights into what election is from each of these elections and from their combined witness.

In Genesis 11:26–12:7 we encounter two seemingly conflicting traditions regarding the departure of Abraham from Haran for the land of Canaan.

> [11:26] When Terah had lived seventy years, he became the father of Abram, Nahor, and Haran. [27] Now these are the descendants of Terah. Terah was the father of Abram, Nahor, and Haran; and Haran was the father of Lot. [28] Haran died before his father Terah in the land of his birth, in Ur of the Chaldeʾans. [29] And Abram and Nahor took wives; the name of Abram's

wife was Sar'ai, and the name of Nahor's wife, Milcah, the daughter of Haran the father of Milcah and Iscah. [30] Now Sar'ai was barren; she had no child. [31] Terah took Abram his son and Lot the son of Haran, his grandson, and Sar'ai his daughter-in-law, his son Abram's wife, and they went forth together from Ur of the Chalde'ans to go into the land of Canaan; but when they came to Haran, they settled there. [32] The days of Terah were two hundred and five years; and Terah died in Haran.

[12:1] Now the LORD said to Abram, "Go from your country and your kindred and your father's house to the land that I will show you. [2] And I will make of you a great nation, and I will bless you, and make your name great, so that you will be a blessing. [3] I will bless those who bless you, and him who curses you I will curse; and by you all the families of the earth shall bless themselves." [4] So Abram went, as the LORD had told him; and Lot went with him. Abram was seventy-five years old when he departed from Haran. [5] And Abram took Sar'ai his wife, and Lot his brother's son, and all their possessions which they had gathered, and the persons that they had gotten in Haran; and they set forth to go to the land of Canaan. When they had come to the land of Canaan, [6] Abram passed through the land to the place at Shechem, to the oak of Moreh. At that time the Canaanites were in the land. [7] Then the LORD appeared to Abram, and said, "To your descendants I will give this land." So he built there an altar to the LORD, who had appeared to him.

It seems that we have here two opposing traditions regarding the departure of Abraham from Haran for the land of Canaan: According to the tradition in Genesis 11:26–32, Abraham was born in Ur of the Chalde'ans, which is the ancient city of Ur in southern Babylonia. The decision to leave Ur and go to the land of Canaan had already been made by Terah, Abraham's father.

It is not clear why Terah decided to wander from his country to the land of Canaan but he did not succeed in completing his journey and died in Haran, which is located in northern Syria, near the Balikh River, a tributary of the Euphrates. (Historically, Haran was part of northern Syria, today it is in southern Turkey.) According to this tradition, Abraham completed the plan of his father Terah when he went from Haran to Canaan.

The trip to Canaan that began with Terah's journey from Ur of the Chalde'ans to Haran was, according to this tradition, a human decision that was not preceded by a divine command. Abraham never disassociated himself from the household of his father Terah. Quite the contrary, Terah was the one who initiated the journey to Canaan and he took his son Abraham with him.

However, the Book of Genesis also presents another, very different tradition alongside this one. According to this second tradition, Abraham's journey to Canaan was the result of a divine command. He did not bring his father with him but rather was required to disassociate himself from his father's house. This verse does not specify where the homeland and father's house that Abraham was required to leave were located but this is stated later in the same tradition.

> Go to my country and to my kindred,
>   and take a wife for my son Isaac. . .
> The LORD, the God of heaven, who took me from my father's house and
>   from the land of my birth. . .
> He will send his angel before you, and you shall take a wife for my son from
>   there. (Genesis 24:4–7)

Abraham sends his most senior servant to find a wife for his son Isaac. Later in the story, it is stated that the servant went to Mesopotamia, to the home of Bethu'el and brought from there Rebekah, the daughter of Bethu'el and sister of Laban. The home city of Bethu'el and Laban was Haran (Genesis 29:4). According to this tradition, Abraham was born in Haran and not in Ur of the Chalde'ans, and the LORD is the one who took him from his homeland and his father's house.

These two traditions are harmonized already in Genesis.

> And he said to him, "I am the LORD
> who brought you from Ur of the Chalde'ans,
> to give you this land to possess." (Genesis 15:7)

In this source, we find the two traditions combined. As in the first tradition, Abraham's birthplace is Ur of the Chalde'ans, but the words "who brought you from" echo conceptually the second tradition, where it is God's command that is at the root of Abraham's departure from the city of his birth.

Let us ponder the potential differences between these two traditions. Abraham clearly has a special relationship with God. He is called to this relationship. How continuous or discontinuous is this relationship with his earthly personality and human relationships? For the one view, his special relationship with God (with the present emphasis on the move towards the Land of Canaan, that might already point to that) continues from and fulfills a human program and a prior family plan. A special relationship with God is forged through and by means of what seems to be human initiative, possibly motivated by various human and earthly concerns. Still, within this framework, a relationship, or the beginning of a relationship, is forged.

The second view is much more extreme. A special relationship, an election, calls for separation, break, a move away from. Moreover, it is initiated by God. If on the first view, man can chose to go towards God or towards a land associated with him, on the second view, the calling must come from God and must be accompanied by a break, a separation.

We have here *in nuce* two views that will continue to inform the understanding of Israel's election. Over centuries and millennia we will encounter sources and positions that place more of an emphasis on the human choice, Israel's choice of God, or the reverse—the unique choice that God makes when choosing his people. Perhaps related to this is the question of what may be called soft and hard separation, associated with election. The one view that can be presaged here considers election an extension of common humanity, growing from it, perhaps fulfilling it, but not divorcing it. The alternative view sees a rupture, initiated by God, that sets the one who is called and chosen apart from others. These differences will condition Jewish understandings of election, appearing time and again under different guises.

One point should be added here, and it applies to both ways of telling the story, both potential understandings of election. Nowhere in these sources is there a mention of Abraham as religious revolutionary who fights against idolatry. In fact, these sources do not even describe Terah, the father of Abraham as an idol-worshiper.[1] Something else, then, is involved in the special calling and special relationship with God. Either election is to be understood along other lines than those of religious teaching and practice. If so, this would take us in the direction of the establishment of a people, a nation, rather than of a faith and a religious practice. The alternative lesson is that even while one is being chosen, this need not imply rejection of the other. separation and distinct identity—yes; rejection and invalidation—no.

---

[1] The only place in the Hebrew Bible where we find a reference to the fact that Abraham's fathers worshiped idols is Josh. 24:2. However, even in this context, we do not find any reason why God decided to take Abraham from beyond the Euphrates River and to bring him to Canaan. Nor is it stated that Abraham rebelled against the religious practices of his family.

The image of Abraham who shatters his father's idols has ancient roots. It can be traced to the literature of the Second Temple, from where it entered rabbinic literature, and then later Jewish and non-Jewish, especially Muslim, sources. For these later views of Abraham, one could not think of a special belonging to God without it translating to the choice of a proper faith, and the rejection of improper faith. It is telling that the foundational biblical texts do not share this view. For them, election may be meaningful, along the lines just suggested or others, even without rejection of idols, the faith of others.

Looking at all these texts we ask ourselves, then, what is the reason and purpose of Abraham's election? The answer, as far as the biblical sources are concerned, is that there is no answer. The fact is that no reason is given in any of them for the election of Abraham.

We are struck by this lack of explanation. Yet, this gap in the biblical narrative is an invitation for continuing reflection, to be carried out by subsequent generations. Precisely because the biblical text remains mum on this question, later generations have the opportunity to deepen their reflection on what the foundation for Abraham's election is—his person, his lovingkindness, his charity, his faith and so on. And then there is a more fundamental concern that may be the most appropriate. Election may be an act of love and love cannot be accounted for rationally. God may simply show his love in a free way that does not require justification and cannot be justified.

This tension between a love that can be justified and one that is beyond (or before) justification is itself a constitutive dimension of reflection on election, especially Israel's in later Jewish thought. Do we simply accept divine love or do we seek to justify it, making it more rational? Perhaps the need for such justification arises from the presence of others, those who have not similarly been chosen. And perhaps the biblical text itself tells the story with no attempt for it to make sense in the eyes of others, keeping its horizons to the relationship itself.

As stated, Abraham's election shares fundamental dynamics with the election of Israel. The idea just raised, according to which election should be understood as an expression of and in light of divine love, finds clear expression with regard to Israel's election.

> [7:6] For you are a people holy to the LORD your God; the LORD your God
> has chosen you to be a people for his own possession, out of all the peoples

that are on the face of the earth. [7] It was not because you were more in number than any other people that the LORD set his love upon you and chose you, for you were the fewest of all peoples; [8] but it is because the LORD loves you, and is keeping the oath which he swore to your fathers, that the LORD has brought you out with a mighty hand, and redeemed you from the house of bondage, from the hand of Pharaoh king of Egypt. (Deuteronomy 7:6–8)

These verses in Deuteronomy 7 represent the people of Israel as a holy people which was elected by God. Deuteronomy 7:7 emphasizes that the election of Israel by God was not based on a rational calculation. Had God looked for a big nation he should have turned to a big and mighty nation like Egypt or Babylon. The fact that He has chosen a small nation like Israel is proof that he was not acting on a rational basis. Why than did he elect the small nation of Israel? He fell in love with them. As we know well love is an irrational rational feeling, that cannot be accounted for based on rational calculations. Love is a mystery. Thus, the election of Israel, just like the election of Abraham, is a mysterious act of God.

Israel's Sanctity

In the next section I would like to explore another dimension of God's relationship with Israel—Israel's sanctity. The two are not unrelated. As we have just seen and as we shall see in the following source, election and sanctity are closely related.

[1] You are the sons of the LORD your God; you shall not cut yourselves or make any baldness on your foreheads for the dead. [2] For you are a people holy to the LORD your God, and the LORD has chosen you to be a people for his own possession, out of all the peoples that are on the face of the earth. [3] You shall not eat any abominable thing. [4] These are the animals you may eat: the ox, the sheep, the goat, [5] the hart, the gazelle, the roebuck, the wild goat, the ibex, the antelope, and the mountain-sheep. [6] Every animal that parts the hoof and has the hoof cloven in two, and chews the cud, among the animals, you may eat. [7] Yet of those that chew the cud or have the hoof cloven you shall not eat these: the camel, the hare, and the rock badger, because they chew the cud but do not part the hoof, are unclean for you. [8] And the swine, because it parts the hoof but does not chew the cud, is unclean for you. Their flesh you shall not eat, and their

carcasses you shall not touch. [9] Of all that are in the waters you may eat these: whatever has fins and scales you may eat. [10] And whatever does not have fins and scales you shall not eat; it is unclean for you. [11] You may eat all clean birds. [12] But these are the ones which you shall not eat: the eagle, the vulture, the osprey, [13] the buzzard, the kite, after their kinds; [14] every raven after its kind; [15] the ostrich, the nighthawk, the sea gull, the hawk, after their kinds; [16] the little owl and the great owl, the water hen [17] and the pelican, the carrion vulture and the cormorant, [18] the stork, the heron, after their kinds; the hoopoe and the bat. [19] And all winged insects are unclean for you; they shall not be eaten. [20] All clean winged things you may eat. [21] You shall not eat anything that dies of itself; you may give it to the alien who is within your towns, that he may eat it, or you may sell it to a foreigner; for you are a people holy to the LORD your God. You shall not boil a kid in its mother's milk. (Deuteronomy 14:1–21)

As in the previous source, also here, the sanctity of the nation of Israel is connected with its election by God (14:2). In this text, as in the previous, the initial act is divine election. Israel's call to sanctity is an outcome of that election. God takes the lead and a life of sanctity, expressed in obedience to various ritual commandments, is the response to the divine calling and a means of affirming, upholding and expressing divine sanctity, born of divine election. The prohibitions that are connected here with the perception of Israel as a holy nation belong entirely to the cultic sphere: mourning customs and dietary laws.

While both biblical texts establish this clear relationship between election and sanctity, the very juxtaposition of these motives invites reflection as to their relationship. While acting in accordance with divine standards of sanctity is an outcome of election, does it also define election and serve as a condition for it? What is the status of election were Israel to fail to live up to the laws of sanctity? And does the fact that election is grounded in divine initiative and divine love provide a guarantee that upholds the relationship, even if Israel fail in terms of commanded sanctity? These questions are alluded to in the structure of the biblical text. They are potent and generate ongoing discussion throughout the millennia of Jewish reflection on the meaning of election and holiness.

Our text adds a motif, that we have not previously encountered. The new motif is the description of the Israelites as "sons of God" (see also Ex. 4:22; Hosea 11:1). Israel's filial status adds a further dimension to understanding election. It suggests a special, close, intimate relationship. The questions just posed are further enhanced by appeal to this metaphor. Is sonship another means of expressing election? If so, is obedience to the ritual requirements a consequence of this status? And can sonship, like election, be lost on account of failure to live up to the ritual expressions of the special relationship? That later rabbinic authorities can dispute whether Israel's status as sons does or does not depend on their behavior (Bavli Kiddushin 36a) points to the profound and unanswered questions that biblical sources open up for the tradition. These questions generate a long history of reflection, and its dynamism continues to the present day.

The Status of the *Ger*

With regard to the prohibition: "You shall not eat anything that dies of itself" (14:21) the text above distinguishes between different parts of the population: The eating of a carcass is prohibited to the native Israelite but permitted to the *ger* and the foreigner.

This distinction seems to express the conception that the *ger* is not part of the group of the "holy Israelite nation" hence he is permitted to eat the carcass which is prohibited to the members of this group. This is probably connected with the fact that the deep connection between God and Israel is expressed here in family terminology: the native Israelites are "sons of God" but the *ger* seems to be excluded from this "holy family."

Let us consider another testimony to the status of the *ger*.

> [10] You stand this day all of you before the LORD your God; the heads of your tribes, your elders, and your officers, all the men of Israel, [11] your little ones, your wives, and the sojourner who is in your camp, both he who hews your wood and he who draws your water, [12] that you may enter into the sworn covenant of the LORD your God, which the LORD your God makes with you this day; [13] that he may establish you this day as his people, and that he may be your God, as he promised you, and as he swore to your fathers, to Abraham, to Isaac, and to Jacob. (Deuteronomy 29:10–13)

The book of Deuteronomy concludes with the description of the covenant ceremony which took place shortly before the death of Moses in the land of Moab. In verse 13 we hear that the *ger* is part of the covenant community. According to these verses it is only by the making of the covenant that Israel is to be established as "the people of God" (29:13). The *ger* seems to be part of this process, that is, he is part of "the people of God." The same emerges from another passage in Deuteronomy.

> [9] And Moses wrote this law, and gave it to the priests the sons of Levi, who carried the ark of the covenant of the LORD, and to all the elders of Israel. [10] And Moses commanded them, "At the end of every seven years, at the set time of the year of release, at the feast of booths, [11] when all Israel comes to appear before the LORD your God at the place which he will choose, you shall read this law before all Israel in their hearing. [12] Assemble the people, men, women, and little ones, and the sojourner within your towns, that they may hear and learn to fear the LORD your God, and be careful to do all the words of this law, [13] and that their children, who have not known it, may hear and learn to fear the LORD your God, as long as you live in the land which you are going over the Jordan to possess." (Deuteronomy 31:9–13)

Shortly before his death, Moses wrote the book of the Torah and gave it to the priests in order that it would be put inside the "ark of the covenant of the LORD." The placing of the book of the Torah within the "ark of the covenant of the LORD" reflects the perception of this book as the content and basis of this covenant. The priests are commanded by Moses to read the book of the Torah before all Israel. "At the end of every seven years, at the set time of the year of release, at the feast of booths." The aim of this public reading is "that they may hear and learn to fear the LORD your God, and be careful to do all the words of this law." As in the previous source, also here, the *ger* is included within the people. He should listen among the entire nation, to the reading of the Torah and perform the laws of the covenant (29:12).

How are we to reconcile the different views regarding the *ger*? With regard to the prohibition on the eating of a carcass there is a distinction between different groups of the population. The eating of a carcass is prohibited to the native Israelite but permitted to the *ger* and the foreigner. This distinction seems to express the conception that the *ger* is not part of the group of the "holy Israelite nation," hence he is permitted with the eating of the carcass which is prohibited to the members of this group. By contrast, the last two sources, also from Deuteronomy, seem to have a different view about the *ger*. In both of these sources, the *ger* is part of the nation who is established as the "people of God" via entering into the covenant with God.

How should we understand this inner tension within the book of Deuteronomy with regard to the status of the *ger*? Some scholars[2] suggest an historical-critical explanation: According to this view, Deuteronomy 14 is a part of the original nucleus of the book of Deuteronomy while Deuteronomy 29:10–13, 31:9–13 are part of a later edition of the book. The original nucleus of the book of Deuteronomy was written according to the scholarly view in the time of King Josiah, at the end of the seventh century BC. The later additions at end of the book of Deuteronomy were written in the time of the exile to Babylon. According to this view, Deuteronomy 14 reflects the lower status of the *ger* in the pre-exilic period. However, in the time of the exile to Babylon, when gentiles were attracted to Judaism and wanted to join the Jewish people, there was an elevation in the status of the *ger*.

Without rejection of the possibility of this explanation, I would like to suggest here a different one. We can differentiate between two types of congregations within the book of Deuteronomy: The first congregation is that of the holy nation. The sacredness of the Israelite nation is based on the election and on the "family relation" of the Israelites as "the sons of God." It is very much rooted in the past history of the people. The *ger* who does not share this past history is thus excluded from this congregation. It is worth noting that only a few laws, recorded in Deuteronomy 14:1–21, are part of this framework.

The other congregation is the covenant community. The *ger* is a part of this community, since he is included among the people who enter the covenant with God. The greater part of the laws of Deuteronomy are included in the framework of the covenant. Accordingly, the *ger* is called to study these laws and to observe them with the other Israelites.

Election involves us, to some extent or another, in a view of the other, the unelected. The unelected may be the enemy, the strong other, or a more neutral other, simply one who has not been elected. In the case of the *ger* we encounter a third possibility—someone who is partially a member of the community, but not fully. The discussion of the *ger* raises the question of whether there can be partial membership in the community of Israel. This possibility has for a very long time been off the table. The biblical *ger* has undergone a historical transformation and the present-day *ger* is a full-fledged Jew. Indeed, even the permission to eat carcasses that distinguishes the biblical *ger* from the Israelite son of God is denied in other passages in

---

2 Saul Olyan, *Rites and Rank* (Princetion: Princeton University Press, 2000), 63–99.

the Torah. Thus, Leviticus 17:15–16 does not differentiate between the *ger* and the Israelite with regard to the eating of the carcass.

Issues of Israel's election and identity are in today's Israel not simply a matter of religious doctrine. They are issues of civil and legal import, determining citizenship and governing marriage laws and other fundamental aspects of life. Present-day Israel finds itself returning, in some unexpected ways, to biblical realities, in relation to others, who no longer fit the paradigm of the strong contradictory other, but who are also not part of the congregation of the covenant or the congregation of the sons of God.

Might the texts we have seen here concerning the *ger* open up a new way of viewing many members of the society who are not full-fledged Jews and who also encounter difficulties in entering the Jewish people, through formal processes? With this de facto return to the reality of the *ger*, these biblical texts take on a new significance. Do they provide for us a meaningful precedent for operating with different criteria, when it comes to different populations? Can there be a covenant community, understood as distinct from those whose shared historical memory confers upon them the status of sons of God? Might the two versions of the move towards the Land of Israel, involving Abraham and Terah, be a further resource for addressing this situation? Might the conventional Jewish path resemble that of Abraham, chosen at God's initiative for the fuller and more demanding exclusive relationship of election? And might the path of Terah, who leaves on his own volition to journey to the land of Canaan, even without full recognition of the God who would call his son to go there, serve as a precedent for another kind of motivation in coming to the land, living on it, and belonging to its people?

Alon Goshen-Gottstein

A Kingdom of Priests and a Holy Nation

The present essay seeks to explore in depth one thread of the tapestry of ideas associated with election, one particular depiction of what Israel is—a Kingdom of Priests and a holy nation. The designation is taken from Exodus 19:15–16:

> Now then, if you will obey Me faithfully and keep My covenant, you shall be My treasured possession among all the peoples. Indeed, all the earth is Mine, but you shall be to Me a Kingdom of Priests and a holy nation. These are the words that you shall speak to the children of Israel.

Interpretation is a window on to meaning and the history of interpretation is a gateway to exploring a range of meanings associated with a verse. When an idea is grounded in a specific text, the history of its interpretation allows us to explore an idea in its richness and complexity. What does it mean for Israel to be a Kingdom of Priests? How can this condition our thinking and attitude as we think of Israel in relation to other peoples? The designation takes on particular urgency since the establishment of the State of Israel and the possibility of relating to "kingdom" in concrete terms.

Philo—Prayer and Blessing for the Nations

Before setting out to explore different interpretive approaches to Exodus 19:6, I would like to mention what seems to be the earliest interpretive reference to the notion of Israel's priesthood, in the works of Philo of Alexandria. Unlike many of the later interpretations, that will highlight the active, missionary, pedagogic efforts of the priest, we find here an understanding that does not require active interaction with the nations in order for Israel to fulfill its priestly calling in relation to them.

> The reason is that a priest has the same relation to a city that the nation of the Jews has to the entire inhabited world. For it serves as a priest—to state the truth—through the use of all purificatory offerings and the guidance both for body and soul of divine laws. For this reason it is astounding that some dare to charge the nation with an anti-social stance, a nation which has made such an extensive use of fellowship and goodwill toward all people everywhere that they offer up prayers and feasts and first fruits on behalf of the common race of human beings and serve the really self-existent God both on behalf of themselves and of others who have run from the services which they should have rendered.[1]

Israel's priestly service is expressed through its rituals, with special emphasis upon the purification that these rituals effect upon both body and soul. Israel offers prayers on behalf of all humanity. Philo struggles with anti-Judaic claims, especially as these focus upon the isolation of Jews and their being apart from others. Philo clearly points to intentionality as the bridge between behavior that seeks to separate and an orientation of service to broader humanity. Israel are full of goodwill to all people. The offerings are made with the clear intention of being offered on behalf of others. Israel is aware that its service to God is not only on behalf of itself, but on behalf of all of humanity. Israel makes up consciously for humanity's deficiencies in serving God.[2]

Philo describes a fundamental aspect of priesthood. A priest is an intermediary between the people and God. Rituals and prayers are offered on behalf of others. To think of Israel as priests is therefore to think of them as intermediaries between humanity and God. It is a striking fact that with all the riches in the history of interpretation of the notion of Kingdom of Priests, we do not find in any of the sources surveyed below a view of Israel as intermediaries before God on behalf of humanity.

---

1 Philo, *On the Special Laws*, Book 2, 163, 167.
2 The notion that separation is a condition for extending blessing to others appears in various sources, though without the reference to the priestly dimension. See, for example, *Sefat Emet*, Sukkot, 1903.

Priesthood in Relation to God—Expression of Special Status

Moving on to the commentarial tradition on Exodus 19:6, one of the most basic distinctions between different interpretations is between views that understand the term in relation to God, and hence metaphorically, and those that understand it in relation to others, the nations of the world, and hence more literally, based on the point of comparison. The former category is represented by some older interpretations, rabbinic and medieval.

Rashi is the prime representative of this interpretive tradition. He renders Kingdom of Priests simply as "ministers." Radak and Abravanel provide us with typical examples of such an understanding.

> Similarly He said to them when they left Egypt: And you shall be unto me a Kingdom of Priests and a holy nation that is an autonomous nation, and you will be my priests and servants, not slaves to another people, and you will be unto me a holy nation, separated from the impurity of the nations.[3]

The verse points to Israel's independence as a kingdom and to their exclusive service to God. Abravanel considers the titles as honorifics, rather than descriptors of Israel's spiritual vocation.

> When Israel serve God they are to be honored as princes and ministers. Therefore he called them a Kingdom of Priests, for being that they worship Him and officiate in His service, their status will rise to the level of sons of kings, nobles of the land, free men and a kingdom of ministers.[4]

Kingdom of Priests is an expression of status. The status is obtained, in part, in contradistinction to other nations, to whom they are no longer subjugated and who perhaps are to give them the stated honor. The designation is dependent on Israel serving God and cannot be taken as an expression of unconditional status. In thinking of how the expression conditions the psyche, one can readily recognize how an understanding of value and honor, coupled with an affirmation of separation from others, can shape a view of Israel's relation to others that centers upon itself, more than upon its service or calling and that runs the danger of bolstering an attitude of superiority and egotism as negative by-products of a particular view of election.

Later readers were sensitive to these dangers. Among hasidic authors we note several attempts to recast Rashi's commentary in ways that make

---

3   Radak, Psalm 114:2.
4   Abravanel, Exodus 19.

it a spiritual challenge, invitation and mission, rather than simply an affirmation of status. Some have read it as a designation of power to draw grace and blessing, as the priest would.[5] Alternatively, it has been read as empowerment and authority to develop the Torah.[6] One wonderful application speaks of ministers in terms of self-control and mastery.

> To speak of ministers does not suggest [ruling] over others, for Israel never desired to rule over the nations . . . but the meaning is that every person should rule over his spirit . . . his heart should be under his control.[7]

To a certain extent, hasidic tradition is testimony to continuing efforts to read the designation in relation to spiritual processes, rather than simply an honorific or an expression of status.

The alternative hermeneutical tradition highlights responsibility to others and awareness of them. It focuses on Israel's responsibilities, rather than status. While Israel is extolled and valued in this view as well, the broader setting and the focus on responsibility go a long way to moderating the potentially negative uses of Kingdom of Priests.

Priesthood as Teaching to the Nations

The other strand of interpretation of Exodus 19:16 understands Israel's priesthood in terms of the nations. The earliest such interpretation is attributed by Abraham Maimonides to his father.

> The meaning of a "Kingdom of Priests" is that the priest of every community is the dignitary and leader who sets an example for the group to follow in his footsteps and leads them on the proper path. Thus, He says, "by the observance of My commandments you shall be the leaders of the world. The relationship between you and the nations should be like the relationship between a priest and his following. The world will follow in your footsteps, imitate your actions, and walk in your ways." This is the explanation of this verse that I received from my father, my teacher, of blessed memory (Maimonides). Now, this will occur if they (the Israelites) will obey their mandate, as is written, "Observe them faithfully, for that will be proof of your wisdom and discernment to other peoples" (Deut. 4:6). Indeed, God

---

5   *Magen Avraham* of Magid of Trisk, Lech Lecha.
6   *Beer Mayim Chayim*, Ki Tavo 27.
7   *Shem Mishemuel*, Shavuot, 1919.

promised the complete realization of this goal in the future in His words through the Prophet Isaiah, "And many peoples shall go, and they shall say, 'Come, let us go up to the Lord's mount, to the house of the God of Jacob, and let Him teach us of His ways, and we will go in His paths'" (Isa. 2:2). And the secret (i.e. intention) of the statement "you shall be to Me a Kingdom of Priests" rather than just saying "you shall be to Me priests," according to the opinion of our sages this means, "that you shall be aristocrats and in positions of power like kings." However, it appears to me that the intention is "that you shall be kings over the world and rule over them. For those who will follow your example of perfection, to them you shall be as priests. However, if they do not imitate your ways willingly, you shall motivate and coerce them by means of the sword in the mission of Moses to the true faith concerning My Lordship and manner of worship," by which I mean belief in the unity of God and the fulfillment of the seven noachide laws which the Gentiles are obligated to fulfill as explained by tradition.[8]

For R. Abraham, priesthood signifies religious leadership and example. The world is to follow the straight path, traced by Israel, as one follows a priest. Deut. 4:6, the classical proof text for the rationality of the mitzvot, and hence for their universal significance, is brought in this context. So are the eschatological verses that highlight teaching to the nations as the future fulfillment. Israel is to be a world leader in the field of religious teaching.

Abraham Maimonides takes his father's teaching one step further. Maimonides' commentary only accounts for the priestly component of "Kingdom of Priests."[9] Abraham Maimonides points out there are two components in the expression and there is tension between them. The royal component too designates an attitude to the nations. Accordingly, there are two possible ways of influencing the nations. One is by persuasion and example, the other through force and warfare. This provides a biblical proof text for the notion found only in Maimonides, with no talmudic backing, that Israel have a responsibility to disseminate the seven Noahide commandments by force (Maimonides, Laws of Kings 8:10). Thus, Abraham Maimonides draws a direct line between the Bible and his fathers' innovative halakhah.

---

8 Abraham Maimonides, *Commentary on Genesis and Exodus*, ed. E. J. Wiesenberg (London, 1958), 302.
9 Maimonides' own understanding of Ex. 19:6 is found in the *Guide for the Perplexed* 3:32. Knowledge of God is what defines the priestly nation. R. Abraham's passage applies this knowledge to the later stage of teaching others, but does not seem to highlight Maimonides' own core definition.

R. Ovadiah Seforno–Defining Israel's Status as Kingdom of Priests

A major chapter in the understanding of Exodus 19:6 is written by the sixteenth-century Italian Torah commentator, R. Ovadiah Seforno. Seforno, as he is typically referred to, is the single most important contributor, until the modern period, to the understanding of Israel as a Kingdom of Priests. The centrality of the concept can be illustrated quantitatively, by comparison to other Bible commentators. Ibn Ezra does not comment on our verse. Rashi's sole reference in his Torah commentary to Kingdom of Priests is in his short gloss on Exodus 19:6. Nachmanides has two references to our verse, in addition to his commentary on it. However, closer scrutiny reveals he is only commenting on its latter part, a holy nation, and not on the concept of Kingdom of Priests.[10] Contrast this with Seforno's appeal to Ex. 19,6. The verse appears no less than nine times in his Torah commentary. The number of occurrences, all consistent in terms of the key understanding, is doubled, when we take into account his other writings, especially his commentary to the Psalms.[11] This alone already suggests its importance.

The centrality of Kingdom of Priests is also qualitative. A study of the contexts in which reference to Kingdom of Priests appears further establishes its centrality. It is the defining feature of Israel's relationship with God and the focus of the relationship established at Sinai. It is the goal around which the covenant was formed as well as the mission and purpose of Israel. In short, it defines what Israel is. More than anything else, for Seforno the answer to the meaning of Israel's election lies in the formula—Kingdom of Priests.

Further indication of its qualitative centrality is found in how it relates to other key concepts. Israel's vocation as Kingdom of Priests relates to what is the most important notion in Seforno's theological universe–the creation of all of humanity in the divine image. Israel's definition and vocation thus relate to humanity and its fundamental spiritual definition. Finally, its centrality is established also in terms of a reading of Israel's history. Kingdom of Priests is what was established at Sinai, what was lost due to the sin of the golden calf and what will be restored in the messianic future. It is thus a defining feature of Israel's history, as well as its identity. This, in fact, leads

---

10 See commentary to Ex. 25:1 and Deut. 28:9. Similar emphases emerge from the commentary of Rabbenu Bechayey, who follows in the footsteps of Nachmanides.
11 See *Kitvei Rabbi Ovadiah Seforno*, ed. Zev Gottlieb, Moassad Harav Kook (Jerusalem, 1987).

us to a crucial challenge in understanding Seforno's view of Kingdom of Priests–how does the present moment, positioned between former lost glory and future return of that glory, relate to the notion of Kingdom of Priests? Is Kingdom of Priests an expression of status, or a definition? Is it a promise or a vocation? If status or promise, these may be temporarily lost or suspended. If vocation, and even more so definition, these can be at most downgraded, but not suspended. Let us consider these complexities by looking at Seforno's commentaries.

The most fundamental text is his commentary to Exodus 19:6:

> "You shall be unto me a Kingdom of Priests": and in this you will be the treasure amongst all, for you will be a Kingdom of Priests, to teach and instruct all mankind to all call in God's name and to serve him in unison.[12] As will be the situation of Israel in the future, as it says "and you shall be called Priests of God" (Isa. 61:6), and as it says "for from Zion Torah shall come forth" (Isa. 2:3).

The teaching vocation is stated clearly as the core definition. The future prophecies of Isaiah provide the scriptural counterpoint, raising the question of how to relate Exodus 19:6 to the future. Is the status and mission part of the present but its fulfillment a matter for the future, or do the later prophecies contain and thereby limit the relevance of Exodus 19:6 to the future only? One other reference complements Exodus 19:6. That is the commentary to Deuteronomy 26:19. Seforno finds the same message in both places. The importance of both verses is highlighted by Seforno's claim that this message appears at the beginning and at the end of God's revelation, thereby marking it as bookends that define the meaning of all that comes between them.[13] In this commentary we do not find the future oriented context, suggesting that the priestly kingdom is part of Israel's foundational identity and is relevant to the present as much as to the future.[14]

---

12 Allusion to Zefaniah 3:9, one of the key universal biblical messages.
13 See introduction to commentary on Psalms, p. 72 and p. 527 of his works. The description of this core message as appearing at the beginning and the end of the Torah is found only outside the Torah commentary itself. It may be that the Torah commentary is too closely focused on individual verses to offer this broad framing. One could have also seen the parallel between these two verses as an outcome of the same fundamental situation of covenant making, at Sinai and then in the plains of Moav. If so, Kingdom of Priests would have defining status in relation to Israel's covenant with God.
14 The same is true for Psalms commentary, pp. 168 and 230. If David or the Psalms can continue to refer to teaching the commandments to the nations, as a realization of Ex.

In multiple places Seforno considers turning Israel into a "Kingdom of Priests" as the essence of events at Sinai.[15] The problem is that things at Sinai went wrong, with the making of the golden calf. In one way this frustrated the divine plan for bringing Israel to the kind of spiritual perfection that would allow them to realize their spiritual and cognitive status as Kingdom of Priests.[16] At the same time, the divine plan took an alternative course. Rather than omnipresent holiness, available along with the full realization of God's knowledge, holiness is contained in the Temple.[17] The special relationship with Israel is therefore not abandoned. Rather, it takes a detour on its way to ultimate fulfillment, which is postponed to messianic times. With such reconfiguration, some dimension of Kingdom of Priests is preserved. This would accord with those places in which Seforno continues to appeal to the concept as defining of Israel, without deferring it to messianic times. If so, we may read Seforno as upholding Israel's teaching vocation even in the present. What has changed is not the mission, but the circumstances for its realization. Juxtaposing Kingdom of Priests to Israel's condition in exile supports a reading that the core definition and mission remain. The circumstances, however, prevent its full implementation at present, leading to anticipation of a future realization.[18]

It is worth contrasting Seforno with another commentator who considers Kingdom of Priests as something that cannot be realized at present and belongs only to the future. R. Yaakov b. Asher, *Ba'al Haturim* (thirteenth–fourteenth c.), in his commentary on Exodus 19:6 states:

> Had Israel merited, all of them would have been high priests. And in the future it will return to them, as it says (Isa. 68:6) "and you will be called priests of God."

19:6, one cannot consider its vision to have been suspended. In commentary to Lev. 26:45 the mission of Kingdom of Priests is identified as the purpose of the Exodus and the meaning of God being Israel's God. If we were to assume total suspension of the priestly vocation, this would mean that in effect the entire relationship has been suspended, an untenable theological position.

15 Ex. 31:18; Lev. 19:2 and 26:45. In all these cases Seforno relates to the earlier part of Ex. 19:6. The later part of the verse seems to be the focus of his commentary to Num. 15:40.
16 See commentary to Deut. 32:5.
17 Commentary to Ex. 31:18. See also Lev. 19:2.
18 Commentary to Psalms, p. 240, though one could also limit the meaning of election in exile to survival until the future when Israel will be the treasured nation of Kingdom of Priests. See also reference to the remnants, whom God calls, in commentary to Gen. 49:26, which may provide further indication of a historical awareness of Israel's weakened state.

This terse comment states that Kingdom of Priests is not relevant today. Despite apparent similarities, I believe we should distinguish between the two commentaries. R. Ya'akov b. Asher says nothing of Israel's teaching vocation. He therefore stands in continuity with the tradition that considers Kingdom of Priests an honorific. The special status described by it has been lost. Theologically, it is easier to relate to loss of status[19] than it is to loss of identity and fundamental vocation. Given Seforno's understanding of Israel's teaching vocation as constitutive of its election, one would be hardpressed to consider all of history, leading up to messianic times, an interim moment, a holding pattern, until such time that Israel can fulfill its destiny. Seforno is better understood as upholding an enduring universal teaching mission, which, however, can only be realized in the future due to circumstances stemming from sin and its consequences, especially conditions in exile.

One important final consideration in favor of the ongoing validity and relevance of Kingdom of Priests is its place in the theological and philosophical economy established by Seforno. If I had to distill all of Seforno's teaching into two key messages, they would be Genesis 1:26–creation of man in God's image and Exodus 19:6. These two messages are not distinct but interrelated. In order to understand what Kingdom of Priests means and what Israel's teaching consists of, we must consider how Kingdom of Priests relates to God's image, in other words, how Israel's particular status relates to the universal status of the image of God. Tying the two together, as Seforno does, provides us with one additional angle for establishing the enduring relevance of Kingdom of Priests. Just as image of God is a constant reality,[20] so its counterpart, describing Israel's status, remains relevant, interacting with the image of God in humanity. The image of God is man's cognitive potentiality that has to be realized. Seforno is maimonidean in

---

19 This is reflected in various hasidic authors who assume Kingdom of Priests applies only to the future. See *Davar Tov Leyisrael: Hanhagot Hazadiqim*, ed. Chayim Rotenberg (Jerusalem, 1997), 286; R. Zadok Hacohen of Lublin, *Pri Tzaddiq*, Ki Teze, 7; *Imrei Emet*, Hannuka. Affirmation of its enduring relevance need not assume a missionary understanding. It is sufficient that it has some practical consequences in the present. Hence the affirmation by the Imrei Emet's cousin, held in high esteem in the same school, Gur, that Kingdom of Priests applies to all generations. See *Siftei Tzaddiq*, Shavuot. The author relates to self control, rather than to status, hence the enduring relevance of a Kingdom of Priests.

20 There are other views. See my "The Body as Image of God in Rabbinic Literature," *Harvard Theological Review*, 87, no. 2 (1994): 171–95.

his view of the image of God. The image of God is what is common to all of humanity. Consequently, humanity as such has the potential to realize the knowledge of God. However, not all do. Among the nations, a few individuals do. Israel has the calling to realize it as a collective. This is the purpose of the commandments.[21] It has the further calling to spread such knowledge to all of humanity, enabling the realization of the image of God in mankind. Seforno considers this as sanctification of the divine name, through Israel's priestly vocation. Their failure to aid others in realizing their divine image is a desecration of the divine name.[22] This vision of Israel's mission is fully universal. In fact, Seforno states clearly that the difference between Israel and others is quantitative, not qualitative. The commentary on the verse leading up to Exodus 19:6 reads as follows:

> "And you shall be unto me a treasure of all the peoples." Even though humankind is precious to me, more than any of the lowly beings, because it alone (humanity) is their purpose, as the sages said (Avot 3:14) "beloved is man, for he is created in the image of God," nevertheless, you shall be a treasure (or precious) more than all others. "For the entire earth is mine"– and the difference between you [and them] is a matter of more or less, for nevertheless the entire earth is mine, and the righteous of the nations are precious to me, without a doubt."[23]

Read in conjunction with the following verse, we have here the juxtaposition of the two key notions. The difference between Israel and the nations is quantitative.[24] In other words, more individuals within Israel have attained or will attain the knowledge of God, thereby putting them in the situation of facilitating humanity's spiritual advancement.[25] However, once achieved, there is no qualitative difference between Israel and others, as indeed is the case in relation to those few pious among the nations who have already realized that potential.[26] The quantitative perspective is also helpful to affirming the enduring validity of the mission of a Kingdom of Priests. If Israel's

---

21 Commentary to Lev. 26:3.
22 Commentary to Deut. 32:5–6. See further Lev. 26:12. See also Seforno's works, p. 527.
23 Commentary on Ex. 19:5.
24 This still leaves room for a special love of Israel, even if the notion of *segula* is extended to all of humanity. See commentary to Deut. 33:3.
25 Actually, the quantitative advantage may be that in Israel only a few have fulfilled the knowledge, while among the nations none have. See commentary to Lev. 13:47. This conflicts with the text under discussion.
26 The closest to a qualitative distinction is found in commentary to Num. 19:2.

advantage is quantitative and does not represent some higher qualitative being, the loss of the quantitative advantage over the nations need not be a return to zero, any more than in the case of non-Jews, some of whom are also recognized as having fulfilled the divine image. If Kingdom of Priests is a quantitative advantage, then its loss or postponement is also quantitative, suggesting reduced capacity for fulfilling its mission, rather than suspension of its vocation.

One can put forth the view of Israel in relation to the nations not only as a Kingdom of Priests but also as a source of blessing to the nations. While Ex. 19:6 is not tied directly to the notion of blessing, Isaiah 61:6, its complement verse, is related to Israel as blessing.[27] Fulfilling its priestly vocation, Israel is thus a blessing to the nations. In this, it follows the pattern established by Abraham, who similarly spread knowledge of God and His ways.[28]

The description of Israel as a Kingdom of Priests is thickly interwoven with other key theological motifs. Its centrality is affirmed by the web of theological associations. It seems to me that the interweaving of ideas also affirms the enduring validity of the description and calling of Israel as a Kingdom of Priests. Considering the testimony in its entirety, I am led to conclude that rather than seeing the reference to sin as suspending and making the notion irrelevant, we should view the association of Kingdom of Priests, sin, change in divine plan and messianic fulfillment as further signs for its centrality in Seforno's thought. The notion is so central and important to him that it is not simply a static description of Israel's status but a dynamic lens through which the vicissitudes of Israel's history are refracted. Through this refraction we learn of various degrees of realization Israel's calling to be a Kingdom of Priests. The category inspires a vision of activism and contribution to humanity, even as it invites to humility in view of historical failure and the limited degree to which this vision can be realized in present times.

Popularity of Priestly Calling as Teaching Vocation

Seforno's commentary seems to have had very little resonance among later authors. With the exception of one hassidic author, it is not echoed by any later authority. The same is true of Abraham Maimonides' interpretation

---

27 See commentary to Gen. 28:14 and 49:26.
28 On this, see the essay by Eugene Korn in the present volume.

that does not seem to have influenced any later author and is only cited in very recent works, after his commentary was published. Nevertheless, the understanding of Exodus 19:6 as an activisit teaching vocation is a dominant strand of Israel. If it does not owe to earlier precedent, then we must account for the popularity of this interpretation on other grounds. Two points are relevant here. First, the understanding is rather intuitive, considering the teaching ministry of priests. Second, this interpretive strand seems to serve a need for Jewish self-understanding, under particular historical and sociological circumstances.

The reading of Exodus 19:6 with reference to the nations became the default reading especially during the nineteenth and twentieth centuries. The rise in the popularity of this trope corresponds to the integration of Jews in broader society, to increased contact with others and to the consequent need to frame their own religious responsibility towards society at large. The active missionary understanding is closely related to historical circumstances, as it hinges on Israel's contact with nations. Significantly, the past fifty or sixty years have seen a decline in the use of the verse in reflections on Israel. This is telling, inasmuch as it is precisely during this time that Israel has become a "kingdom," with the founding of the State of Israel, and therefore the invitation to and the potential for being a "Kingdom of Priests" could have played a greater role. This gap presents us with a challenge and a theological invitation for today. The history of interpretation of the verse suggests why it is a notion that should be relevant particularly at the present point in time, and raises the query of why it has largely fallen into disuse in contemporary preaching and teaching.[29]

Let us consider some highlights from this tradition of activist-missionary interpretation. The following teaching comes from the sixteenth-century Karaite Isaac Troki.

> It is well known that Israel is the chosen nation concerning whom it is recorded in Exodus (19:5), "And ye shall be unto me a peculiar people from among all the nations for mine is the earth." All this tends to prove, that the Almighty revealed His law to Israel for the purpose that they should learn to walk in the right way, and to perform righteous deeds. With this

---

[29] To be sure, an idea never falls into total disuse, especially as it is cited by followers of an earlier teacher for whom it was central, such as Rav Kook. Still, based on earlier uses and on what one might expect to find under circumstances of Israeli sovereignty, one is struck by the scarcity of appeal to the category.

distinguished gift for themselves, He has coupled the noble mission that they should become useful to other nations; "For His mercy extends to all His creatures." With a view to Israel's instrumentality in His Divine government, we find (in Exodus 19:6), "And they shall be unto me a Kingdom of Priests and a holy nation." And to the same purport says Isaiah (61:6), "And ye shall be named the priests of the Lord; ye shall be called the servants of our God." "Ye shall eat the riches of the Gentiles, and in their glory ye shall triumph." In numerous parts of the Scripture, the people of Israel are called priests, it being the duty of that class to inculcate religious duties and precepts, and to "teach Jacob judgments, and Israel the Law." Thus, it is our vocation to instruct, in the law of the living God, the Gentiles, among whom we are dispersed; and as the Psalmist says (Psalms 96:3), to "relate His glory among the Gentiles, His wonderful works among the nations." All future felicity of the Gentiles will proceed from Israel, as has been assured to our patriarchs, (see Gen. 12:3) "And in thee all the nations of the earth shall be blessed"; and (Gen. 28:14) "And through thee and thy seed all the families of the earth shall be blessed."[30]

This text is by a Karaite author. Written as an anti-Christian polemic, it has enjoyed broad influence and has impacted rabbinic authors, beyond its originally Karaite origins. The text focuses on Israel, while citing verses that relate to Abraham. It describes Israel's relations to the nations by appeal to the priestly metaphor. Just as priests are teachers to the people, so Israel are teachers to the nations. The understanding is active and missionary. Israel has a role to go out and teach the nations. Israel's election is grounded in divine compassion. Because all of humanity needs to be taught, Israel is chosen as teachers for humanity and their dispersion serves that purpose. The contents of teaching are left broad enough to sustain multiple understandings. We note that the exile is cast in positive terms, as an opportunity to teach the nations. Troki's concluding statement refers to all blessing coming to the nations through Israel. It would seem this blessing is a consequence of the teaching rather than being identified with the teaching itself.[31]

A similar appreciation of exile in terms of realization of Israel's vocation as a Kingdom of Priests is found in the following source.

---

30 Isaac Troki, *Faith Strengthened*, trans. Moses Mocatta (London: Kessinger Publishing LLC, 1851), 114–15.
31 Compare this to Abravanel on Genesis 12:2, where both aspects are mentioned.

> The matter is well-known to the observer, that the destiny of the Jewish nation as decreed by the King of the World, is not that they alone should serve God and be unto Him a cherished nation, but rather that they should also serve as intermediaries to make His glory, power, and providence known in the eyes of the nations who will learn of Him through them, and will eliminate evil and destroy idolatry from the midst of the land. Regarding the strength of its purpose, it was said to her, "you shall be to Me a Kingdom of Priests and a holy nation" (Exodus 19:6). And it is written: "For a priest's lips shall guard knowledge, and teaching should be sought from his mouth, for he is a messenger of the Lord of Hosts" (Malachi 2:7) . . . .
>
> Thus, through Israel they will recognize and acknowledge the Kingdom of the Lord and His sovereignty over the nations, as she (Israel) girds herself with strength to perform this task even in the days of her poverty and oppression. Hence, in every place that she set her foot the ancient nations learned from her the belief in the First Cause, may He be blessed, and most of the principles of faith pertaining thereto. Even though they have sinned, and the trustfulness of hope that our Father in Heaven had from her (regarding the fulfillment of His expectations) was not realized, for he hoped to produce grapes and instead he produced spoilt fruit, nevertheless, many nations have joined us in the faith of God and His goodness, as most nations believe in Him, may He be blessed, and in the stories of the Holy Torah, for our life and continued existence testify to their veracity. There is no doubt in my mind, that this is the intention of the saying of our sages, "The Holy One, blessed be He, did not exile Israel among the nations save in order that proselytes might join them, for it is said: And I will sow her unto Me in the land" (Pesachim 87b), meaning, that although the nations did not convert and become part of Israel, nevertheless, they have the status of a resident alien, since they do not worship idols. All this came about as a result of our exile and dispersion throughout all the corners of the earth.[32]

This author too sees Israel's charge in active missionary terms. It has the responsibility of making God and His providence known to all nations. Israel is described as an intermediary, but its function as an intermediary is directed from God to humanity in a teaching capacity. The classical verses describing Israel's ideal vocation are enlisted to make the point. Israel is considered to have succeeded in fulfilling this vocation. This has been made possible precisely due to Israel's exile. In fact, as the continuation of this passage suggests, Israel has succeeded in this task more than

---

32 R. Yosef Kara, *Solet Lemincha*, Avot, 1847, ch. 1, 9–10.

it has in the charge of being faithful to God and His commandments. The talmudic statement that sees converts as the purpose of exile is reread by him. Rather than focus upon converts to Israel, the author employs the category of another kind of convert, the *ger toshav*, a kind of half convert who is removed from idolatry, while not fully entering Israel, to describe the religious reality of other religions that teach the same God, share the same story, but nevertheless have not become part of Israel. Israel's exile is thus for the sake of other peoples and other religions, reread as a type of convert to truth, through whom Israel's vocation is fulfilled in exile.

It is worth juxtaposing this positive view of exile, with an alternative view, that considers exile an impediment to the fulfillment of the command to be a Kingdom of Priests.

> The purpose for which God chose the Jewish nation is not just realized within themselves, but rather, "you shall be to Me a Kingdom of Priests and a holy nation" (Exodus 19:6) to instruct the nations of the earth in the ways of God, "and nations shall walk by your light" (Isaiah 60:3). However, this is only possible at a time when God has exalted the horn of His people and there is glory for all His faithful ones (cf. Psalms 148:14). At that time, nations will come and cleave to the House of Jacob (cf. Isaiah 14:1). This is not the case when Jacob is subjected to plunder and Israel to despoilment (cf. Isaiah 42:24). The upshot of this is that the destruction of our Holy Land affects the entire world. However, when the time will come that the will shall arise before the Throne of His Glory (i.e. when it will be God's will) that all the inhabitants of the globe shall recognize and acknowledge their creator and maker, at that time, "the Lord's house shall be firmly established at the top of the mountains, and it shall be raised above the hills, and all the nations shall stream to it" (Isaiah 2:2).[33]

This passage is by a nineteenth-century Hungarian rabbi. The purpose of election is for the sake of humanity and Israel are a nation of teachers. However, they cannot fulfill their destiny under conditions of exile. One's status must be more elevated if one is to serve as teacher and inspiration to others. The destruction of the Land of Israel is thus of universal significance, as Israel's progress, along with that of the rest of humanity, is impeded until the messianic future. The demand to be a Kingdom of Priests

---

33 Rabbi Feivel Floit, Eulogy for Rabbi Abraham Sofer, *Zekhor LeAvraham: On the Occasion of 100 Years of the Passing of Rabbi Abraham Sofer* (Jerusalem, 1972), 301 [Hebrew].

and the fulfillment of Israel's vocation must thus await the future fulfillment of the *eschaton*.

A similar understanding of exile and how it impedes Israel's fulfillment of its task is echoed in the following text. However, this text is composed in Israel, following its establishment. We do not find the theology of Israel's mission and the assessment of its condition in the present historical moment changed as a consequence of the recent declaration of Israel's independence.

> And so we say to Hashem, may He be blessed, didn't You promise us, "And they shall be unto me a Kingdom of Priests" (Exodus 19:6), (this means) that we will not be poor priests but rather a priestly kingdom of leaders and rulers of the highest stature. In such circumstances, we can definitely have an influence on the world. However, this is not possible now that we stand as paupers and are an object of scorn and mockery among the nations, (sadly proclaiming) what are we? What is our glory? Therefore our Father, our King (we beseech you to) shine upon us the light of Your face to uplift and elevate us, so that the nations will behold our glory and they will all go to the House of the Lord and learn our good ways.[34]

Until we have achieved a measure of dignity and respect in the eyes of others, we cannot fulfill our ultimate spiritual vocation as humanity's teachers. Because the interpretive tradition considers Kingdom of Priests as a point of encounter between Israel and the nations, taking stock of historical circumstances is inevitable, either in affirming Israel's successful realization of this command, or conversely in justifying its inability to live up to the task. Framing the issue in these terms raises in even clearer terms the challenge for today, when this idea can be studied from the safety and framework of the State of Israel. Is there more respect for Israel, and is this the moment when Israel can fulfill its vocation to be a Kingdom of Priests? Is Israel, the state, able to live up to this ideal, or at the very least provide a framework for those who seek to fulfill it to do so?

Comprehensive Appeal to Kingdom of Priests—Rabbi S. R. Hirsch and Rabbi A. I. Kook

There are two teachers for whom the notion of Kingdom of Priests seems to have played a very significant role. The term is cited with greater frequency

---

34 Rabbi Levi Yitzhak Derbermediger, *Lenefesh Chaya* (Tel Aviv, 1960), 157.

than is common in the literature and the lessons derived from it are varied. The dynamism, relative breadth and variety suggest how central the notion is. Very often Kingdom of Priests serves as a default designation for Israel. The two teachers are Rabbis Samson Raphael Hirsch and Abraham Isaac Kook. If the former appeals to the term thirty times and more in the course of his writing, the latter doubles the number, indicating how central the notion is for his reflection on Israel. Both teachers basically ascribe the same meaning, or range of meanings, to the term. Both of them associate it with Israel's ideal of teaching to the nations and with Israel's serving as a model for an ideal religious community and an ideal society.[35] Both grow out of the Ashkenazi tradition of the nineteenth and twentieth century, that ascribed much importance to Exodus 19:6, as it sought to articulate Israel's responsibility to the nations. Given the significant overlap, it is possible that Rabbi Hirsch exerted an influence on Rav Kook, who was familiar with the former's writing.[36] At the very least, we can affirm that both thinkers belonged to the same interpretive and theoretical tradition, in framing Israel's own task in relation to the nations in terms of a Kingdom of Priests.

Against this broad commonality, it is interesting to consider the very different circumstances under which the two were writing. If Rabbi Hirsch was formulating an ethos for Jews living in exile, seeking to be integrated into broader society while affirming their own collective value, Rav Kook sought to articulate the meaning of Israel's particularity and mission in the framework of Israel's revival on the international stage, in the context of his view of history and metaphysics and the role Israel played in it. Despite the different contexts, the challenge is quite similar—identifying the meaning of Israel's vocation in a broader framework. That both teachers make similar moves suggests how Kingdom of Priests can be developed, if we seek to make it a cornerstone of a vision of (contemporary) Israel. At the same time, some fundamental differences illustrate the different theologies, and these in turn are also relevant for the challenges of a contemporary application of Kingdom of Priests.

As stated, the greatest commonality between these two figures is the consistent reference to Israel and its vocation in terms of a Kingdom of

---

35 Rav Kook also relates the term to dimensions of Israel's being that can be understood independently of its mission to the nations. See *Shmona Kevazim* 7:291.
36 For positive appreciation of Rabbi Hirsch in Rav Kook's letters see *Igrot Reaya* 1:144, 2:363 and more. In the first source Rav Kook refers to himself as engaging in the same project as Rabbi Hirsch, except under different circumstances.

Priests. The quantitative dimension translates to a deepening of understanding. As far as I have been able to identify, this conceptual centrality is unique to these two authors. Both specify that the ideal of a Kingdom of Priests should extend to the life of the individual and form part of his aspirations and not be limited to the collective.[37] It seems there is a correlation. Extensive usage of Exodus 19:6 leads to the formulation of an ideal which is then implemented in the life of each and every individual.[38]

Rabbi Hirsch's commentary on Exodus 19:6 is foundational:

> And you shall be unto Me—for the selfsame purpose of "the entire earth"—A Kingdom of Priests and a holy nation.[39]
>
> A Kingdom of Priests—each and every one of you will be a priest, by accepting upon himself my kingdom, in every deed he does, and by accepting upon himself the yoke of the kingdom of heaven and realizing it, and spreading the knowledge of God and submission to Him, through his speech and the example of his deeds. And so Isaiah states "And you shall be called priests of God, servants of our Lord" (Isa. 61:6).

---

37 One would think that hasidic authors would have made the same point. I was surprised to learn that not a single one of the nearly four hundred hasidic texts that engage Exodus 19:6, consulted using the DBS database, makes a similar move. While many of them do extend the implications of Kingdom of Priests to the individual, they do so as some alternative spiritual lesson, rather than as part of a conscious aspiration for realizing priesthood in relation to the individual. For example, each individual must accept the yoke of Heaven (*Bat Ayin*, Shavuot); individual self-control (*Shem Mishemuel*, Yitro, 1913). The great exception to this characteristic of hasidic literature is the Habad school and in particular the Lubavitcher Rebbe, who will be studied below.

38 Indeed, from the said survey of hasidic texts one can conclude that Kingdom of Priests is not an ideal. Discussions of it do not take place outside the immediate interpretive context, which requires some kind of commentary and understanding. Whatever that understanding is it does not function as a major force in shaping religious thought with reference to Israel. The reason is obvious. Kingdom of Priests gains prominence where Israel are viewed in social and political contexts involving relations with the nations, in ways other than a contrast.to the detriment of the latter. Hasidic literature has other ways in which it features Israel's significance, and these do not include an active mission or understanding Israel's purpose in relation to the nations. The sociological context of Eastern Europe, and the broader positioning of the hasidic movement that does not seek integration nor sees Israel's purpose in relation to the nations, make the appeal to Exodus 19:6 unnecessary.

39 Reference to Exodus 19:5, where, in Hirsch's reading, God seeks to educate all people and nations to be his. The thematic juxtaposition thus suggests that Israel's purpose as a Kingdom of Priests is for the sake of all of humanity. Rav Kook offers basically the same understanding of the verse in his *Midbar Shur* (Jerusalem, 1999), 312–13.

A holy nation—Just as within each and every one of you will be a priest, so the appearance of your collective facing outward will be an appearance of sanctity for God. One single and unique nation among the nations, that does not live for its own glory, greatness and splendour, but in order to establish the kingdom of God and its glory upon earth. This people will not seek greatness in its power, but in the absolute rule of the divine law-morality, and this is the meaning of holiness.[40]

Two main points emerge from Hirsch's commentary on the verse. Kingdom of Priests is core to Israel's vocation and it relates to the nations and the testimony that is brought by each and every individual who is himself a priest. The tradition of sharing teaching with the nations is augmented by appeal to the yoke of God's kingdom, apparently in order to make sense of the combination of kingdom and priesthood, with the latter component pointing to the mission of spreading and teaching God's teaching. While the reference to Kingdom of Priests seemed to be geared inward, the latter part of the verse, relating to a holy nation, seems to focus the meaning of Kingdom of Priests externally, with "holy nation" delivering the same message with reference to the collective and its relation to the nations. Perhaps Rabbi Hirsch creates an amalgam between the missionary understanding of Exodus 19:6 and the inward facing understanding. This amalgam, created for the sake of juxtaposing the two parts of the verse, accounts for the duality of his interpretation of Kingdom of Priests. It makes sense to distinguish between the individual priestly impact facing within while the outward-facing impact belongs to the entire people. While in context the juxtaposition of Kingdom of Priests and holy nation works well as a distinction between internal and external projection, in fact the very understanding of Kingdom of Priests is already indebted to the missionary and outward facing understanding of the verse. The continuity between verses 5 and 6 further points to the understanding of Kingdom of Priests as relating to the nations. The fluidity in understanding between internal and external perspectives suggests a twofold dimension of realization, that can be pitched either way, depending on the interpretive context.[41]

---

40 My translation from the Hebrew.
41 This fluidity accounts for the alternative reading, offered by Hirsch in *Horeb*.

> As the priest among the people, so should they among mankind uphold the vision of God and humanity and by so doing be a holy nation, raised above every injustice, profaneness and hardheartedness, as becomes the bearers of such a message.

The two components of the verse are seen as a continuum, rather than juxtaposed with one

Returning to the extension of Kingdom of Priests to the individual, Hirsch can speak of an individual member of Israel sanctifying his entire personality to aspirations of and to a life of priesthood, as befits a member of a Kingdom of Priests.[42] Every person has *tchelet* (azure) on his *zizit*, as a reminder of his being a priest, azure being the color of the high priest.[43] Seen from the other perspective, the high priest himself is a representative of the Kingdom of Priests, serving as sign and model for the entire people.[44]

Let us consider the same motif in the teachings of Rav Kook:

> Just as the general priest within the people of God has been prepared in order to teach the Lord's commandments and laws, to manifest concretely the substance of a pure and holy life, in order to be a model for the entire people, so there is in every individual in Israel a dimension of priesthood, because in their collectivity they are a nation of priests and a holy people. The inner desire for the holiness of life and for the knowledge of Torah and going in its ways is hidden in the depth of the Israelite heart. And we have already explained regarding the purpose of the second tithe (*ma'aser sheni*), that is eaten by the owner[45] that it comes to awaken the foundation of essential priesthood, that is admixed in the soul of every person in Israel.[46]

The designation is more than metaphoric. It relates to a specific aspect of each individual Israelite. Multiple dimensions intersect in the definition of priesthood. They include the teaching vocation that we have seen, but also relate to the quality of a pure and holy life and to being a model for others. Rav Kook moves from action to the interior life—the inner desire, the depth of the heart and the soul of the Israelite. There is thus an important added dimension in Rav Kook's teaching, compared to that of Rabbi Hirsch. Where the latter relates to Kingdom of Priests in a behavioral way, seeking to create an ideal society, for Rav Kook the designation is essential. It describes part of the being of the Israelite, his heart and more importantly his soul. In this reading, Kingdom of Priests seems to be a description of

---

another. The same is actually true of the commentary on Exodus, and this accounts for the slight inconsistency. See Hirsch, *Horeb: A Philosophy of Jewish Laws and Observances* (London: Soncino, 1962), 465.

42 Commentary to Lev. 19:23.
43 Samson Raphael Hirsch, *Hamitzvot Kisemalim* (Jerusalem: Mossad Harav Kook, 1997), 92.
44 Commentary to Lev. 21:10–12.
45 Making this an offering that is eaten by an Israelite, and not by a priest.
46 *Ein Aya Shabbat* I:65 on Shabbat 21a.

soul. The collective designation of a special soul then extends to the individual, who partakes of that special priestly reality as a characteristic of heart and soul. The designation of a Kingdom of Priests therefore describes a mission of teaching, but even more so a dimension of being.[47]

Like Rabbi Hirsch, Rav Kook extends the significance of Exodus 19:6. However, true to his soul-orientation and perspective, he considers the meaning of this attribute not only in terms of mission and action, but in terms of heart, soul and being. This suggests a significant difference between the two authors. If for Rabbi Hirsch, it is possible to speak of some periods when Israel was not/did not realize its calling as a Kingdom of Priests, for Rav Kook the designation seems to be essential, rising above the vicissitudes of Israel's behavior.[48]

The potential conflict between inward facing and outward facing values and how these relate to the two parts of our term is worked out in different ways also in the writings of Rav Kook. The key to reconciling competing formulations may lie in Rav Kook's recognition that "Israel has a twofold purpose, following God's will, and both are included in the two designations by means of which we were described by our heavenly father at the time of giving the Torah—A Kingdom of Priests and a holy nation."[49] The twofold purpose relates to Israel's value in and of itself, to attain perfection in their relationship with God, and to their mission of teaching the nations. The key to conflicting readings of Exodus 19:6 lies in a twofold mission, that can itself be variously pitched in relation to the two key terms. In some places, Rav Kook states that the value of Israel's own spiritual status and attainment is greater than the value of bringing others to their perfection.[50] In other passages a distinction is drawn between different time periods—the Exodus and the messianic future, with Israel's purpose shifting from self-perfection to the perfection of others.[51]

While sharing the same broad interpretive tradition, struggling with the same questions and making similar moves, there are several factors that distinguish Rav Kook's perspective. The first is the concern for Israel's own

---

47 The soul dimension is relevant also for a view of Israel among the nations. Kingdom of Priests can be one way of recognizing Israel's true being and its relation to humanity as soul to body. See *Shemona Kevatzim* 7:169.
48 For Kingdom of Priests as a designation of some periods and not others in Rabbi Hirsch's teaching, see commentary to Lev. 1:5.
49 *Midbar Shur*, loc. cit.
50 *Ibid.* 313.
51 *Meorot reaya, geulat mizrayim ugeula haatida.*

status. While Rabbi Hirsch is concerned with the internal realization of Israel's obligations, he does not exhibit the same concern for Israel's status in and of itself. Rav Kook has a much higher "Israelology."[52] This corresponds to Rav Kook relating not only to actions and to mission but also to being. This concern for Israel's very being, their soul, conditions his overall approach. It is telling how this dimension seems to push his interpretation away from the interpretive baseline that he shared with Rabbi Hirsch. The more common understanding shared by both, which grows out of the said Ashkenazi tradition, understands Kingdom of Priests as a mission to the nations. That this mission also implies Israel's holiness does not in and of itself entail an essentialist view of Israel's status. This is certainly the case for Rabbi Hirsch, and it can be seen in Rav Kook also in statements such as: "And you shall be unto me a Kingdom of Priests and a holy nation—exalted teachers and guides for the entire world, holy in their exterior and interior life, private and collective."[53] Such a formulation is close to that of Hirsch's commentary to Exodus 19:6, and it sees holiness as an extension or a complement to the first part of the verse.

Given the potential, recognized by Rav Kook, for shifting interpretations of these two components of the verse, it is important to note the departure from this baseline interpretation and how concerns for Israel's status and a high "Israelology" lead to a reversal of meaning in the following striking passage.

> The highest most secret knowledge is not destined to spread in the world in a quantitative way, so that many will come to know it, for that is an impossible matter. . . . However it should penetrate all those in whom is found a lofty quality of high contemplation. And these individuals, in their spiritual heights, elevate the world from its baseness through their very being, not through their recognizable influence. The interior secrets they do not reveal and cannot reveal. But what the great light causes in essence in all its force, through the spreading of its sparks also upon all that is revealed. . . .
>
> Also the general intention (or: tendency) of Israel's influence in the world is not the spreading of knowledge of proper religious teachings,[54] by means of teaching and the simple and manifest influence. But when this

---

52 A neologism that seeks to parallel ecclesiology.
53 *Ein Aya Shabbat II*:171 to Shabbat 86b.
54 Literally: opinions. The term harks back to *emunot ve'deot* as a medieval term for proper religious teaching.

nation holds its special essence well within itself, the entire world is already elevated, by virtue of having such special interior essence (*segula*) in the treasure of humanity.[55]

The acts and directives envisioned by the prophets are on a lower level relative to the higher level of interior activity. Whereas the unclear prophecy[56] says "many nations shall say Let us go and rise to the mount of the Lord and to the house of the Lord of Jacob and He will teach us of his ways and we shall walk His paths, for from Zion Torah will come forth and the word of God from Jerusalem" (Isa. 2:3), which suggests a degree of activity that is recognizable, which is the second degree, the clear prophecy, which is the Torah of Moses, states: "If you listen to my voice and observe my covenant, and you shall be unto me a treasure from all the people, for the entire earth is mine, and you shall be unto me a Kingdom of Priests and a holy nation, these are the words you shall speak to the children of Israel." (Exodus 19:5–6)[57]

Unlike many of the other texts we have seen that appear as commentaries or public facing essays, this text is taken from Rav Kook's mystical diaries, that may have never been intended for publication. These diaries are marked by a strong appeal to his mystical experience and approach. This is particularly relevant to the present text. Its starting point contrasts outward teaching with mystical teachings. The latter is beneficial not because of the knowledge it spreads, but because of the being an energy is disseminated by masters of the secret knowledge. As such, they are higher. As such they are higher, even if many are unaware of their beneficial impact on the world. The same is true of Israel. Israel, in this reflection, are the world's secret, spreading their light to the world, by virtue of their being. We note here the concern for being vs. action and teaching. Israel are still for the nations, but their influence is mystical, rather than practical. Rav Kook is not removing Israel from their task as teachers. Rather, he is raising them to a higher position in the hierarchy of teaching, corresponding to the teaching of the secrets of Torah, that influence by emanation, rather than by understanding. In a rendition of Exodus 19, Rav Kook highlights the word *segula*, special attribute, unique essence, special treasure, all of which refer to Israel's very being, if it lives its true essence properly, in accordance with its destiny. In this reading, "Kingdom of Priests" is reconfigured to represent the hidden

---

55 In other words—by virtue of the fact that Israel, this special treasure, is part of humanity.
56 That of other prophets, except for Moses.
57 *Shmona Kevazim* 1:253.

influence Israel has. Unlike the emphasis of Hirsch on internal vs. external perfection, Rav Kook contrasts hidden and visible impact. Kingdom of Priests retains its meaning in relation to the nation, but is understood as a radiation of being, rather than a dissemination of teaching. That view of Israel's vocation as teachers is relegated to a lower level, corresponding to the lower level of other prophets in relation to Moses. By contrasting other prophets and Moses and contrasting the external and secret dimensions of Torah, Rav Kook privileges the hidden impact of the *segula* upon any active engagement in teaching. We see here the genius of Rav Kook and how he is able to transform an interpretive tradition, to which he himself belongs, in light of an interior mystical vision, and how he buttresses this view with associations that justify it.

There is a third dimension that distinguishes Rav Kook from Rabbi Hirsch. It relates to their context and to their conceptualization. Rabbi Hirsch seeks to provide meaning for Judaism in the framework of broader German society, with full awareness of engagement, vision, and mission as these relate to the nations. Rav Kook is a thinker of Israel's redemption in Israel. The vision he offers is therefore the foundation for a people rebuilding itself in the land. He is not oblivious to the relationship between being a Kingdom of Priests and the concrete efforts at rebuilding a kingdom as part of contemporary nationalist movement. In this context, a Kingdom of Priests suggests something of the collective, beyond individual holiness.[58]

To speak of a Kingdom of Priests also points to Rav Kook's messianic concerns. Accordingly, Rav Kook not only sees in Kingdom of Priests a definition of Israel's vocation, but also a dimension of messianic fulfillment. Only in the messianic future will Israel be truly a Kingdom of Priests.[59]

Rav Kook is the great synthesizer. His appeal to Kingdom of Priests includes essence and manifestation, Israel's status and vocation, corresponding to the two fundamental interpretive strategies. It includes a view of the present, with Israel as Kingdom of Priests in their being, but also a vision of the future, where the priestly vocation will be realized. This view incorporates a strand of thinking that we have ignored thus far and to which we now turn.

---

58 See *Ma'amarei Reayah*, Jerusalem, 1984, 174-75.
59 For the association of Kingdom of Priests with Israel's return and with messianic processes see *Shemona Kevazim* 7:45, *Ein Aya Berachot* I:68.

Interior Impact and Elevation—The Mystical Tradition

It would be a mistake to consider the only two options for interpreting Kingdom of Priests as praise of Israel or Israel's mission to the nations. Rav Kook has shown us that influence may be active, as in a teaching vocation, or more hidden, a function of being, a transfer of energy and being. Rav Kook combines both dimensions and in so doing draws on and synthesizes two schools of thought. The philosophical orientation is more outward, emphasizing teaching. By contrast, the mystical tradition—Kabbalah and Hasidism, reflects an interior orientation, that shows far less concern for Israel's relations with the nations. The majority of views articulated in this school do not consider the nations as recipients of what Israel has to give, as a Kingdom of Priests. However, even within this tradition, we find various articulations of what it means to be Israel as a Kingdom of Priests that are relevant to Israel and its relations to the nations. Here too, this emphasis will come to light under particular historical circumstances that invite reflection on Israel as a people in relation to others.

A wonderful illustration of the inward looking approach as the opposite of the missionary perspective is found in R. Levi Yitzhak of Berdichev's *Kedushat Levi* to Exodus 19:5-6. On Israel being a treasure among the nations, he makes the following observation: "It should have said: you should be a treasure to me more than all the angels, for when we do God's will, we are on a higher level than the angels!" Israel should be contrasted with the angels, their natural counterpart, not the nations. The axis of comparsion is not horizontal—Israel vs. the nations, but vertical—Israel vs. the angels. This continues the trajectory of reading the verse as an expression of honor for Israel. Here this honor is contextualized in the view that Israel have the power to act on high. Accordingly, A Kingdom of Priests is understood as the power that Israel have to annul negative and harmful decrees. Israel's status is not simply a matter of honor, but of power. The implications of the power do not extend to the nations. However, as we shall shortly see, the theurgic way of thinking can readily open up to a view of Israel's impact on the nations by means other than a teaching vocation.

The most popular Torah commentary among hasidim is R. Chaim ibn Atar's (eighteenth c.) *Or Hachayim*. His commentary to Exodus 19:6 suggests how little currency the verse has for kabbalistically oriented readers. His first commentary suggests that the recipients of the promise are Moses and Aharon, not all of Israel, thereby affirming Moses and Aharon's continuing superior status, compared to Israel. This commentary totally does away with Kingdom of Priests as a designation of Israel and their value. However, he also offers alternative readings. One of them is in line with R. Levi Yitzhak's query. Israel, rather than the angels, is to be the Kingdom of Priests. The third commentary is closer to our concerns. Israel elevate sparks of divinity that are cast throughout creation, in accordance with kabbalistic teaching. They have authority, power, and kingship over the beings whom they elevate. The view is cosmic, and to a large extent obscures the universalist perspective of the missionary school. Israel acts upon the cosmos by its being and by fulfillment of the commandments, not by actively seeking to transform society and the world around it. Nevertheless, if the second commentary is vertical, the third is horizontal and has some significant overlap with the orientation of the missionary understanding. Israel as Kingdom of Priets impacts other beings and other parts of reality.

This provides us with an introduction to an amazing configuration of Kingdom of Priests by a twentieth-century kabbalist. In this configuration, the mystical raising of sparks and the universal vision to the nations combine. Moreover, more than a passing gloss on a verse, what follows represents a major theological statement of what could be meant by Kingdom of Priests. If the notion rises to such prominence, especially within the kabbalistic tradition, this is best accounted for by an awareness of the times, their challenge and opportunities. Once again, Kingdom of Priests is revealed in its fullness as circumstances invite and permit.

The following early twentieth-century appeal to Kingdom of Priests was formulated in inter-war Israel, with conscious awareness of the circumstances of the time and in dialogue with contemporary socialist idealism. The following teaching of Rabbi Yehuda Leib Ashlag not only contextualizes the meaning of Kingdom of Priests as part of an invitation to construct an ideal spiritual society. Ashlag offers an original and comprehensive picture of what it means to be a Kingdom of Priests, following his own social vision of collaborative and selfless living. Israel are to live as a Kingdom of Priests: a model for a higher form of living, that will transform the nations spiritually by extending the power and spiritual light they have attained to others. Israel serves as a model and a paradigm to the nations, who are destined to attain the same spiritual heights. Ashlag portrays Israel as more than teachers and role models to humanity, and integrates the teaching-based view of Israel's vocation with a kabbalistic understanding of mediating energy, bounty, and blessing.[60]

> A Kingdom of Priests means that all of you, from youngest to oldest, will be like priests. Just as the priests have no land or any corporeal possessions because the Creator is their domain, so will the entire nation be organized so that the whole earth and everything in it will be dedicated to the Creator only. And no person should have any other engagement in it but to keep the mitzvot of the Creator and to satisfy the needs of his fellow person. Thus he will lack none of his wishes, so that no person will need to have any worry about himself. This way, even mundane works such as harvesting, sowing, etc. are considered to be precisely like the work with the sacrifices that the priests performed in the Temple. How is it different if I keep the mitzva of making sacrifices to the Creator, which is a positive mitzva, or if I can keep the positive mitzva, "Love thy friend as thyself"? It turns out that he who harvests his field in order to feed his fellow person is the same as he who sacrifices to the Creator. Moreover, it seems that the mitzva, "Love thy friend as thyself," is more important than he who makes the sacrifice....
>
> And you can see that in the words "Kingdom of Priests" comes to expression the entire form of service on the pole of "love they friend as thyself." That is—a kingdom made up entirely of priests, for whom God is their lot, and they have no self-possession of all material possessions. And we are forced to admit that this is the only possible definition that one may understand regarding this Kingdom of Priests. Because we cannot interpret it with reference to offering sacrifices on the altar, for this may not be said with reference to the entire nation.... Similarly with reference to receiving priestly gifts, who will be giving them? And also to interpret it with reference to the holiness of priests [is not possible], for it already states "holy nation."[61] So perforce, the meaning of the matter is that God is their lot, that they lack any material possession for themselves, and this is the measure (or: lesson) of love thy friend as thyself, that encompasses the entire Torah.
>
> Now we fully understand the previous words, for he says, "Now therefore, if ye will hearken unto My voice indeed, and keep My covenant," meaning make a covenant on what I am telling you here, that ye shall be

---

60 Rabbi Gottlieb (Rabbi Yehuda Leib Aschlag, *Sefer Matan Torah*, with comments by Avraham Mordechai Gottlieb, Bene Berak, Or Baruch Shalom [2007], 107n122) suggests Rabbi Ashlag's views are synthetic and include teaching-based (Hirsch) views as well as the understanding (not referenced) of Israel's priestly vocation as blessing humanity.
61 And one cannot assume both expressions mean the same.

Mine own treasure from among all peoples. This means that you will be My treasure, and sparks of purification and cleansing of the body shall pass through you onto all the peoples and the nations of the world, for the nations of the world are not yet ready for it. And at any rate, I need one nation to start with now, so it will be as a remedy for all the nations. And therefore he ends, "for all the earth is Mine," meaning all the peoples of the earth belong to Me, as do you, and are destined to cleave to Me. But now, while they are still incapable of performing that task, I need a virtuous people. And if you agree to be the remedy for all the nations, I command you to "be unto Me a Kingdom of Priests," which is the love of others in its final form of "Love thy friend as thyself," which is the axis of all the Torah and Mitzvot.[62]

This is an outstanding text. This is perhaps the most explicit attempt in the literature to articulate the point of the comparison with priests and to give it meaning. Rabbi Ashlag rejects various possible meanings that would make the point of comparison too literal, and prefers instead the sense of total offering of love, made by the priest on behalf of others. The priest is the model for total dedication to service and love of the other, in all aspects of life. Implicitly appealing to Maimonides, Laws of Shemita and Yovel 13:13, Ashlag highlights the fact that priests do not own property. They have no share in physicality, represented by inheritance of the land. God is their share. A priest is someone dedicated exclusively to God. Such dedication is mirrored by selfless service and loving actions to the other. Seeking to fulfill the other's needs, priests ground their awareness in God and in the other, but not in themselves.

Israel are priests through their spiritual achievement. Any action carried out with selfless intention, in the service of God and the other is a priestly action. Israel are a Kingdom of Priests because all their actions are supposed to be carried out with such high priestly intentions. This is a universal vision and all nations are to attain it. However, the nations are not ready, and Israel is asked to serve as the harbinger, through whom the rest of the world will attain the same spiritual heights. Israel's service is not only a model, but actually transmits purifying energy to the nations of the world, who slowly advance towards this ultimate goal of universal service of God.

---

62 This is taken from an essay titled "*Haarvut*," meaning mutual responsibility and vouchsafing, included in the volume *Matan Torah* (Bene Berak, 2008), 106–7. The essay appeared first in 1933. English translation in part based on *Kabbalah for the Student*, trans. Michael Laitman (Toronto, 2008), 258–59.

The characteristic of priesthood is total love. While in all likelihood Ashlag describes such total love as taking place within the Kingdom of Priests, the overall structure of his thought suggests that this love extends from Israel to the nations. As the goal of Israel's election is to help advance humanity, and as advancement is in selfless love, it seems that all of humanity is included in the priestly vocation of selfless love.

This text was authored in the 1930s as a Jewish society in the land of Israel was forming. It is clearly part of an attempt to formulate an ethos for the society in formation. Reading this text nearly one hundred years later, from the vantage point of more than seventy years since the foundation of the State of Israel, poses the question of how close or far we have come to realizing this ideal of a Kingdom of Priests. The notion, for Rabbi Ashlag, is based on altruism, lack of possession and the quest to express love and service to all in all actions. It is sad to consider how far we are from realizing the kind of vision expressed here. If for R. Kara cited above, successful fulfillment of Israel's priestly teaching vocation compensates for their own failures in other domains, the high bar of priesthood projected by Rabbi Ashlag leads to a negative view of present-day reality, which in turn casts doubt on the possibility of realizing a vision of such high aspiration. Unlike the prayerful demands of Rabbi Dermediger, of reestablishing Israel in its home, shortly after the establishment of the state, in Rabbi Ashlag's works we realize that simply removing the obstacles of *galut* are not sufficient. Until Israel achieves this great spiritual height, it cannot be a Kingdom of Priests.

Hasidic Appeal to Kingdom of Priests

The theurgic dimension of Kingdom of Priests is representative of the kabbalistic approach. Hasidism is less theurgic and tends to focus more on the personal experience and transformation of the individual. Coupled with its overall interior social orientation that does not advocate for active contact and outreach beyond the community of the faithful, we can expect to find little development of Kingdom of Priests in hasidic literature. As noted above, several hasidic authors pick up on the comment of the *Ba'al Haturim*, according to which Kingdom of Priests is an eschatological reality and not part of present day understanding of being Israel. It is only in the framework of commenting on earlier sources, that profile the term as an honorific, that hasidic understandings emerge that profile virtues such as self control.

Against this background, I would like to introduce two hasidic authors for whom Kingdom of Priests is significant. The first is Rabbi Yaakov Friedman, in his *Oholey Yaakov*.[63] Rabbi Friedman was grand rabbi of the Husyatin dynasty, one of the offshoots of Rizhin. He is known for his expansive horizons and more particularly for his support of the Zionist movement. Rabbi Friedman lived through World War II and through the founding of the State of Israel. Reading his sermons offers us a window on to how a thoughtful religious personality lives historical transitions with deep faith and spiritual vision.[64] While his hasidic teachings typically follow classical hasidic emphases, seeking to elevate the awareness and feeling of the individual, we find in his work also a strong collective awareness. This relates to the state under formation, the attitude of the world's nations to it and its long term aspirations and responsibilities. In this context, it is striking to find Seforno echoed time and again. In fact, as far as my searches reveal, Rabbi Friedman is the only author to echo the Seforno on Kingdom of Priests in any way. This singular appeal must be credited to the historical circumstances of reestablishing a "Kingdom," for which Seforno provides theoretical foundations. Rabbi Friedman quotes Seforno on Exodus 19:6 as a current vision for Judaism and, in the broader context of his thinking, for the emerging state. Any doubts we may have had regarding the applicability of Seforno during the interim period between Sinai and Messiah appear to have not troubled him. The vision of a Kingdom of Priests is relevant and contemporary circumstances bring the potential of this notion to the forefront.

There is one important difference between Seforno and *Oholey Ya'akov*, and here Rabbi Friedman upholds a view similar to that of Rav Kook.[65] As noted, Seforno does not assume any fundamental distinction between Israel and the nations. The difference is, as we suggested, quantitative. A hasidic author cannot uphold such a view. Therefore, alongside affirmation of Israel's calling as a Kingdom of Priests teaching the nations, he also affirms the enduring additional value that Israel will have over the nations. To make the point, he stands Seforno's argument on its head. Reference to a future priestly status is proof of the special status that Israel will enjoy in

---

63 Tel Aviv 1962 and 1984.
64 See Yehuda Brandes, *In the Kingdom of Holiness: A Visit to the Palace of the Rebbe of Husiyatin—A Zionist Rebbe in Tel Aviv* (Tevunot: Alon Shevut, 2006) [Hebrew].
65 I have not been able to find any reference of Rabbi Friedman to Rav Kook, even though his writings would have been available to him.

the future. Combining the views of *Ba'al Haturim* and of Seforno into one eschatological affirmation, he deduces from this eschatological perspective that Israel's special status will endure in the *eschaton*, even once their teaching vocation has been successfully fulfilled.[66]

The way Rabbi Friedman understands Ex. 19,6 is less theological and more moral. We must perfect ourself morally, not only for our own sake, but also for the sake of the nations, for whom we serve as a model.[67] Conceptually, this is close to the notion of Kiddush Hashem that we also saw in Seforno, where Israel's perfect moral behavior becomes basis for appreciation by others and invitation for them to follow suit. Reading the Seforno, and unlike Seforno's own focus, he emphasizes that teaching does not take place through words, but through actions. Our actions must serve as a model for others, thereby fulfilling our vocation of teaching the nations. In this way, he is able to provide an ethos for the emerging nation. Its goal is not to set up active teaching for the nations. Rather, its entire being, expressed in its actions, is a form of teaching the nations. "Your way of living in your kingdom shall be so holy and pure, so full of morality and justice, that you shall serve as a model and guide for other nations."[68]

The second hasidic author to draw heavily on Exodus 19:6 is Rabbi Menachem Mendel Schneerson, the late Lubavitcher Rebbe. It is beyond the scope of the present study to enter into detailed analysis of the dozens of references to Ex. 19,6 in his vast corpus of teachings. The Rebbe does not seem to have initiated the appeal to the concept. It seems to have a significant history, beginning with the Alter Rebbe, and continuing with the Middle Rebbe.[69] The frequency of the Rebbe's usage therefore has to be understood as an expression of the particularity of this hasidic lineage. Even though the Rebbe has a broad universal vision, unlike many hasidic authors, and even though he actively engaged in projects of outreach to the nations, it does not seem that these were inspired by Exodus 19:6. Moreover, even though the Rebbe had strong interest in the State of Israel, its course and policies, this contemporary context does not seem to drive the appeal to Kingdom of Priests. In other words, if throughout this essay we noted that rise in appeal to Exodus 19:6 is related to concern with contermporary

---

66 Part I, p. 313.
67 P. 155.
68 P. 312.
69 For a theurgic understanding of Israel's performance of mitzvot as benefiting the nations, see *Ma'amaerei Admor Haemtzai* (N. Y, 1986) and Bemidbar, p. 122.

historical realities and Israel's contribution to them, this does not seem to be the case for the Rebbe. His use is to be understood as interior to the particular school he represents.

The Rebbe's usage is best characterized as a continuation of the honorific tradition,[70] applied individually and used as a means of inspiring to further spiritual advancement. Preaching the value of each and every individual Jew is a fundamental message of Hasidism and a hallmark of the teaching of the Rebbe. If reference to Kingdom of Priests is already established in the Habad lineage, the Rebbe seems to make several important advances in its application. Basing himself on the *Ba'al Haturim*, he affirms that priests means high priests.[71] Reading the Lubavitcher's homilies we would not know that the *Ba'al Haturim* has deferred this status to the future. The Rebbe takes from *Ba'al Haturim* the affirmation of high priestly status and considers it an ongoing feature of being Israel. Moreover, much as Rav Kook and Rabbi Hirsch did,[72] he extends it to every individual.[73] This yields the statement that each individual Jew is like a high priest. The foundations of the claim are honorific. However, the Rebbe turns it into a demand for action and a call to rise to the designation. For every Jew to be a priest, even more so—a high priest, is a call to be consumed by the idea that in all his actions and in all his being a person serves God.[74] It is a demand to rise and advance in God's service, level by level.[75]

There is one striking and unparalleled application found in his teachings. The entire literature, and therefore the entire history of applying Exodus 19:6, suffer from a strong gender bias. One rarely thinks of women in this context. The priestly analogy makes application of Exodus 19:6 to

---

70 This is evident throughout, but especially as the Rebbe cites Rashi's commentary. See *Sefer HaMa'amarim* תשיח (New York, 2002), 174.
71 *Matan Torah Be'Or Hahasidut* (Ufarazta: Kefar Habad, 2002), 18; 168–69.
72 There are no references that would suggest direct dependence. Given the Rebbe's encyclopedic knowledge of all things Jewish, one cannot exclude the possibility of his having encountered these ideas in the works of these teachers. One can equally consider the move a classical hasidic move towards individualization of a collective concept that does not require external precedent.
73 *Matan Torah Be'Or Hahasidut*, 26.
74 Ibid., p. 42.
75 Ibid., 169. For a theurgical understanding of Kingdom of Priests, see *Sefer HaMa'amarim* תשיז, p. 185. That all Israel are priests means that they all have the power of blessing. See *Sefer HaMa'amarim* תשמב, p. 171. Note, however, that this blessing is not addressed to the nations. While the elements are the same as in Seforno's identification of priestly vocation and blessing, the application is different, and more in keeping with general hasidic orientation.

women most unlikely, considering priests were men. It is most striking therefore to discover that one of the Rebbe's original applications of the verse is to extend the status of Kingdom of Priests to women.[76] If the category is essentially a description of the collective, which is then extended to the individual, such extension is as relevant to women as it is to men. The concrete implications are that the vocation of holiness and transforming life in its physicality, in light of a higher spiritual calling, are as relevant to women as they are to men.[77]

Kingdom of Priests—Invitation to Reflection and Humility

Kingdom of Priests provides an excellent prism for reflecting on Israel's particularity, especially in a contemporary context. It contains one of the fundamental tensions in understanding election—the tension between a status that is inherent unto itself and a mission that sees Israel's particularity as a function of its service to others. Kingdom of Priests is not a hackneyed expression, such as "the chosen people," "a treasured nation" (*am segula*) and other terms. It is employed far less and the present essay holds a key to understanding why that is so and what are the challenges in its application. It can therefore serve as an invitation to think of Israel's election and status through its particular complexities.

In many ways, the category is a promise, an ideal, but one that is so far from realization that it invites us to humility with regard to Israel, rather than to the potential boasting of status. Certainly, the tradition that is generated by Rashi's understanding that sees in Kingdom of Priests an expression of honor and status does not, in and of itself, support the humble approach. It is therefore important to appreciate that very tradition in light of the efforts of hasidic masters to move away from the potential boasting and to find in it an invitation to self-mastery and spiritual excellence. If so, it represents a spiritual opportunity and invitation, rather than a statement appa. Can we boast being a Kingdom of Priests if we lack the self-discipline of which the *Shem Mishemuel* speaks, or if we fail to proclaim God's kingdom fully? Inasmuch as the designation is a collective one, the question is

---

76 Ibid., p. 43.
77 This fits with broader patterns relating to his vision for women, their education and their role. See Ada Rapoport-Albert, "From Woman as Hasid to Woman as 'Tsadik' in the Teachings of the Last Two Lubavitcher Rebbes," *Jewish History* 27, nos. 2/4: 435–73.

all the more powerful. Can we speak of a Kingdom of Priests, when large parts of the people do not follow the priestly vocation of dedication to God?

The question of the degree of success in implementing a spiritual ideal applies to the interpretive approaches that see in Kingdom of Priests an invitation in relation to the world at large. Is Israel fulfilling a mission of teaching to the world? The sources we have reviewed assume a pious Israel and a world that knows neither God nor morality and needs Israel to provide such teaching. If we consider the historical long run, perhaps Israel has fulfilled this role historically. But if we consider Israel today, it is hard to consider its vocation in relation to the world as one of teaching. Do we possess a unique spiritual and moral teaching? What is it? Are we offering it to the world? Can we use the designation "Kingdom of Priests" before we are able to provide unequivocal answers to these questions?

The point is significantly complicated when we consider the new historical reality that faces Israel. If, as argued, Kingdom of Priests becomes a central category defining Israel's relations to the nations only under historical circumstances of interaction, what are the ramifications of the founding of the State of Israel for Israel's vocation, promise, and it being a Kingdom of Priests? Rav Kook would have hoped to see in Israel the ideal society that offers the entire world the teaching of God. Rav Ashlag would have aspired to an ideal society, founded upon love and altruistic service. Rabbi Friedman imagines the newly found state as a model of justice and righteousness to the nations. The more one emphasizes spiritual and moral fulfillment, the farther these ideals seem to be from the concrete historical reality of the State of Israel. Israel's struggle for survival, its divisions, and how far it is as a whole from the realization of these great ideals make it nearly impossible to speak of it as a Kingdom of Priests. Indeed, no one does. In fact, it seems the notion has far less currency today than it did over the two hundred years preceding Israel's establishment. A combination of uncertainty as to its meaning and of disappointment in relation to the realization of whatever meaning is ascribed to it in the framework of contemporary Israel would account for the little appeal the category has.

While it has been a minority position in the history of interpretation, the view of the *Ba'al Haturim*, and to a certain extent of Sforno as well, that it is a category we have missed out on due to our sins and one that will only become operative in the messianic future is one we should bear in mind as we consider what Kingdom of Priests means. It may require the fullness of a proper kingdom, stable in ways Israel is not yet stable, for it to also become a Kingdom of Priests.

Balancing this perspective is the view of Rav Kook that recognizes in Kingdom of Priests both a vocation and a depth dimension of being. If so, perhaps we ought not give up on the category and postpone it to a distant future. Perhaps it should be part of a quest and discovery of true self, of the yearning of heart, the power of soul, the depth of being. Perhaps such depth is required for the recovery of true vocation, of Israel's mission and of what teaching it may offer the world at large.

Seeing Kingdom of Priests not only in terms of vocation but in terms of being, rather than leading to boasting and glorifying in Israel, could serve as an invitation to quest and recovery, integrating such quest in the rich web of complementary understandings that were brought together by Rav Kook, balancing being and doing, interior and exterior, collective and personal. Rather than boast Kingdom of Priests as a collective status, it can also serve as an invitation to the discovery of personal meaning, individual priesthood and the kind of true spiritual life that points to holiness and suggests a vision for society and a message for the world. The Lubavitcher Rebbe's appeal to the category as a way of driving his listeners to greater spiritual heights is one way of putting it at the service of the interior spiritual quest.

One of the consequences of the decline in thinking of Israel as Kingdom of Priests is the overall attitude to the nations. Within contemporary Israel, certainly within contemporary *religious* Israel, there is very little interest in others. This is in part a consequence of ongoing existential struggles, but even more so an outcome of no longer being in the same society as non-Jews. If earlier authors were divided over whether Israel's priestly vocation could be best fulfilled in exile or in the security of homeland, the present witness seems to favor the former option. With the decline in consciousness of duty towards the nations as part of Israel's calling, it seems that raising such awareness as part of the very meaning of Israel is an urgent educational and spiritual need.

Given the relative lack of contact and the uncertainty as to what teaching Israel has to offer the world at large, there does seem to be one pathway that could raise awareness and keep the vision of a Kingdom of Priests alive. This is prayer. Praying on behalf of others places Israel in an intermediary role that simultaneously upholds its status and offers a vision of care for others. It does not assume the kind of active engagement that a teaching vocation does, nor does it raise the theoretical questions of what Israel's message to humanity is. Historically, the view of Israel praying and making offerings, as priests for the nations, has had little currency. When the view of Israel as teachers was expanded, its expansion related to Israel's being, as we see in Rav Kook's writings, or to the impact of its spiritual life, as we see in Rav Ashlag's. An expansion from Torah to prayer for the nations does not seem to have occurred.[78] Yet, there is much to commend it as a pedagogic and spiritual approach. We noted that the earliest reference to Israel's priestly vocation, in Philo, relates to Israel's prayer for and beneficial intention on behalf of humanity.[79] Such prayer does not contradict the need for self-identity and the possible demand for separation that attaches to it.[80] Implementing practices of prayer for the world would go to the heart of Jewish vocation and what it means to be Israel, as well as inspire and open paths towards other possible ways of realizing the promise of a Kingdom of Priests in the contemporary setting of Israel. If Israel are not only priests, but high priests, as the Lubavitcher Rebbe affirms, then the high priest's prayer for the world should surely be part of Israel's practice.

The possibility of describing Israel as an intermediary[81] may have not arisen over the course of the history of Jewish thought due to a general reticence to think in terms of intermediaries. However, beyond acknowledging the reality of priests as intermediaries, our religious thinking on the whole is much more receptive to the notion of an intermediary in view of the rise of intermediary figures within the hasidic movement. One wonders whether the deep rooted patterns of hasidic thought might have not pointed that way, had the teachers of Hasidism shown a greater interest in the nations and their spiritual welfare in the present. Perhaps the time has

---

78 There are multiple factors that could account for this. These include the lower place of prayer in the overall religious economy of Judaism, compared with Torah study, and the agonistic relations between Jews and non-Jews that do not lend themselves easily to prayer for non-Jews. Menachem Kallus' contribution in this volume opens the door to revisiting this particular inhibition.

79 Interestingly, an expectation of priestly prayer for the world is part of some Christians' contemporary view of Israel. See *L'attitude des Chrétiens à l'égard du Judaïsme, Orientations pastorales du Comité épiscopal pour les relations avec le judaïsme* (1973), section 5b. The text is available at https://www.paris.catholique.fr/391-L-attitude-des-chretiens-a-l.html.

80 See Rav Kook, *Midbar Shur*, 22nd Sermon (Jerusalem: Orot, 1999), 203; *Pinkesei Hareaya*, part 3, 55 (Jerusalem, n.d.), 102; *Sefat Emet*, Sukkot 1903.

81 I am grateful to my wife Tirza for raising in conversation the question of Israel's priestly status as intermediaries and pushing my thinking in this direction.

come to consider what contribution Hasidism might make to a more universal awareness within Judaism. Reflecting on the role of the Tzaddiq and Israel's priestly vocation is one suggestive possibility.

There is one final lesson that emerges from the diversity of understandings of Kingdom of Priests, the deliberations regarding its application and the challenges of the present moment in history. The lesson points in the direction of humility. To reflect upon what it means to be a Kingdom of Priests is an invitation to humility, given our failure, our inability to identify its meaning, or to apply it. As such, it is a wonderful antidote to other categories that could generate the contrary attitude. And it is this very humility that also makes this category a promising category for recovery of meaning and of attachment to a reality of being with God that can ultimately ascend to the greatest mystical heights, bringing blessing and understanding to Israel and the entire world.

Eugene Korn

Israel as Blessing: Theological Horizons

Israel and the Biblical Blessing

Blessing appears in the Bible's account of the birth of the Jewish people as well as its destiny in human history:

> Be a blessing.... I will make of you a great nation, and I will bless you; I will make your name great, and you shall be a blessing. I will bless those who bless you and curse him that curses you; and all the families of the earth shall bless themselves by you. (Genesis 12:2–3)

The nexus between Abraham and blessing is not limited to this one textual reference nor to Abraham alone. Blessing as part of God's promise appears twice more to Abraham, in Genesis 18:18–19:

> Since Abraham is to become a great and populous nation and all the nations of the earth are to bless themselves by him. For I have singled him out that he may instruct his children and his posterity to keep the way of the Lord by doing what is just and right, in order that the Lord may bring about for Abraham what He has promised him.

and in Genesis 22:17–18:

> I will bestow My blessing upon you and make your descendants as numerous as the stars in the heaven and the sand on the seashore.... All the nations of the earth shall bless themselves by your descendants because you have obeyed My command.

In Gen. 26:4 it is extended to Abraham's son, Isaac:

> I will make your heirs as numerous as the stars of heaven, and assign to your heirs all these lands, so that all the nations of the earth shall bless themselves by your heirs.

And then to Isaac's son Jacob in Genesis 28:14:

> All the families of the earth shall bless themselves by you and your descendants.

Curiously, however, the theological idea (*theologoumenon*) of Israel as blessing does not appear again in the remainder of the Pentateuch. In the remainder of all Tanakh the blessing's reference to the Jewish people after Jacob appears *explicitly* only in the later prophets.[1] Nevertheless, the blessing's application to the post-patriarchal Jewish people is mentioned explicitly in the Genesis 18 verse ("his children and *his household after him*"), in the Genesis 22 passage ("All the nations of the earth shall bless themselves *by your descendants")* in the Genesis 26 reference ("all the nations of the earth shall bless themselves *by your heirs*"), as well as in the passage in Genesis 28 ("All the families of the earth shall bless themselves *by you and your descendants.*"). Importantly Genesis 28 is directed at Jacob, and hence must refer to Jacob's progeny down through the generations.

It seems clear that blessing is also implicit in God's charge to the entire Jewish people at Sinai to become a "kingdom of priests" (Exodus 19:6)[2] and the prophetic call for Jews to function in history as a "light for the nations" *(or lagoyim)* (Isaiah 42:6 and 49:1–6). A primary function of the priest—particularly in the post-Temple life of Israel—is to be a conduit of God's blessing to the community, in which case the call to become "a nation of priests" implies bestowing blessing on the world community. "Light for the nations" also carries the undeniable connotation of providing goodness and understanding to the gentile world. If so, the bestowal and predictions of blessing apply to the Jewish people over the sweep of their history, just as rabbinic tradition assumed that God's covenant with Abraham applies to Abraham's Jewish descendants in perpetuity. If these assumptions are warranted, blessing constitutes an intrinsic part of the Bible's understanding of

---

1 Zachariah 8:13, Ezekiel 34:26, Jeremiah 4:1–2, and Isaiah 19:24–25, all of which will be discussed later in the essay.
2 For a full discussion of "*mamlekhet kohanim*," see "A Kingdom of Priests and a Holy Nation" by Alon Goshen-Gottstein in this volume.

Israel's theological calling and destiny. And as Abraham's progeny are called upon to extend blessing to "all the families of the earth," it should play a central role in defining the Bible's covenantal conception of the Jewish people's relations with the gentile world.

Despite these Pentateuchal and Prophetic references, the *theologoumenon* of Israel as blessing has not played a prominent role in past rabbinic biblical and talmudic interpretation. This may be due more to the trauma the Jewish people experienced throughout its diasporic history rather than to that the idea that blessing was not a central motif in the Torah's vision of covenantal theology. Jewish interaction with gentile powers have often been tragic, thereby causing rabbinic commentaries to pass over the Bible's theological calling for the Jewish people to enter world history by influencing the gentile nations. Another possibility for why these texts have not enjoyed wide circulation is that it is primarily in modernity that Jewish readers are interested in developing the theological concept of Israel as blessing. Reading texts is not only about what the texts say but also about the interaction between what they say and what the reader seeks to find or is able to recognize. If so, different texts and themes may naturally belong to different periods. Some generations may have been less interested, or less able, to hear the notion that Israel is to be a blessing unto others. This points to a challenge of contemporary interpretations in our times. To develop a theology of Israel that offers possibilities for how Israel should relate theologically to other peoples and religions, modern thinkers may be in a better position than were previous generations to hear messages in Jewish sacred texts and later rabbinic writings.

In order to preserve the coherence and integrity of the above texts, blessing should be understood as a constituent element of Israel's mission and election. Identifying the centrality of the biblical concept of blessing and how its uses were limited to specific contexts presents the theological challenge of developing the principles and applications of the concept.

The Bible provides few details regarding the nature of this blessing and the dynamics of its transmission. However rabbinic tradition does provide a number of sources regarding these subjects, and they have significant implications for Israel's role in sacred history and its ideal relationship to gentiles. Studying these sources allow us to reveal important conceptions of Israel's covenantal mission, to engage in constructive theological thinking and to explore some of the covenantal challenges before Jews today.

This essay will survey the rabbinic interpretations of Israel's blessing, outlining their implications for different theological approaches to Jewish self-understanding as well as Israel's relationship to humanity. The different theologies, attitudes and practices that emerge from this variety all find expression in contemporary Jewish self-definition, behavior, and attitudes toward other religions. The goal of this survey is to promote fresh thinking that can contribute to future constructive Jewish theology.

The texts under consideration come from a broad range of sources representing different periods and schools of Jewish thought. The essay's use of eclectic sources is designed to achieve several purposes. It makes us aware of the broad range of options available for Jewish theology. It allows us to revisit the fundamental dynamics of Jewish thought and the inherent tensions in performing the task of constructing a contemporary Jewish theology. Finally, it allows us to recover voices sometimes overlooked in Jewish religious discourse, and thereby broaden the theological possibilities at our disposal.

Prophetic Conceptions of Israel as Blessing

A number of prophetic texts mention the idea of blessing as essential to Jewish identity. Despite the existence of these texts, it is striking how little attention they have received in the history of interpretation and commentary, and how most students of the Torah are unaware of them and their significance. Certainly no Jewish theology has been built around the centrality of blessing in Israel's covenant.

Israel as blessing appears in the prophets Zachariah, Ezekiel and Jeremiah, as well as Isaiah:

> And just as you were a curse among the nations, O House of Judah and House of Israel, so, when I vindicate you, you shall become a blessing. Have no fear; take courage! (Zachariah 8:13)
>
> I will make these and the environs of My hill a blessing, I will send down the rain in its season, rains that bring blessing (Ezekiel 34:26):

Rabbi David Kimchi (Radak), a primary rabbinic commentator on the prophets, relates the promises of blessing that appear in Zechariah and Ezekiel to the specific blessings to Abraham as recorded in Genesis 12:2–3.[3]

---

3   See Radak's commentary on those verses.

This reinforces the idea that Abraham's blessing also applies to all of Israel in her relation to the nations. However we understand the meaning of being a blessing in relation to Abraham, these prophets extend it into a continuation of the promise for salvation. This might be understood as indicating that *the purpose* of salvation is Israel continually striving to function as a blessing to the nations over the course of history, or alternatively, that the blessing will not occur within normal history, but only in the *eschaton*, that is, only at the end of history (the messianic era) when salvation is fully realized will Israel become a blessing—but not before. And when the messianic era is understood to be a rupture or discontinuity with pre-messianic history, then Israel need not strive to be a blessing to the nations prior to that time. In effect, consigning blessing to the *eschaton* is an effective way of undermining the normative force of the biblical responsibility of blessing. As we shall see, these two interpretations represent two radically opposed understandings of how Israel should live out its covenantal responsibilities as it relates to the gentile nations.

The mandate or prediction to function as a blessing in Zachariah is couched between the promise of salvation and the encouragement to be fearless. This detracts from the force of the categorical message of blessing appearing in Genesis. Is this due merely to the literary style of the prophetic texts, or is it essential to prophetic visions and theologies? In either possibility the de-emphasis may have contributed to the blessing prophecy failing to achieve great popularity in rabbinic tradition.

Radak again sees Ezekiel's reference to blessing as an extension of Genesis 12. However he appears to emphasize the divine bestowal of rain as the result of (or constituting) blessing with the actions of Israel functioning as the conduit for the blessing. This can easily elude the reader and thus relegate the prophecy of Israel as blessing to the background.

Israel as blessing also appears in Jeremiah 4:1–2:

> If you return, O Israel—declares the Lord—if you return to Me, if you remove your abominations from My presence and do not waver, and swear, "As the Lord lives," in sincerity, justice, and righteousness—nations shall bless themselves by you [lit. "him"] and praise themselves by you.

R. Shlomo Yitzhaki (Rashi) interprets the meaning of this verse similar to his interpretation of Genesis 12:2–3: "If you [Israel] does so, [i.e. return to the Lord] then nations will bless themselves by Israel. Every non-Jew will say to his son, "You shall be like So-and-So the Jew." Thus Israel seems to stand almost as an introverted religious model to be seen and emulated by the gentiles of the world.

Radak comments on this verse in Jeremiah: "Nations will bless themselves by him and will glory in him. There will yet come a time also when the other nations will bless themselves in Him and will take pride in Him and not in idols. It is also possible that the words 'in him' refer to Israel—i.e., if Israel will do all of this, then the nations will bless themselves by you, as it is written, 'All the nations of the earth shall bless themselves by your heirs' (Genesis 26:4)." Similar to Rashi, this latter interpretation seems to imply that Israel's active return to God will occasion the blessing to the nations, with Israel's direct relationship with the gentile nations being secondary.

Rashi's strong reading of Jeremiah 4:1–2 suggests that *all* nations will be blessed through Israel. (Radak also recognizes this reading.) Similar to his reading of Genesis 12:2–3, Rashi highlights how Abraham serves as a model for others. In Genesis 12:2–3, as in his interpretation of Jeremiah, Rashi understands the verse to indicate that gentiles will say to their sons, "be like Abraham," even though there is nothing in the biblical text to indicate that this blessing/role modeling should be in the framework of father-son relations. It maybe that Rashi implies here that Israel's relationship to the nations should be regarded as parallel to that of a parent to a child: role model and teacher by example. In his second interpretation Radak appears to agree with Rashi, but his first interpretation suggests that God is the one who is being blessed, not Israel. That the verse can be read in more than one way may have contributed to the limited influence that this verse has had over the generations in expressing the notion of Israel as a blessing to the nations.

Lastly, Isaiah announces blessing in 19:24–25:

> In that day, Israel shall be a third partner with Egypt and Assyria as a blessing on earth; for the Lord of Hosts will bless them, saying, "Blessed be My people Egypt, My handiwork Assyria, and My very own Israel."

These verses in Isaiah are unique in the Bible in that they appear to extend the covenantal blessing of Israel to Egypt and Assyria, thus implying that those nations have achieved (or will achieve) theological parity with Israel. They imply that at some future time, Israel will share its status with Ashur and Egypt, the two reigning empires of Isaiah's time. Terms of status and endearment hitherto exclusive to God's relation with Israel are now shared with other peoples. They may suggest theologically that Israel's status and election are but instrumental, that is Israel will influence Egypt and Assyria, who will in turn bestow blessing on other gentile nations. Thus ultimately God's design is for others to enjoy the same elected status and relationship that Israel enjoys. Since this diminishes Israel's unique character and religious calling, these verses also have not been stressed in rabbinic tradition and Jewish thought. Yet they may be fertile grounds for understanding Israel's instrumental role in shaping Christianity and Islam and these later religions in turn influencing humanity.

Radak comments on these verses:

> In that day, Israel shall be a third partner. They will share a third in the faith of God, and they will be a blessing in the midst of the land. For they will enjoy an advantage of blessings over the other nations for as long as they maintain their faith in God.

Here Radak introduces the notion of faith in God as the foundation for the new status of Assyria and Egypt. Faith—presumably knowledge of the One God of heaven and earth—is the basis for shifting relations between Israel and the nations. One could reconstruct an understanding of this idea according to which Israel's goal is to spread the knowledge of God in the world. When Israel is successful, others will share in Israel's special status and enjoy its particular blessings.

According to Radak, blessing is what the nations receive from God as a consequence of their true faith. This interpretation does not seem to have the rich understanding of "blessing" that characterized the interpretations of Genesis 12. While Radak emphasizes the three nations enjoying the advantage of blessings, one can also imagine that blessing conveys the idea of spreading the faith in God's to others and seeing Israel's special status as instrumental to the task of teaching humanity about God. This has obvious ramifications for Jewish understandings of other religions, and raises the questions for Jewish theology of identifying which conditions are necessary for others to recognize God, whether the other faiths must mirror the Jewish concept and worship of God, and whether other nations can be considered as sharing Israel's blessings and Abraham's covenant. It also leaves open the question of how faith itself leads naturally to blessing understood biblically as peace, security, and human flourishing.

Blessing as Active Universal Engagement: Teaching Theology and Morality

How aware is Jewish thought, both throughout the generations and particularly today, of the idea of being a blessing to the nations? This question is related to the diverse understandings of what it means to be a blessing. Traditional interpretations of the biblical blessing oscillate between active understandings that promote Jewish engagement with gentiles and their culture, and more passive ones that restrict blessing to introspective Jewish modeling that naturally engenders gentile emulation. Thus we can imagine different degrees of activity, awareness, and intentionality of the biblical blessing. Each of the understandings represents a paradigm for contemporary relations between Jews and gentiles, and for ideal Jewish interaction with humanity.

Nor is this strictly a theological or "metaphysical" question since different educational and social initiatives follow from the adoption of particular interpretations. Should Jews be "out there" doing good and striving to influence gentiles? Should they seek to share the knowledge of God as a way of being a blessing? If so, should they seek to convert gentiles, either minimally to the Noahide commandments or maximally to the Mosaic covenant? Should Jews keep gentile humanity as part of their spiritual intention, even as they face God and practice their particular Mosaic covenant within the Jewish people? Alternatively, perhaps Jews need do nothing other than function as a model worthy of other's praise, emulation and blessing. Ought Jews to focus inward exclusively with role modeling taking place without Jewish concern for the presence of others, or does it also involve some degree of intentionality toward others?

This presents a two-fold behavioral and spiritual challenge: What does blessing imply regarding ideal Jewish action and to what extent should Jews direct their actions toward others to extend blessing to them? Second, how closely should the rest of the world be present in Jewish thoughts and intentions, even as we serve God in the context of our particularistic covenant?

One major understanding of the biblical blessing and charge sees blessing in active terms. God has challenged Abraham, and consequently Israel, to share their theological understanding with the nations. Thus teaching is a form of creating universal blessing. According to this view Abraham is the prototype of a teacher who shares Judaism's message with others. By emphasizing teaching, we begin to move from blessing peoples to recognition of their religions. This is most evident in Maimonides' statements about the theological and historical function of Abraham to bring theological truth, values and human flourishing to gentile nations and individuals:

> He [Abraham] began to call in a loud voice to all people and inform them that there is one God in the entire world and it is proper to serve Him. He would go out and call to the people, gathering them in city after city and country after country, until he came to the land of Canaan—proclaiming [God's existence the entire time]—as [Gen. 21:33] states: "And He called there in the name of the Lord, the eternal God." When the people would gather around him and ask him about his statements, he would explain [them] to each one of them according to their understanding, until they turned to the path of truth. Ultimately, thousands and myriads gathered around him. These are the souls of Abraham's house. He planted in their hearts this great fundamental principle, composed texts about it, and taught it to Isaac, his son. Isaac also taught others and turned [their hearts to God]. He also taught Jacob and appointed him as a teacher. (*Mishneh Torah*, Laws of Avodah Zarah 1:4)
>
> "You shall love God," i.e. make Him beloved among the creatures as your father Avraham did, as it is written, "The souls that he made in Haran." (Gen. 12:5) Avraham, as a result of his deep understanding of God, acquired love for God, as the verse testifies, "Avraham, who loved Me" (Isa. 41:8). This powerful love therefore caused him to call out to all mankind to believe in God. So too, you shall love Him to the extent that you draw others to Him. (*Book of Commandments*, Positive Commandment 3)

In Maimonides' understanding Abraham is a Socratic instructor who dispenses blessings to the world by teaching the pagans around him about the true nature of God and correct faith. Aside from Abraham's correct metaphysical understanding that God is unique and non-physical, Maimonides believed that Abraham was aware only of the moral Noahide commandments, the commandment of circumcision and possibly the commandment to pray. It is likely, therefore, that Maimonides believed that Abraham taught those around him about the moral commandments as a necessary means to understanding theological truth. If so, according to Maimonides, the mission of Israel includes teaching humanity about the accurate nature of God and divine moral law. In fact, Maimonides acknowledged that these truths were spread to the nations of the earth partially by both Christians and Muslims, whose religions were derived from Judaism.[4] Thus this idea of "blessing" has implications for how Jews should understand Christians and Muslims theologically in the context of sacred history.

In his commentary on Genesis 12:2, the medieval exegete, Don Isaac Abravanel (fifteenth-century Spain) also understands blessings this way:

> The purpose of the process referenced here and the phrase "You shall be a blessing" that God commanded him [Avraham] is that when he travels he should be a blessing among the nations in teaching and informing them about the true faith in a way that will complete the world through him and his teaching so that divine providence will extend to those who accept his teaching and study His faith. Regarding this it says, "I will bless those who bless you."

According to Abravanel, Abraham's success is measured by the fact that so many consider themselves to be his heirs, even though they are not genealogically related to him. This bold statement appears to be made without reservation, and likely constitutes an acknowledgement that Christianity and Islam—the religions to which Abravanel was exposed—were also carriers of a true teaching sourced in Abraham.

There is another more behavioral interpretation of "being a blessing." Some sources highlight the cognitive knowledge of God, while others, highlight the path of righteous and moral living—*tsedekah* and *mishpat*—as emphasized in the reference to blessing in Genesis 18:18–19.

Whether God's charge to Abraham to function as a blessing to the world connotes teaching the world about the reality and metaphysical character of God or basic moral norms of righteous and justice, under this conception of blessing Israel has an active mission toward gentiles. Its mission consists in sharing this teaching and following in the footsteps of Abraham, who is the first one to both share his theological awareness with others as well as acting as a defender of justice and righteousness (Genesis 18) and thus functioning as a model of ethical relations toward others. Hence Israel actively brings blessing to the nations in two ways. Teaching faith in God itself is an act of blessing, while the moral consequences of that theological sharing are also a blessing to humanity as it leads to individual and social flourishing.

---

4   See *Mishneh Torah*, Laws of Kings and Their Wars, 11:4 (uncensored edition).

A third instance of interpreting the election of Israel as blessing to the world is offered by R. Naftali Berlin (Netziv): "While not using the term blessing, he sees the Book of Exodus as the theological extension of the Book of Genesis. Sinaitic revelation is the culmination of God's creation of the universe that proceeds from Genesis 1 through the covenantal blessing bestowed upon Abraham in Genesis 12 through Exodus 20:[5]

> It thus emerges that the giving of the Torah is the completion of creation, and this is identical with the Exodus from Egypt, as then Israel were fit to accept the Torah and to complete the Creation, and to come through it to the *telos* of their formation, in relation to the People of God This is analogous to the function of human reason and forthright qualities in the Torah of Humanity, regarding which even though the land and what fills it did not reach this completion until after a long time after the creation of Heaven and Earth, and even nowadays there are many human beings that have not reached this height, nonetheless the nations of the world comprehend that only this is the telos for the raised status of the human being. Similarly we have reason to believe that even though Torah and her principles were not given until after the Exodus from Egypt, and even now there are many of Israel who have not achieved a Torah mind-set, nonetheless the Torah is the sole reason for the raised status of Israel, who were formed to be a covenantal people for a light for the nations. Thus the book of Exodus is the second book of the first book (Genesis), as if they are one subject separated into two books of the book of creation.... The general completion of the world is that there will be a nation who will be God's people. This was not achieved until Israel left Egypt and arrived at its goal that it be fit to be a light for the nations and to establish the knowledge of God in the world.

Rather than understanding revelation at Sinai in parochial or national terms, Netziv proceeds in the opposite direction, insisting like Isaiah (49:6) that Sinai revelation has universal value. The purpose of Sinaitic election is for the Jewish people to serve as "a light for the nations" by teaching the world the true knowledge of God. According to Netziv, Israel's religious identity cannot be understood without Israel's connection to the gentile nations because Israel's election is the center of a universal strategy for disseminating divine truth to humanity. In other words, the world was not created for Israel; rather Israel was created for the world.

---

5   Commentary to the Bible, *Ha-Ameq Davar*, Introduction to Book of Exodus.

It should be noted that understanding Israel's blessing as active teaching (or universal mission) is an instrumentalist conception of election, and this, in turn, leads to a theological and national paradox: When Israel's uniqueness consists in its mission to bless and teach others, the very success of that blessing entails the loss of Israel's uniqueness. By succeeding in its mission Israel would no longer enjoy the benefits of its unique relationship with God. Isaiah's prophecy in 19:24–25 approaches this idea, and Maimonides and his rationalist theological followers developed this understanding of Jewish religious identity most fully and downplayed the meaning of Jewish election.[6]

Blessing as Passive Modeling

We saw how Rashi and Radak often understood Genesis' blessing to Abraham as providing a model whose influence naturally spreads to the nations ("They [the gentiles] will say to their sons, 'be like Abraham'") without entailing any necessary Jewish intentionality toward gentiles. This is a significant difference between the first concept of blessing as active engagement with gentiles and this more passive modeling interpretation of blessing. Even in this model of blessing, however, it is clear that Jews need to be aware of the presence of gentiles and the impact of Jewish behavior on others, albeit that such awareness need not be the primary element in Jews leading their religious lives. Moreover, this model may function as an important stimulus for Jews to evaluate themselves in their spiritual and behavioral lives. It may demand that they continuously ask themselves, "Am I an admirable model? Are my actions worthy of emulation by others?"

The interpretation of blessing by Ovadia ben Jacob Seforno in sixteenth-century Italy represents an integration of these disparate conceptions. For Seforno, ideal Jewish religious intention is toward God, yet ultimately being a blessing to God results in human flourishing because God finds joy in correct human belief and progress. Focusing on God's joy is thus coupled with action in relation toward others. Relating to Genesis 12:2, Seforno offers a synthesis of religious intention toward God and concrete action in relation to gentiles:

---

6   Maimonides' *Guide for the Perplexed* does not mention Jewish "election." The end of his *Mishneh Torah* describes the fullness of the messianic era—i.e., when Israel's mission and blessing has been fully realized—in thoroughly universalistic terms. See Laws of Kings and Their Wars, 12:5 (according to Yemenite ms).

> The blessing of God is that He should rejoice in His creation, as our sages have said, "(God said to me,) 'Ishmael, My son, bless Me.' I replied, 'May it be Your will that Your mercy may prevail over Your other attributes'" (BT, *Berakhot* 7a). Therefore He (God) says, "become a blessing to Me by (your) deep understanding (whereby) you will acquire perfection, and teach knowledge (of God) to the people."[7]

Seforno here couches his understanding of blessing in terms that relate to God directly: Being a blessing means being a blessing to God, so the correct understanding of Genesis 12 is that God challenged Abraham and his descendants to be a blessing for Him. God finds joy in His creation—specifically when His human creatures achieve spiritual perfection. Abraham is commanded to reach spiritual perfection, through attaining the perfected understanding of God who acts toward His human creatures with the moral attribute of mercy. He takes this interpretation a step further by asserting that perfected knowledge is the basis for teaching others and hence Abraham is to share his knowledge with others. In the end it is this activity of teaching that makes Abraham a blessing to God.

Seforno's cited the talmudic passage in which a righteous person (R. Ishmael) gains the upper hand over divine justice, implying that blessing increases divine joy because it allows for the continued existence of God's children who will withstand divine justice with the aid of divine compassion. Thus, anything that advances the project of maintenance, evolution and perfection of creation can be considered a divine blessing. Unique to Seforno's reading is that Abraham—and by extension all Israel—are simultaneously a blessing to themselves, to God, and to the world.

Yet who are the others that Abraham is bidden to teach and perfect spiritually? While it is possible that in Seforno's mind Abraham is to teach his offspring exclusively (as suggested by Genesis 18:19), it is more likely that because the Jewish people had not yet been formed and according to rabbinic tradition Abraham converted the "strangers" around him, the others who Abraham was commanded to teach are those "souls" outside his biological family.

Blessing as Non-Relational Theurgic Agency

While philosophical and rational schools of interpretation emphasized blessing as active teaching or influencing (either theologically or morally)

---
7   Commentary on Bible, Genesis 12:2, Pelcovitz edition, 64.

and the medieval biblical exegetes emphasized passive modeling, still others stressed more solitary dimensions of blessing, and thereby avoided the possibility Israel's losing its unique status and covenantal role. One specific mode of this interpretation that is popular among kabbalistic thinkers is blessing that is directed toward, and connecting with, the supernal world. This is achieved through ritual and religious intent that draws the divine flux into the physical, human plane. Blessing refers to the drawing of a celestial reality to the human realm—almost exclusively to the life and experience of the Jewish people. The covenantal blessing emerges as an important concept in this spiritual transfer. Abraham's specific blessing is understood in the context of the broader kabbalistic understanding of blessing, and thus biblical and classical sources are reread in light of the particularities of the kabbalistic understanding of how the celestial realm above relates to the human realm and below.

Drawing blessing from above focuses exclusively on the relationship between Jewish faith/behavior with the celestial world, and is divorced from any conscious or direct Jewish interaction with others. That this type of theurgic agency could, in principle be achieved in complete Jewish isolation from the rest of humanity highlights the fact that this understanding eliminates the need for Jews to be concerned with gentiles while they lead their religious and spiritual life. Blessing is thus the natural effect of living in accordance with the divine commandments between Israel and God—a radically more introverted way of generating blessing than either active engagement or passive modeling.

This is concept is expressed by the kabbalist R. Joseph ben Abraham Gikatilla of thirteenth-century Spain:

> This is the secret of the blessing that God, blessed be He, granted to Abraham. For the abundance of bounty and emanations that are drawn from the Supernal Eden, which is called *keter* (crown), and subsequently flow through the conduit of *tiferet*, which is called *nahar* (river), are all gathered into the tenth pool which is the secret of *malkhut* (kingship), and this is the pool that the stories of the wells of Abraham and Isaac refer to. God entrusted Abraham with this pool through which all the nations shall be blessed. This is the meaning of what He said, "I will make of you a great nation, and I will bless you; I will make your name great, and you shall be a blessing" (Genesis 12:2). What is the meaning of "be a blessing"? That the *shekhinah* (the immanent presence of God) that is the pool shall dwell in you.... Even

> though God gave Abraham the pool He did not give him nor Isaac the gate, because their progeny contained dross, i.e. Ishmael and Esau; but He did give the gate to Jacob whose progeny did not contain any dross. The meaning of God's words to Abraham, "and all nations of the earth shall be blessed in you" is clear and well-understood, for the seventy families attach themselves to Abraham and Isaac. This is the meaning of the word ברכה ("blessing"), which comes from the word והרכבה הבריך (to graft unto), i.e. that the seventy nations are grafted unto and spiritually connected to Abraham and Isaac.[8]

The author here plays on the Hebrew words *berakhah* (blessing) and *berekhah* (pool). The tenth sphere of *malkhut* (divine kingship) is the pool, into which all higher blessings gather and which is also associated with the notion of blessing. The divine grant of blessing to Abraham means that God provided him with access to *malkhut*. As *malkhut* is responsible for the drawing forth of all blessings to the physical world, it is also the source of sustenance and bounty for gentiles. God granted this to Abraham so that the nations may also receive blessings. Hence blessing for the nations is inherently linked to this *sefira*, and it is only through the access entrusted to Abraham that blessing is available to others. Blessing is a form of spiritual graft, of extending spiritual power from God to Israel to the nations. Only Abraham's blessing keeps gentiles connected to the divine.

Note that blessings to the nations stem from the metaphysical endowment God bestowed upon Israel rather than from any knowledge that Israel possesses or actions that Israel manifests. This concept does, however, stress the importance of Israel maintaining a high spiritual state to remain connected to "pool" of divine kingship of *malkhut* and hence blessing.

R. Menachem Mendel Schneerson, the Rebbe of Lubavitch in twentieth-century America, follows a related line of thinking:

> This is the meaning of the verse, "Praise the Lord, all you nations; extol Him, all you peoples, for great is His steadfast love toward us" (Psalms 117:1–2). . . . How is the demonstration of God's love to us [Israel] a reason why other nations should praise Him? The explanation is well known; the intensification of God's love toward us causes a purification, refinement, and elevation among the Gentiles and nations, to the extent that they visibly recognize its effects and as a result, they extol and praise God. This process is accomplished through the offering of the seventy oxen and similarly through

---

8   *Gates of Righteousness*, First Gate.

the service of "Instead of bulls we will pay [the offering of] our lips" (Hosea 14:3), i.e., prayer.[9]

This teaching provides a further proof for Israel's continuing obligation to serve as a blessing for the nations. Gentile nations rejoice because whatever God's grace is shown to Israel also extends to the nations. Israel, then, becomes a—perhaps the exclusive—spiritual conduit of blessing for the nations. Because the blessing is fully observable to the nations, it induces them to offer praise to God. However this interpretation again omits any explicit reference of Jewish mindfulness toward gentiles when experiencing God's love. Israel "earns" God's blessing through ritual (the sacrifice of seventy oxen on the festival of Tabernacles) or through prayer—both of which are actions directed toward God alone.

This raises an important theological question: To what degree should the energetic transfer of blessing to gentiles be conscious and intentional in Jewish spiritual life? One possible interpretation of this teaching is that throughout the religious life of the Jewish people, Israel and the nations engage in a conscious exchange of blessing, an extension of divine love that reaches out to all humanity, in turn leading to the praise of God. And this extension of divine love should be a spiritual aspiration for Jews not only annually during the festival of *Sukkot* (Tabernacles), which anticipates the era of complete blessing for all nations,[10] but also every day as Jews engage in daily prayer.

A third expression of blessing as theurgic agency is provided by R. Elimelech of Lizhensk, the influential hasidic master in eighteenth-century Poland:

> This is the meaning of the verse, "See. . . I set before you blessing and a curse" (Deut. 11:26): The word "see" hints at and refers to the righteous ones [*tsaddikim*] who are on the level of (serving God with) love, which

---

9   *Torat Menachem*, pt. 1, 131.
10 When the Temple stood in Jerusalem, seventy oxen were sacrificed on the festival of Sukkot. That Talmudic rabbis (BT Sukkah 55b) understood these oxen to correspond to the seventy gentile nations of the world. This conception continues in Jewish religious life today when prayer has replaced animal sacrifices and the Musaf prayer of the Sukkot festival refers to the seventy sacrificial oxen. The prophetic reading for that festival (Zechariah 14) describes the ascent of the nations to worship God in the Temple. Thus Sukkot becomes a time of praying for the gentile nations as well as an intimation of the messianic era when all nations will recognize God and be blessed to offer sacrifices in the rebuilt Temple in Jerusalem.

is also identified with sight. "I set before you a blessing and a curse," refers to the curse which is placed upon the nations, and the blessing consists of compassion for Israel. All this is delivered in your hands (i.e. is in your power); by virtue of your righteousness, you will be able to accomplish the foregoing.[11]

Unlike the two earlier sources that highlight blessing between Israel and the nations, R. Elimelech portrays Jewish-gentile relations in diametrically opposite terms, corresponding to good and evil and similar dichotomies. This counterpoint of Israel and gentiles is not uncommon in kabbalistic and hasidic writings, in which blessing to Israel carries a theological concomitant of curse for gentiles. The righteous (Jewish) *tsaddikim* are on the level of love and they extend that love, expressed through compassion, upon Israel. In contrast, they stimulate the opposite of blessing—"curse"—upon the nations. The duality of blessing and curses is paralleled by the duality of Israel and the nations. Gentile curse is the dialectical concomitant of Israel's blessing, rather than as a conduit to universal blessing, as Genesis 12:2–3 indicates. It also ensures Israel's enduring uniqueness and superiority.

It may well be that historical circumstances led to this polarized worldview. Whatever its genesis, it is now firmly entrenched in a number of rabbinic writings and presents contemporary Jews with the challenge of understanding, evaluating, and potentially adopting this worldview.

With its active and missionary emphasis, the philosophical tradition allowed for natural sharing between Abraham and the world, between Israel and humanity. By contrast, kabbalistic tradition largely focuses on ritual and interior spiritual life as the arenas of religious activity, with its correlative de-emphasis of Jewish-gentile relations. The first interpretations present the flow of blessings from Israel to the nations, a desirable sharing in divine bounty. The latter present a discontinuity and limit, positing the nations as polar opposites of Israel. The extreme version of this theology is R. Elimelech's teaching in which divine intent of blessing for the nations is replaced by a curse upon them. The spiritual depth of that theology is matched by oppositional, even hateful, statements concerning gentiles, projecting Jewish-gentile relations as theologically undesirable and to be strenuously avoided.

How should we evaluate this strand of interpretation? Do we accept it as a permanent truth of Jewish theology and spiritual life, merely as a

---

11   *Noam Elimelech, Re'eh.*

temporary insight resulting from difficult historical circumstances, or as a denial of the biblical aspiration for Jews to spread the divine blessing all God's children, and hence to be rejected?

In summary we have seen that interpretations of the concept of Israel as blessing run the gamut of Jewish-gentile relations—from proactive and potentially harmonious relations offered by interpreting blessing as active engagement, to the possible indifference and potential self-critiquing function posed by the passive model interpretation, to possible obliviousness and perhaps adversarial relationship posed by the theurgic interpretation of blessing.

Since these three modes of interpreting blessing demonstrate sometimes contradictory ways of relating to the gentile "other," a fundamental challenge for theological Jews today is to consciously choose one understanding of blessing over the others—with both its spiritual and behavioral implications. We are thus forced to examine varying motifs within Jewish tradition and make critical choices that yield the most fruitful results for our given social, cultural and spiritual circumstances. In the process we come to understand that the tradition is neither monolithic nor consistent, and that some aspects of tradition need to be reinterpreted constructively. The act of favoring one theological motif over another can also be an important way of purifying tradition from within.

Blessing, History, and the State of Israel

The introverted understanding of blessing, that is, the theurgic agency model, may be interpreted as Israel standing outside the realm of history and political life. In such a view Israel is a source of blessing to the world because of its spiritual life and religious observance. However, by the same logic, Israel's flawed worship stemming from its exile and the Temple's destruction might be considered an impediment to fulfilling the divine biblical mandate to the Jewish people to share its blessing with the nations. In the more extrovert understanding (active engagement), the harsh historical reality of exile proved to be a hindrance to Israel's fulfilling its blessing mission realized as its vocation to teach the human family. When diaspora Jews experience oppression and exclusion, these historical conditions undermine the theological value of activism prescribed by this interpretation of blessing. Thus the more passive or introverted understandings of blessing flow more naturally.

During times of Jewish flourishing, optimistic Jewish thinkers taught that exile held the greater opportunity for Israel's active fulfillment of blessing because it affords the Jewish people positive interaction with gentiles and their cultures. This was particularly true in Jewish homiletical, rabbinic and philosophic writings following the Emancipation and the European Enlightenment,[12] as it is true in America today, where the theme of *tikkun olam* has become commonplace among centrist and liberal American Jews. It is no accident that following the post-Emancipation era the question of the Jewish people's role for the nations surfaced as a more conscious theological direction. When Jews live in relative harmony among gentiles, the question of positive Jewish relations toward gentiles become sharper and more desirable.

Analyzing the concept of Israel as blessing relating to the changing historical and political conditions of the Jewish people requires us to examine the *theologoumenon* in light of the existence of the State of Israel and Jewish sovereignty. This theological task flows from the recognition that today Jews are living in a new moment in history. Its novelty derives not merely from modern developments in interreligious relations and global interdependency—with the recognition that "no religion is an island"—but also from the reality that with sovereignty and independence the State of Israel has become the primary representative of the Jewish people to the world community. These transformed political conditions require us to reassess Israel's relationship to gentile nations, which takes on new importance when "Israel" is not only a people, but also a state. Hence it seems clear that the current Jewish existential and political conditions mandate new thinking, or at least new implications of prior theological options. Moreover, these theological ideas are not limited to theory but have dramatic political, cultural and historical consequences today.

Today's State of Israel generates a theological paradox: On the one hand Israel's prolonged continuous fight for survival in a threatening region where the majority of its neighbors refuse to acknowledge its *de jure* legitimacy and its *de facto* existence naturally fosters a Jewish inward turn that focuses on self-concern. In this condition the theological option stressing internal religious values without primary consciousness of their effect on the world, that is, passive modeling, has great currency. Further still, the

---

12   The nineteenth-century German rabbi, Samson Raphael Hirsch and the early twentieth-century Jewish German philosopher, Hermann Cohen, are examples. For Hirsch, see the essay by Alon Goshen-Gottstein in this volume.

state affords a significant percentage of Israelis the freedom to be fervently Orthodox Jews (*haredim*), and to go about their religious lives based on the model of non-relational theurgic agency. Their theological orientation is to live outside of history and politics, convinced that only isolated spiritual immersion and individual Torah study will bring blessing and security to the Jewish people. If the gentile nations achieve blessing it will only be directly initiated by God in the *eschaton*, not in empirical history as we know it. As one would expect, kabbalistic theology, with its portrayal of Jews and gentiles as polar opposites, is popular in this group.

Yet Israeli sovereignty and independence also provide the Jewish people with unprecedented voice in the family of nations and influence in world events. It has led to the recognition of Jewish dignity and equality in Israel's relations with others. One need only contrast the acceptance of the full dignity and influence of Jewish people today with the Jewish conditions in medieval Christian Europe or during the Shoah in the twentieth century to see that Israel represents an unparalleled historic opportunity for the Jewish people to exercise influence on and foster progress for the nations of the world. Whether it be through its technological and security achievements, its democratic and humanistic values that are unique in the Middle East, its demanding military ethics or its academic prowess, Israel today plays a significant role in world culture and events. Never before has the Jewish people had such an opportunity to teach and influence others on a global scale, and with it the opportunity to spread blessing by contributing to the cultural and economic flourishing of human life.

For the first time in 2,000 years, Israeli sovereignty allows Jews today to play a role similar to that of the biblical Abraham, to whom the first blessing mandate was given. The Bible and rabbinic tradition portray Abraham as actively engaged with his surroundings, a man of action and influence. His landedness, wealth, status and military prowess enabled him to exercise influence on the people around him, to dispense "blessing" to his neighbors.[13] While persecution and anti-Semitism have not disappeared today, the success of modern Zionism has bestowed upon the Jewish people many of those same biblical conditions and opportunities. As it was for Abraham, it appears that the active engagement model of blessing is a realistic and fruitful interpretation for the Jewish people today.[14]

---

13   Gen. 12–18.
14   The overwhelming majority of Jews today reside in Israel and the United States of America. In America too, Jews have prospered and exercise significant influence on

Yet as the rabbinic sources divide on the meaning of Israel as blessing and how that blessing is best achieved, so also do contemporary Jews divide on how their lives can realize this *theologoumenon* and the means to achieve this blessing. Do Jews and the State of Israel have a universal mission to teach the world? If so, is that teaching exclusively theological or does it also include the keys for moral, political, and technical progress? Should Jews ignore the gentile nations and attend only to their own spiritual and physical security, leaving it up to God alone to spread blessing? Lastly, should Jewish religious life connecting to divine blessing be above all history and politics, focusing instead on exclusively spiritual and theurgic matters?

In sum, what should the religious, moral and political aspirations of the State of Israel and the Jewish people be? Many options exist, both religious and secular, but for Jews who measure their individual lives and the life of their people in spiritual terms, the answers to this question cannot be divorced from the theological reflection that the Bible charges the children of Abraham be a blessing, and "that through them all the families of the earth be blessed." And for those Jews, Jewish destiny and Jewish mission will be driven by what theological interpretation they give to the central covenantal notion of Israel as blessing.

---

nearly every aspect of American culture and politics.

Jerome Gellman

Jewish Chosenness—A Contemporary Approach

Introduction

The last half-century has seen an important shift in the attitude of the Catholic Church, and of several Protestant churches, to Judaism and to Jews. The landmark event was the proclamation of *Nostra Aetate* on the Church and the Jews, by Pope Paul VI at Vatican II, on October 28, 1965. Since then, traditional Christian demonizing of Jews and Judaism has been giving way to a more respectful attitude toward Judaism than in the past. And strides have been made in rolling back the age-long teaching of anti-Semitism in Christian Churches. Christian theologians have been creating new, friendly theologies on the Jews and Judaism.

In July 2009, the *Berlin Declaration*, "A Time for Recommitment," issued by the International Council of Christians and Jews, called upon Christians to continue the trajectory of this change. It also called upon Jews to "To re-examine Jewish texts and liturgy in the light of these Christian reforms." Jews were to respond in kind to the Christian awakening by scrutinizing their own theologies and liturgies for anti-Christian and anti-Gentile content. What follows here is a positive response by a religious Jew to the call to Jews to examine our theology and its attitude toward other religions.

Specifically, I offer a new understanding of the doctrine of the Jews as God's chosen people. Spinoza pointed out long ago that the Jewish self-identity as God's chosen people has created resentment and enmity toward the Jews for centuries. Particularly, Christianity claimed for its followers the title of "The New People of God," thereby replacing the Jews' claim to the title, which resulted in severe religious competition for the place of honor at God's table.[1] The Synagogue, so it was said, was blind to the fact that it no longer housed God's chosen people. This attitude is now changing, yet remains a lingering source of inter-religious acrimony.

What demands a revised theology of chosenness is the ever-present danger of Jews interpreting the doctrine of chosenness in ways that endorse ethnocentric supremacy, cultural isolation, and the defamation of other religions. Such a rendering of the doctrine in our times signifies not only an agonistic stance toward other peoples and other religions, but a serious spiritual shortcoming within Judaism itself.

The task I set myself here is to advance internal Jewish religious renewal and mutual religious understanding by presenting a new approach to the doctrine that the Jews are "the Chosen People."

I am not the first Jew to undertake this project. Jewish thinkers before me have written much that is worthwhile in advancing new ideas on Jewish chosenness.[2] However, for reasons I cannot enter into here, I believe that what has gone before is not yet fully adequate to the task. I hope that my proposal will advance us toward a fully adequate conception of Jewish chosenness for our times.

In treating the "Chosen People" theme I will not be trying to explain why God chose *specifically* the Jewish people, rather than, say, the Hittites. Instead, I will be offering an explanation why *any* "Chosen People" might exist in God's world, whether that people be the Jews *or* the Hittites.

Before I begin I offer the following formal definition of what it means to say that the Jews are "*the chosen people.*" It means that:

(1) God has created a permanent, non-revocable, relationship with the Jews that God has not created with any other nation.

---

1   For a study of the notion of the Church as "the people of God" in contemporary Catholic theology, see Angela Kim Harkins, "Biblical and Historical Perspectives on 'the People of God,'" in Franklin T. Harkins, ed., *Transforming Relations, Essays on Jews and Christians throughout History* (Notre Dame, IN: University of Notre Dame Press, 2010), 319–39.
2   These include: Michael S. Kogan, *Opening the Covenant: A Jewish Theology of Christianity* (New York: Oxford University Press, 2008); Jonathan Sacks, *The Dignity of Difference, How to Avoid the Clash of Civilizations* (London, Continuum Books, 2002); and Michael Wyschogrod, in *The Body of Faith, Judaism as Corporeal Election* (Minneapolis: Seabury Press, 1983).

(2) This relationship is of supreme value relative to any relationship God has created or will create with any other *specific* nation.

And,

(3) The religion of the Jews is integrally related to this relationship between God and the Jews.

This is a formal definition that does not say just *what* the relationship is between God and the Jews that makes the Jews into the chosen people.

Freedom and Joy

In his *Philosophical Fragments*, Soren Kierkegaard presented a poignant parable about a king who falls in love with a humble maiden. The king fears he will overwhelm the maiden with "all the pomp of his power," thereby depriving her of her autonomy and sense of self-worth so necessary for their mutual love. So the king limits himself and himself becomes a humble servant, so as to join with her in love freely given. Just so, says Kierkegaard, "God picks His steps... lest he trample human beings in the dust." And just so, God limits Himself so that people will come to him freely. For Kierkegaard this thought leads into a kenotic theology of the incarnation, where God becomes a humble man so as to enter into relationship with other human beings in "freedom and joy." God becomes the man Jesus who walks and talks among humanity as one of them, fostering a love that God could not get in any other way. This is not a pose or a trick, for God really does become a man, becomes a humble servant to be, as it were, with the maiden.

A number of Christian philosophers agree with the spirit of Kierkegaard's parable. They argue that God must be "elusive" and not overwhelm so as not to rob people of their morally significant response to the Divine. Thus, Ronald Hepburn wrote that,

> If God were incontrovertibly revealed, then our belief would be constrained, our allegiance forced, and no place would be left for free and responsible decision whether to walk in God's ways and to entrust oneself to him in faith. Divine elusiveness is a necessary condition of our being able to enter upon properly personal relations with God.[3]

---

3   Ronald W. Hepburn, "From World to God," *Mind* 72 (January 1963), 40–50.

And Michael Murray wrote,

> To preserve the exercise of robust, morally significant free will, God cannot provide grand-scale, firework displays in an effort to make His existence known.[4]

Recently, C. Stephen Evans of Baylor University has expressed an idea in this spirit in a principle he calls the "Easy Resistibility Principle."[5] According to this, God makes it easy for people to resist Him. Says Evans,

> Those who do not wish to love and serve God find it relatively easy to reject the idea that there is knowledge of God. The plausibility of this principle stems from the assumption that God wants the relation humans are to enjoy with him to be one in which they love and serve him freely and joyfully.

In this way, Evans explains why God does not provide strongly indicative natural signs of God's presence in the world. God abides by the principle of Easy Resistibility. Yet, says Evans, God does make His presence accessible to those who wish to know him. Evans makes of this the "Principle of Wide Accessibility," according to which God makes it *possible* at least for humans to come to know his existence. But the signs have to be read and a person must enter freely into relationship with God.

These Christian philosophers, as well as others, testify to the fundamental way God relates to the world.[6] The same idea surfaces in Jewish thought at times. The *Sefer Hachinuch* gives the following explanation for the Biblical commandment to keep a fire burning on the altar in the Tabernacle. (Mitzvah 132):

> We and every wise person knows that in great miracles which God performs with His goodness to people, He will all ways do them in a way of hiddenness, so that it appears somewhat as though they are plainly natural, or nearly natural. Even with the miracle of the parting of the Red Sea, which was a demonstrative miracle, it is written that God moved the sea by way of an easterly wind the entire night, making the sea dry. For that reason, we are commanded to burn a fire on the altar, even though a fire would

---

4   Michael Murray, "Coercion and the Hiddenness of God," *American Philosophical Quarterly* (January 1993), 30, 37
5   In C. Stephan Evans, *Natural Signs and Knowledge of God: A New Look at Theistic Arguments* (Oxford: Oxford University Press, 2010).
6   See also John Hick, *Faith and Knowledge* (Ithaca: Cornell University Press, 1957), especially 178–85.

descend from heaven, in order to hide the miracle [of the fire descending from heaven], so that the fire that came from heaven would not be visible in its descent.[7]

The idea of this passage is that God does not want to overwhelm us, does not want to trample us in the dust, with His miracles. In order to give us the space for choosing Him freely, God hides his miracles just enough to give us a hint of his activity as well as the opportunity for us to respond to God freely.

I take this teaching of God's elusiveness to be included in the opening chapter of Genesis. For six days, God creates, pouring God's creative energy into the world, the world directly impacted by God's overbearing presence. On the seventh day, God rests. For God to "rest" is for God to withdraw God's overwhelming presence from the world so as to create the conditions for humanity to come to God in freedom. That God rests is the precondition for Eve to choose to eat from the forbidden tree and share the fruit with Adam. What it means, in Genesis 1, for the seventh day to be holy, is for it to hold the conditions for coming to God freely. (This is not yet the Jewish Shabbat. See below.)

God Overwhelms the Jews

I am fond of this idea that God wants people to come to Him in freedom and joy and for that reason leaves them room for resistance or indifference. I take the opening chapter of Genesis to be imparting this teaching. For six days, God creates, pouring God's creative energy into the world, the world being directly impacted by God's overbearing presence. On the seventh day, however, God rests. For God to "rest" means for God to withdraw God's overwhelming presence from the world, so as to create precisely that degree of distance in which humanity can choose to come to God in freedom.

I hope to convince you, however, that *the* formative Jewish experiences of God are a radical exception to this idea. And this exception colors the Jewish experience of God even today. The determining Jewish experiences of God are of *God overwhelming the Jewish people to accept Him and His Word*. God overwhelms the Jewish people, with an embrace than which none is stronger. No mere "wooing" or "invitation" for the Jews. Here is why I say this.

---

7   My translation.

(1) A basic category of Judaism is "God's command." In Judaism, God issues 613 commands to the Jewish nation, and these are expanded into a great many more laws. "Commandment" is such a central concept in Judaism that even the fear of God and the love of God are *commands* in Judaism!

In Rabbinic literature, God's many commands to the Israelites are a sign of God's great love of them. So attests the following rabbinic source:

> Rabbi Hananya ben Akashia said: "God wished to confer merit on Israel. That's why God gave them such an abundance of Torah and commandments. (Tractate Makot, 23b)

God displays most vividly and powerfully His love of and desire for the Jewish people in the great many commandments God "bestows" on them.

(2) God redeems the Israelite slaves with numerous, shattering violations of nature in the form of plagues upon the Egyptians. God then spectacularly splits the sea to save the Israelites, following which the Bible testifies that they "feared the Lord and put their trust in him and in Moses his servant." God burrows into the Israelite consciousness with an overpowering pyrotechnic display of God's activity on their behalf.

(3) God makes Mount Sinai shake, and fire and thunder drive the fear of the Lord into the Israelite nation (Exodus, 19–20). Then, God reveals the Ten Commandments not just to a leader who must then convince the people of their having been revealed by God. No. God *sears* the Ten Commandments into the consciousness of the Israelite people by revealing the commandments directly to the entire nation all at once in a shattering event. God leaves no room for doubt about the testimony of others or doubt about the authority of the leader. God's presence and God's will are as manifest to the people as is their own breath.

(4) Take a look at this Talmudic passage:

> Said Rabbi Dimi: [At Mt. Sinai] God turned the mountain over above them like a bowl and said to them: "If you accept the Torah fine. But if not, here you will be buried." (*Avodah Zarah* 2:2).

This looks like raw coercion, not God letting the Israelites come to God "in freedom and joy." God veritably "tramples them in the dust," to use Kierkegaard's phrase.

Actually, though, I prefer a softening of the harshness of this passage offered by a hasidic interpretation. That interpretation turns it from a coercive threat into an overwhelming act of love. I can do no better than to quote the Hasidic Master, Rabbi Shneur Zalman of Liadi (1745–1812):

> God's love for us is greater than our love [for God]. The Rabbis said, "God turned the mountain over above them like a bowl." This means that because of the intensity of God's love for us [the Jewish people] He acts to arouse in us love of Him, so that we should not want to separate ourselves from Him. It is like a person who hugs a person [from behind] and turns him around face to face and won't let him go, because the love of the hugger is greater than that of the hugged, and so that the hugged will not forget the love of the hugger.[8]

On this interpretation, God is not threatening the Israelites, but is concerned that they will not carry with them a strong enough love of God. Then they would end up spiritually dead ("*there*," later, elsewhere, will be your spiritual "burial place."). So God overwhelms them with God's own love to make it harder for them to resist. God hugs them tightly (the "bowl"), hoping that the impression of God's overwhelming love will stay with them for ever after. True enough, later the Israelites then rebelled over and over again. But God was making resistance a perverse response to His manifest presence.

(5) The sense of being overwhelmed by God is reinforced further by the fact that people are *born* Jewish. No baptism, acceptance, or initiation by parents or oneself is required. In the eyes of Jewish law, you are Jewish whether you like it or not. And there is no way out. If you are born Jewish, you can become a Jesuit priest or a Buddhist nun, yet Judaism will consider you a Jew until the end of your days. Of course someone can choose to convert to Judaism. But in doing so one chooses to join a people whose central experience is of a divine bear hug. And as long as the conversion was sincere there is no way back. The convert will remain Jewish and commanded until the day she dies, no matter what! Thus does the fact of just *being* Jewish reinforce the experience of God's overwhelming the Jews in choosing them.

I do not mean to suggest that God does not also want the Jews to choose God in joy and freedom. On the contrary, this is God's fervent desire. The covenant's very existence attests to this desire. And according

---

8   Rabbi Shneur Zalman of Liadi, *Mamarei Ha-Admor Ha-Zaken*, section 196. My translation. I am indebted to Yehuda Zirkind for leading me to this text.

to one traditional source, the Jews freely chose God later in history, after the story of Esther.[9] They freely accepted what they had earlier received. After a long period of God's overwhelming the Jews with His presence, God pulls back and wants the Jews to react in freedom in accepting Him. Indeed, most contemporary Jews are not likely to feel themselves coerced by God to keep the Torah. But my point is not that all feel so compelled. Rather, my emphasis is that when confronting traditional Judaism, what confronts a contemporary Jew is *this* sense of the Jews' relationship to God, reinforced by the lack of choice of having been born Jewish. The foundational Jewish sense of God as overwhelming the people remains the predominant lens through which to view Jewish history and Jewish experience.

All of this tells of God's relationship to the Jews. When addressing the non-Jews, however, God does not overwhelm. Here God does woo, does invite, issuing a *call* to come to God in freedom, a call that can be accepted or rebuffed. Look at this Talmudic passage:

> Rabbi Yochanan said, "Every word that God said [at Mt. Sinai] divided into seventy languages." (*Shabbat* 88b)

Now, in rabbinic literature, the "seventy languages" are of the proverbial seventy nations of the world. Hence, this statement declares that God proclaimed the Ten Commandments to all the nations of the world. On my understanding, in uttering these words to all nations, God exhibits his desire for all to come to God in freedom. However, God does not *compel* the non-Jews as God did the Israelites. Significantly, God's call to the other nations of the world comes concurrently with God's choosing the Israelites. The Divine choice of the Jews simultaneously reverberates as a *call* to all of humanity. And God's call continues even today, as a rabbinic Midrash says that daily God proclaims from Mt. Sinai, "I am the Lord your God," translated, I would add, into the seventy proverbial languages of humanity.

---

9 "Said Rava: 'Nonetheless, [even though they accepted the Torah under duration] they accepted it once again in the time of Ahasuerus'" (Talmud, Shabbat, 88a). Bruce Rosenstock has suggested to me that the return of the exiles in the time of Ezra and their acceptance of the law marks a new freely given acceptance of God and His law. See also David Weiss Halivni, *Breaking the Tablets, Jewish Theology After the Shoah* (Lanham, MD: Rowan and Littlefield Publishers, 2007), ch. 2.

The Meaning of Jewish Chosenness

Given this radical distinction between God's approach to the chosen people, the Jews, and God's approach to the non-Jews, here is my proposal as to why God would single out one nation to robustly *induce* them to accept God, while acting with self-limitation toward the rest of humanity:

(1) God wants humanity to come to Him freely, and God must be restrained in relation to them in order to make that possible. As a result, the world is left with no unambiguous indication, no obvious expression, of God's strong love for them. God is in danger of being perceived as not sufficiently interested in humanity, as not particularly anxious for humans to recognize God's love for them, as not very loving of humanity. God must do something to prove his love to all human beings.

(2) In God's behavior toward the Israelite nation, God provides a real-life demonstration, a figure, a picture, of God's desire for intimacy with *all* humanity. In God's intensity toward the Israelites to accept God and the Torah, God's says to the world: "See my passionate desire to be God to the Jewish people. For here, in my turning to the Jews is a concrete figuration of my desire for all of humanity. Keep this before you when you discern my presence as non-compelling. Keep this in mind when I call to you but do not compel you. Don't take that as insufficient interest on my part. Here, in the Jews, is proof of my wanting all of you with me."

(3) Thus, every act of God's love toward the Jewish people also speaks to all peoples. Each such act is an invitation, a call, an offer, by God to all peoples to receive God's love, as demonstrated by God's relationship to the Jewish people. In this way, God is able to provide a demonstration of God's fervent desire for humanity while allowing humanity the requisite space to choose God in freedom.

(4) In this way do the Jewish people serve God as God's witness to humanity that God desires the hearts of *all* peoples. And this is *my* understanding of the verses in Deuteronomy that God chose the Israelites because God loved them. God's love of the Israelites serves as a sign of God's love for all humanity.

This is *not* the way Jewish chosenness has been interpreted historically. Instead, most often God's love of the Jewish people was taken by the Jews to signify God's exclusive love of the Jews, or indicative at least of God's greater love of the Jews. I am proposing telling a new story from traditional texts. On my view, God's choice of the Jews will not be mistaken as being due to God's special love for the Jews, because the complete story I tell will be propagated. Not only will we present God as overwhelming the Jews with His love, leaving God's motive to be guessed. We will tell my story about why God does this and what God hopes to accomplish thereby.

Jewish history is a complex response to God's decision to choose the Jews both by overwhelming them and God's granting them an enhanced capacity to respond to God with love. On the one hand, Jewish history is a story of Jews responding in love to God in light of the initial overwhelming experiences. On the other hand, it is a story of resistance born of the struggle against God's intensity, and of being born Jewish, and thus being commanded, with no choice in the matter. It is a story of struggle for freedom. In that sense, the Jewish people have been and continue to be a *sacrifice* for God, participating in all of the joy, and all of the tragedy, of being—God's Chosen People.

The continued existence of the Jewish people, through all of its triumphs and sufferings, is a living reminder to the world of the formative experiences of the Jews. That continued existence should signify to the nations of the earth God's steadfastness in staying by those to whom God has turned.[10] This is the promise implicit in the story of the Exodus from Egypt.

But more. The history of the Jewish people serves as a mirror of all of human existence. Human existence has a good share of loss and failure, of anguish and disappointment, of suffering and defeat. This truth about human existence is mirrored in the history of the Jewish people. Jewish history has been a long litany of persecution and suffering, restrictions and isolation. But through it all Jewish history has been punctuated by God's grace shining through the tribulations of a people. In this way, the Jewish people serve as a model for how to understand one's life and how to maintain hope in the darkest of nights. Thus do I invert the Augustinian position, as ordinarily understood, according to which God keeps the Jews in existence in perpetual suffer for their rejection of Jesus, so as to be witness

---

10   Augustine, *City of God* 18:46.

to what befalls his deniers. I turn Jewish survival and suffering to into a positive, rather than a negative, testimony to God's grace.

The controlling image here is of the burning bush, which burns but never is consumed. This image has served Jewish commentators at least since the time of the ancient Jewish philosopher Philo, who wrote:

> For the bush was a symbol of those who suffer the flames of injustice, just as the fire symbolized those responsible for it; but that which burned did not burn up, and those who suffered injustice were not to be destroyed by their oppressors.[11]

The Jewish role as God's chosen people implies a sacrificial existence that configures, but does not atone for, the fiery side of human existence with the promise of God's redemption. Hence, the Jews in their sacrificial mode are not a Christ figure of atonement, but are rather the Israelites who endure bitter enslavement only to be redeemed in an archetype of a divine promise of redemption for all of humankind.

Each of God's acts of love toward the Israelites and the Jews becomes a promise to the Gentiles if they will come to God in freedom. The Exodus from Egypt speaks of a promise of redemption for all peoples in God. The giving of the Torah to the Jews signifies the possibility for all peoples to be guided by God's light if they will choose it.

The Jewish Sabbath subverts the seventh day of creation of Genesis 1 when God rested, thereby having created the space for humanity to come to God in freedom. The Jewish Sabbath is a sign of the especially close intimacy between God and the Jews, bound to God in the covenant: "The Children of Israel shall keep the Sabbath for all their generations, as an everlasting covenant. For between me and the Children of Israel it is a sign forever." (Exodus 31:17) Thus does the *Shabbat* bear a duality for the world: a movement by God to create freedom for the Gentile to come to God in joy, and a movement by God to bind the Jews to God as the chosen people.

Of course, the sacrificial nature of Jewish existence is but one side of the Jewish experience, balanced with the joy and sublimity of being Jewish and following the Jewish religion. Yet, for a Jew the joy and freedom must come through and be the result of living the sacrificial mode of service to God. It would take us too far from the task at hand were I to enter into how

---

11 Philo, *Life of Moses* 1:65–67, as quoted in James L. Kugel, *How to Read the Bible, A Guide to Scripture, Then and Now* (New York: Free Press, 2007), 213.

this complexity works itself out in Jewish religious life. But I do mean to suggest a phenomenology of Judaic religious consciousness rooted in the sense of being commanded, and overwhelmed by being God's chosen people. A sense of sacrificiality redeemed.

The continued existence of the Jewish people, through all of its triumphs and sufferings, is a living reminder of the formative experiences of the Jews. And, the continued existence of the Jewish people is a mirror of all human existence. When one looks into this mirror what one sees is that within the dire vicissitudes of life God's covenant will remain.[12]

In saying that God only *calls* to the non-Jews and does not compel, I must issue a slight qualification. I am aware that sometimes non-Jewish individuals have felt that God had taken hold of them tightly and would not let them go. Teresa of Avila comes to mind as an outstanding example of this. *The Catholic Encyclopedia* writes about her, "The more she endeavored to resist, the more powerfully did God work in her soul." I recognize this as a possibility for a non-Jew, and admit that this would violate Evans' Principle of Easy Resistance. However, I doubt that this phenomenon reflects a true Divine activity on a large scale. In contrast, it is the Jews as a people who have carried this sense of God's overbearing overtures to them into an entire religion, as a permanent presence in the world.

---

12 This does not address the question of why God allows the vicissitudes of life such free reign in the first place. I will not take up that question here. It is the classic question about God and life and most poignantly about God and the Jewish people. In what I write here there is a partial, but *very* partial, attempt at a theodicy concerning Jewish suffering. That is that given the fact of human suffering, Jewish suffering together with Jewish survival against all odds testifies to the world of God's grace within the afflictions of life. This is a dimension of the sacrificial role of the Jews in God's world.

I do not pretend for a moment, however, that this thought justifies the horrendous evils the Jewish people have endured in their history. Neither do I address why there is human misery in the first place. Here I must be silent.

Menachem Katz

Aleinu—A Prayer Common to Jews and Gentile God-Fearers*

Introduction

In this paper I will explore different meanings attributed to the first section of the *Aleinu* prayer, the liturgical poem recited at the conclusion of each of the three daily Jewish services. I will also examine modern theological and educational applications of the interpretations of this prayer. I will address the question of the historical circumstances in which the ideas may be realized, in particular in relation to contemporary theological challenges arising out of the special conditions of our time, including the founding of the State of Israel as well as advances in interfaith dialogue.

The texts cited in this paper come from a broad range of sources, representing all periods and schools of Jewish thought.

The Scope of Israel's Prayers

Most Jewish prayers that were coalesced and formulated in the Tannaitic period (after the destruction of the Second Temple, in the Yavneh generation and following it), refer mainly to the Jewish people (such as the *Amidah*). Let us look at examples from these central prayers:

---

* I lectured on this topic at the Fifteenth World Congress of Jewish Studies, 3rd August 2009.

In the blessings accompanying the recitation of the *Shema*, the daily declaration of faith, God is praised for loving and watching over the people of Israel: "הבוחר בעמו ישראל באהבה" "who has chosen His people Israel with love" (*Shaharit*, morning service); "אוהב עמו ישראל" "who loves His people Israel" (*Arvit*, evening service); "גאל ישראל" "who has redeemed Israel"; "שומר עמו ישראל לעד", "who guards His people Israel forever"; "תֶכֶס שֶׁרוּפָּה סֻכַּלְשׁוּרִי לָעוּ לָאֲרֹשִׁי וּמַע לָךְ לָעוּ וּנִיָלָע סוֹלָשׁ" "who spreads over us a shelter of peace and over all His people Israel and over Jerusalem."

In the *Amidah*, or standing prayer, which is the core of all Jewish prayer services, the stress is consistently on the Jewish people.

The prayer opens:

> Blessed are *You*, **Lord our God and God of our fathers, God of Abraham, God of Isaac and God of Jacob**, ...

Its closing words are:

> May it please You to **bless your people Israel** with peace at all times and hours. Blessed are You, O Lord, who blesses **His people Israel** with peace.

This also applies to the critical closing phrases of other blessings in the *Amidah*, including those of general human concern, such as the blessing for healing, where the reference is solely to the people of Israel: "who heals the sick among your people Israel."

The particularity of prayer and its relation to the Jewish people is clearly expressed in the *Mekhilta*, that speaks about "the occupation of Abraham, Isaac, and Jacob" in contrast to the other nations:

> *And They Were Sore Afraid; and the Children of Israel Cried Out unto the Lord* (Ex. 14:10). Immediately they seized upon the occupation of their fathers, the occupation of Abraham, Isaac, and Jacob....
>
> And in this sense it also says: "Fear not, thou worm Jacob, and ye men of Israel" (Isa. 41:14). Just as the worm has only its mouth to smite the cedar with, so Israel has only prayer. And thus it says: "Moreover, I have given to thee one portion above thy brethren, which I took out of the hand of the Amorite, with my sword and with my bow" (Gen. 48:22). And did he really take it with his sword and bow? Has it not already been said: "For I trust not in my bow, neither can my sword save me" (Ps. 44:7)? Hence, what must be the meaning of the words: "With my sword and

with by bow"? "With my sword"—this is prayer, "with my bow"—this is supplication.[1]

Likewise, David said to Goliath: "Thou comest to me with a sword and with a spear and a javelin, but I come to thee in the name of the Lord of hosts" (I Sam. 17:45).

And it is also written: "Some trust in chariots, and some in horses; but we will make mention of the name of the Lord our God. They are bowed down and fallen; but we are risen and stand upright. Save, Lord; let the King answer us in the day that we call (Ps. 20:8–10)...

What did it say of Moses? "And Moses sent messengers from Kadesh unto the king of Edom..."

"Our fathers went down into Egypt ... and when we cried unto the Lord, He heard our voice" (Num. 20:14–16). The Edomites, however, said to them: You pride yourselves upon what your father Isaac bequeathed you, "The voice is the voice of Jacob," "And the Lord heard our voice" (Num. 20:16).

And we pride ourselves on what our father Isaac bequeathed us, "The hands are the hands of Esau," "And by thy sword shalt thou live" (Gen. 27:40) ...

And so here you also interpret: "And they were sore afraid; and the children of Israel cried out unto the Lord"—they seized upon the occupation of their fathers, the occupation of Abraham, Isaac, and Jacob.[2]

While in theory Israel could also pray for the nations, a fact that is of obvious relevance for the continuation of the *Aleinu* prayer, in the present context the focus is on Israel engaging in prayer in relation to their enemies, and therefore both as the subject and the object of prayer.

The majority of prayers that took shape and consolidated their language in the tannaitic period refer to the Jewish people, as indeed described by Menachem Kahana:[3]

> An examination of the *Shemoneh Esreh*, which was formulated at Yavne after the destruction of the Temple, indicates that one of its central themes, if not the main one, is the **redemption of Israel**.... A blessing for the redemption of the world and its rectification within the kingdom of the Lord was not

---

[1] The midrash completely turns around the meaning of the words of Jacob. Jacob spoke about sword and bow, while the midrash turns them into prayer and supplication; *bekashti* (with my bow)—*bakkashah* (supplication), sound similar; *herev* (sword)—perhaps because prayer is a kind of symbolic sword that cuts through to beyond.
[2] *Mekhilta de-Rabbi Ishamel,* Beshalah, Parshah Bet, 206–9.
[3] M. Kahana, "The Attitude to Non-Jews in the Tannaitic and Amoraic Period," *Et ha-Da'at* 3 (2000): 22.

interpolated into the daily prayer service, but this idea is expressed in the Rosh Hashanah *Malkhuyyot* series (verses describing God's kingship) ... Only very much later, in the Middle Ages, did it become customary to recite the *Aleinu le-Shabbe'ah* prayer, which was taken from the *Malkhuyyot* series, after the Amidah prayers during the three daily prayer services, *Shaharit* (Morning), *Minhah* (Afternoon), and *Ma'ariv* (Evening). In this way the *Amidah*, which focuses on the redemption of Israel, gained a kind of permanent complement concerning the redemption of the entire world, even though the initial motives for this completion apparently stemmed from other reasons.

Kahana is referring to the second part of the *Aleinu* prayer, which expresses and stresses the kingship of God in the world (*Malkhuyyot*) at the end of days:

> We hope therefore, Lord our God, soon to behold thy majestic glory, when the abominations will be removed from the earth, and the false gods exterminated; when the world will be perfected under the reign of the Almighty.[4]
>
> And all mankind will call upon thy name, and all the wicked of the earth will be turned to thee,
>
> May all the inhabitants of the world realize and know that to thee every knee must bend, every tongue must vow allegiance.
>
> May they bend the knee and prostrate themselves before thee, Lord our God, and give honor to thy glorious name;
>
> May they all accept the yoke of thy kingdom, and do thou reign over them speedily and forever and ever.
>
> For the kingdom is thine, and to all eternity thou will reign in glory, as it is written in thy Torah: "The Lord shall be King forever and ever."

Aleinu Leshabeach—History of Research

The present discussion focuses on one ancient prayer that, I believe, departs from the common focus of rabbinic prayer, described above. This is the *Aleinu Leshabeach* prayer. Following is the text of the prayer:

---

4 Whereas in our version we read *le-taqqen* לְתַקֵּן (to perfect), in the Yemenite and Rabbi Saadiah Gaon versions the term is read as *le-takken* לְתַכֵּן (to establish).

> It is our duty to praise the Master of all, to proclaim the greatness of the Creator of the universe, for He has not made us like the nations of the earth; and has not emplaced us like the families of the lands; for He has not assigned our portion like theirs, nor cast our lot like all their multitude. For they bow to vanity and emptiness and pray to a God which helps not.
>
> But we bend our knees, bow, and acknowledge our thanks before the King Who reigns over kings, the Holy One, Blessed is He.
>
> He stretches out heaven and establishes earth's foundation, the seat of His homage is in the heavens above and His powerful Presence is in the loftiest heights. He is our God and there is none other.
>
> True is our King, there is nothing beside Him, as it is written in His Torah: "Know therefore this day, and consider it in thine heart, that the LORD he is God in heaven above, and upon the earth beneath: there is none else."

A number of exegetes and scholars have discussed this prayer.[5] The most common approach focuses on "He has not made us like the nations of the earth," stressing that the set Jewish prayers are for the Jewish people alone. Another view, in medieval Europe, was that the prayer was directed against Jesus with the verse "For they bow to vanity and emptiness" (the numerical value of וריק [emptiness] being equal to that of ישו [Jesus]); In this approach the contrast is not between the Jewish people and the nations but between the Jews, who do not accept Jesus as the Messiah, and the people who do.[6] This is why this verse was deleted from the prayer in the Ashkenazi prayer rite from the Middle Ages in Christian Europe. In what follows, I will propose an alternative. Let me turn first to other explanations that can help us better understand the prayer.

The scholar of liturgy, Aharon Mirsky believes the *Aleinu Leshabeach* prayer was formed during the Second Temple period. He reached this conclusion on the basis of linguistic and stylistic considerations, which, in his opinion, reflect the period between the Bible and the Mishnah, as he argues here:

> For the poem *Aleinu le-Shabbeʾah* ... the language of the poem and its style are reminiscent of the Written Law as well as the Oral Law. As for the

---

5 See Sh. Bar-On and Y. Paz, "The Lord of All" and "The Creator of the World" (below, n11), n6.
6 See, for example, Ismar Elbogen, *Jewish Liturgy: A Comprehensive History* (Philadelphia: Jewish Publication Society, 1993), 63–64.

> Written Law—when the poet comes to praise the Holy One blessed be He, the Creator of all, he interpolated into his poem the rhetoric of Isaiah 51[:13] with the verse: "who stretched out the skies and made firm the earth" ... and [concerning] the manner of the Oral Law—here we find the names, such as the Holy One blessed be He, *Shekhinah* (presence) ... not only does the poem have the characteristics of biblical style and characteristics of mishnaic style, but you find them mixed and melded into each other.[7]

In terms of both style and content, *Aleinu Leshabeach* stands in the era between the Bible and the Mishnah, an era with a character of its own, a blend of styles, corresponding to the way it was formed and shaped by the Torah and the general thought of those days. It is a precious style in Hebrew literature.

Joseph Heinemann discusses the link between the *Aleinu* prayer and the Temple service:

> There remains one more prayer found among the statutory prayers whose style clearly proves its *Bet Midrash* origin,[8] but concerning which there is no ready explanation why it was formulated in a pattern which does not fit the general style of the synagogue liturgy. We are referring to the first part of *Aleinu Leshabeach* which originally formed the opening passage of the *Malkiyyôt* in the *Amidah* on the New Year, viz., part of one of the statutory prayers *par excellence*....
>
> All this strongly suggests that *Aleinu* was composed against the background of the Temple service. Only while the Temple stood could it be stressed that the Divine Presence dwells "up on high" without explicitly stating that it also dwells in the Holiest of Holies. On the contrary, when its presence in the Temple could be taken for granted, it was necessary to caution against a simplistic faith that might see the Temple as God's actual dwelling place, insisting rather that His presence also dwells in the heavens and that the Temple below is only a mirror image of the one above. Only at the time when the Temple existed could the Kingdom of God be understood as a fact rather than as an eschatological hope.
>
> However, having connected the origin of this prayer with the Temple, we have yet to account for its *Bêt Midrāš* pattern. We would suggest that the *Aleinu* prayer came into being in connection with the service of the "Men

---

7 A. Mirsky, *Ha-Piyyut* (Jerusalem, 1991), 72–73.
8 Prayers that were created following public Torah study, in particular in the course of public discussion.

of the *Ma'ᵃmād.*" This service took place in the Temple ... The service of the *Ma'ᵃmād* centered around the repeated reading from the *Tôrāh* of the account of Creation (Gen. 1) ... There could be no more fitting conclusion to such an exposition of the Creation chapter than the *Aleinu* prayer, which, starting with praise of God as the Creator of the universe, proceeds to emphasize at length the sole recognition of his Kingdom and his omnipotence by his people Israel and its worship of him in his Temple in the Holy City.[9]

Heinemann, as well as other scholars, are of the opinion that it is precisely when the Temple stood that such theological clarification is required, in contradistinction to how pagan temples would have been understood. There was significant need at that time to warn against superficial faith, which considered the Temple as God's actual dwelling place and to stress that His presence also dwells in the heavens, while the Temple below is only a mirror image of the one above. His hypothesis is that this prayer was created as a result of the repeated reading of the Creation chapter by the "Men of the *Ma'ᵃmād.*"

The scholar of Talmudic and Rabbinic literature, Israel Ta-Shma agrees with Heinemann's opinion and on the basis of the latter's statements he explains the history of the transformations in the recitation of this prayer in the course of the Middle Ages and why it is now said at the close of our prayers and at other times. Ta-Shma also takes notes of the *Rishonim* having praised this prayer at great length and having exaggerated the very antiquity of *Aleinu*, to the days of Moses and Joshua bin Nun:

> I shall summarize these ideas in brief... In the early Middle Ages individual Jews in Ashkenaz and France customarily recited at the end of their prayers, after "*u-va le-Tziyyon,*" a series of daily *ma'madot* (passages) ... *Aleinu* was one selection among the passages in this series, and that was its position before it appeared in the prayer books among the conclusionary chapters of the regular prayer service. With the gradual decline of this series, parts of it were interpolated into the set daily prayers in various positions: before, during, and at the end of the prayer service. The *Aleinu le-Shabbeʽah* piece, and others of a similar nature, should be considered in light of this distribution.[10]

---

9 Joseph Heinemann, *Prayer in the Talmud: Forms and Patterns* (Berlin & New York: de Gruyter, 1977), 270–73.
10 I. M. Ta-Shma, *Ancient Ashkenazi Prayer* (Jerusalem, 1983), 143–44.

I wish to underscore that while Mirsky, Heinemann and Ta-Shma spoke of the age of the prayer and its link to the Temple, through the *Ma'amadot* connected to the Temple, they did not refer to the germane point of the current discussion, namely, that the prayer was intentionally formulated in language that would befit both Jew and non-Jew, members of the Jewish people as well as others. From these scholars' statements, particularly Heinemann's, we see clearly that they perceive this prayer as emphasizing the difference between those who belong to the people of Israel and those who do not.

Shraga Bar-On and Yakir Paz discuss the meaning of the *Aleinu* prayer and when it was compiled in their recent article: *"The Lord of All" and "The Creator of the World": Aleinu le-Shabeach as an Anti-Binitarian Prayer*.[11] Their main argument is that this is a polemical, clearly anti-Binitarian prayer. It seems to me that in their article they succeeded in showing convincingly the anti-Binitarian stance of this prayer, and that it is a lively debate against various early beliefs. Yet, their argument for the composition of the *Aleinu* between the second century and the first half of the third century CE does not seem to me necessary. While anti-Binitarian polemic did exist during this period, it also existed previously in the first century CE, during the period of the Temple.[12] It is even more difficult for me to accept the reading of the *Aleinu* prayer according to which this prayer holds that distinguishes and differentiate between the People of Israel and others and that "the prayer has a distinctly national character."[13] As they take a particular understanding for granted, their discussion does not advance the argument for such an understanding.

Aleinu Leshabeach—A New Suggestion

I would like to propose that the first part of *Aleinu* is a very ancient prayer that was composed prior to the destruction of the Second Temple and that served as a common prayer for all who came to the Temple, both Jews and

---

11 Shraga Bar-On and Yakir Paz, "'The Lord of All' and 'The Creator of the World': Aleinu le-Shabeach as an Anti-Binitarian Prayer," *Jewish Studies* 52 (2017): 19–46 [Hebrew]. See also their article "'The Lord's Allotment is his People': The Myth of the Election of Israel by Casting of Lots and the Gnostic-Christian-Pagan-Jewish Polemic," *Tarbitz* 79 (2010–11): 23–62 [Hebrew].
12 For references to earlier instances of anti-binitarian polemic see Bar-On and Paz, "'The Lord of All' and 'The Creator of the World,'" notes 27–30.
13 Ibid., 26.

non-Jews, who were called "God-fearers" or "fearers of Heaven." My interpretation contrasts with the common understanding of this prayer, *Aleinu Leshabeach*, as emphasizing the difference between the Jewish people and the other nations. The dating of the prayer as prior to the destruction of the Temple is relevant to the present argument. I propose that this is not a prayer that contrasted between the Jewish people and other nations, as portrayed by the common interpretation, but rather—as I see it—that it served as a common prayer for all those who came to the Temple, both Jews and gentiles, those who are called God-fearers or fearers of the Heavens. The contrast is between pagans and all those who accept God as the Creator, Jews and non-Jews. In other words, those who accept God as Creator of the world: Kohanim (the house of Aaron), the people of Israel and those who fear God.

That the Temple served as common ground for a common faith of Jews and Gentiles emerges already from the Psalms. Thus we read in Psalm 115:

> (2) Let the nations not say, "Where, now, is their God?" (3) when our God is in heaven and all that He wills He accomplishes ... (9) O **Israel**, trust in the Lord! He is their help and shield. (10) O **house of Aaron**, trust in the Lord! He is their help and shield. (11) O you **who fear the Lord**, trust in the Lord! He is their help and shield. (12) The Lord is mindful of us. He will bless us the **house of Israel**; He will bless the **house of Aaron**; (13) He will bless those **who fear the Lord**, small and great alike. (14) May the Lord increase your numbers, yours and your children's also. (15) May you be blessed by the Lord, Maker of heaven and earth.

It can be said of all of these people, in the words of Aleinu, that they are not like the other "nations of the earth" or "families of the world."

I believe a distinction is made here, but not between the people of Israel and others, but between those who believe in one God, the Creator of the world (including God-fearers), and others, be they idolaters or believers in the twoness of God. There is no reference here to the people of Israel, but rather between those who believe in a (single) creator of the universe and those who do not. This is a special prayer created precisely so that Jews and non-Jews could recite it together in Jerusalem. What we have then is a prayer that stresses the unfathomable difference between idol worshippers and those who believe in one God, creator of the world, "Master of all," and "Creator of the universe." Following the logic we saw above, according to which the Temple occasioned the need to distinguish pagan from true religious understanding, such emphasis is featured in a prayer to be recited by all at the Jerusalem Temple.

Biblical Foundations for *Aleinu's* Worldview

The *Aleinu Leshabeach* prayer is unique in relation to the majority of Jewish prayers, where there is clear mention of the Jewish people, in one way or another.[14] Here we find no reference to the people of Israel. This, in my understanding, is intentional, so that all those who frequent the temple will feel equal in this declaration of faith. This is in keeping with a prophetic ideal that is realized in this prayer. For example—"As for the foreigners who attach themselves to the Lord ... I will bring them to My sacred mount and let them rejoice in My house of prayer ... **For My house shall be called a house of prayer for all peoples**" (Isa. 56:6–7).[15]

In Psalm 134, the same approach can be found:

(1) A Song of Ascents, now bless the Lord, **all servants of the Lord**, who stand nightly in the house of the Lord.
(2) Lift your hands toward the sanctuary and **bless** the Lord.
(3) May the Lord, maker of heaven and earth, **bless you** from Zion.

It is not clear to whom the salutation at the beginning of the psalm is addressed to *kohanim* (priests) who are servants of the Lord or to all servants of the Lord, not necessarily *kohanim*, nor is it clear at the end of the psalm whom the Lord will bless. It is noteworthy that a number of expressions in the psalm allude to the *kohanim* as the object of the address. This is seen in expressions "who stand ... in the house of the Lord," "servants of the Lord," and particularly "lift your hands," which can be associated with what is stated concerning Aaron the high priest, "Aaron **lifted his hands toward the people and blessed them**" (Leviticus 9:22), especially in light of the sentence in our psalm, "**Lift your hands** toward the sanctuary and **bless** the Lord."

However, not only is it not clear that the appeal is to the *kohanim*, but apparently it is stressed that it is not only *kohanim* who are being addressed but rather all servants of the Lord. After the opening appeal, "Now bless

---

14 In addition to "Israel," there are other terms or phrases such as "Lord our God and God of our fathers," "God of Abraham, God of Isaac, and God of Jacob."
15 See also Psalm 117 and Psalm 115.

the Lord," the speaker finds it necessary to explain to whom his words are addressed—"**all** servants of the Lord," with the emphasis on "all." In the continuation as well "who stand ... in the house of the Lord," ostensibly refers to *kohanim*, but the entire phrase, "who stand **nightly** in the house of the Lord," is difficult to understand as speaking precisely of the priests. We know that the service of the Lord in the house of the Lord, the Temple, took place during the day and that the Temple gates were locked at sunset. Thus, even though at first glance it seems that the psalm is directed to the *kohanim*, on second reading one realizes that it addresses all servants of the Lord. If that is the case, we have here a psalm that stresses that not only the *kohanim* but rather all servants of the Lord are those who bless the Lord, and the Lord will bless them, not necessarily through the priests, for it is the Lord who is "Maker of heaven and earth."[16]

This was precisely the concept that was central to those who formulated the *Aleinu* prayer, and it stands in contrast to the "priestly" approach in which the *kohanim* are the ones who perform the service before the Lord and who approach him, and they are also the ones who bless the people (but not the Lord!).

Rabbinic Parallels to *Aleinu's* Universalism

As noted earlier, Prof. I. M. Ta-Shma argued that the *Aleinu* prayer was recited following the Torah readings of the *Ma'amadot*. What distinguishes this service is that it universal in nature, consisting of scriptural readings from the *chapter of the creation of the world*, as the Mishnah attests (Ta'anit 4):

> *What are the* Ma'amadot? [...] And the Israelites of that selfsame Course came together unto their own cities *to read the story of the Creation.* [...]
>
> > On the first day they read from: *In the beginning ...* to *Let there be a firmament*, and on the second day, from *Let there be a firmament ...* to *Let the waters be gathered together*,
> >
> > and on the third day, from *Let the waters be gathered together ...* to *Let there be lights*,

---

16 Perhaps there is a similarity between the psalm and the blessing by Melchizedek, that is, to the blessing of a non-Jew. Note that the phrase "Creator of heaven and earth" (Genesis 14:19) is similar to the expression "Maker of heaven and earth" (Psalm 134:3).

and on the fourth day, from *Let there be lights* ... to *Let the waters bring forth abundantly*

and on the fifth, from *Let the waters bring forth abundantly* ... to *Let the earth bring forth*

and on the sixth, from *Let the earth bring forth* ... to *And the heaven and the earth were finished.*

Another rabbinic parallel may be found in the different blessings for the reading of the Torah. These reflect different understanding of the Torah in relation to Israel. While some of the blessings do stress the "chosenness" of the Jewish people, the blessing recited after the Torah reading does not have such a dimension. And it may be that this is not unintentional. Blessings on the Torah can be dated back to the time of Nehemiah and we have testimonies to their recitation during Second Temple times.[17] Based on various criteria, it may be suggested that the reference to Israel in the blessings on the Torah represent a later stratum, while the earlier stratum may contain a more universal perspective with reference to the Torah. Accordingly, the proposed later blessing before Torah reading states:

> Blessed art thou, Lord our God, King of the Universe, *who hast chosen us from all peoples*, and hast given us thy Torah. Blessed art thou, O Lord, Giver of the Torah.

In contrast, the [apparently] more ancient blessing, after the Torah reading, presents a universal approach:

> Blessed art thou, Lord our God, King of the Universe, who hast given *us* the Torah of truth, and hast planted everlasting life in our midst. Blessed art thou, O Lord, Giver of the Torah.

This "us" reminds us of the "us" of the *Aleinu*, and is similarly open to a reading that transcends ethnic boundaries, and constitutes a congregation of common faith, beyond the boundaries of Israel.

Finally, in the following (perhaps the latest of these blessings), the emphasis is most clearly on the Jewish people:

---

17 See D. Henshke, *Festival Joy in Tannaitic Discourse* (Jerusalem: Magnes Press, 2007), 201–3 (Hebrew); D. Flusser, *Judaism of the Second Temple Period: Sages and Literature* (Jerusalem: Gefen Books, 2002), 191–97; M. Weinfeld, *Early Jewish Liturgy* (Jerusalem 2004), 204–5 (Hebrew), M. A. Friedman, "'He Planted Eternal Life in Our Midst'—In the Past; 'May He Plant His Torah in Our Hearts'—In the Future," *Tarbiz* LX (1991), 265–68 (Hebrew).

> Blessed are you, Lord our God, King of the Universe, who has sanctified us with your commandments, and commanded us to study the Torah. Lord our God, make the words of thy Torah pleasant in our mouth and *in the mouths of your people, the house of Israel*, so that we and our descendants and the *descendants of the people, the house of Israel,* may all know they name and study the Torah for its own sake. Blessed are you, O Lord, who teaches Torah *to your people Israel.*

The possibility of a Torah blessing that is not centered on Israel may conform to an understanding that sees the Torah itself as suited for all people, beyond Israel's ethnic boundaries. This is indeed how Menachem Hirschman reads this blessing and he provides a broader conceptual framework from within which it can be appreciated in a consistent manner.[18]

Hirschman points to various sources, associated with the school of R. Ishmael, where the Torah's universal potential is featured. The very name of his book was taken from an expression appearing in *Sifre Bamidbar*, "The crown of the Torah ... for all those who come into the world." A similar notion, even more pronounced, is found in *Mekhilta d'Arayot*, "Even a Gentile who 'did' Torah, behold he is like the high priest":

> "By doing, a person shall live" (Lev. 18:5).
> R. Yirmiya was wont to say, "whence do you say that **even a Gentile who 'did' Torah, behold he is like the high priest?'** Scripture teaches 'by doing this a person [shall live].'" Priests, Levites, and Israelites are not specified here (rather scripture says a person); and likewise it says "this is the Torah ...." The Priests, Levites, and the Israelites are not specified; rather "This is the Torah of a person, my lord God" (2 Sam. 7:19); ... you see **even a Gentile who "did" Torah, behold he is like the high priest.**[19]

If that is the case, we may speak of a general approach—Torah and prayer for all humans. Such a view is also echoed in the following fourfold breakdown of groups relating to God:

---

18 Hirshman, Marc, *Torah for the Entire World* (Hebrew. Tel Aviv: Hakibbutz Hameuchad Publishing House, 1999); Hirshman, Marc G., Rabbinic Universalism in the Second and Third Centuries, *Harvard Theological Review* 93,2 (2000): 101–115
19 L. Finkelstein and M. Lutzki, ed., *Torat Kohanim* (New York: JTS, 1956) (Facsimile edition of Codex Assemani 66 of the Vatican Library), 373–74.

And you find them also among the four groups who respond and speak before Him by whose word the world came into being:

"One shall say: 'I am the Lord's, and another shall call himself by the name of Jacob, and another shall subscribe with his hand unto the Lord, and surname himself by the name of Israel" (Isa. 44:5).

"One shall say: 'I am the Lord's" (Isa. 44:5), that is: "All of me is the Lord's and there is **no admixture of sin in me**."

"And another shall call himself by the name of Jacob" (ibid.), these are the **righteous proselytes**.

"And another shall subscribe with his hand unto the Lord" (ibid.), these are **the repentant sinners**.

"And surname himself by the name of Israel" (ibid.), these are the **God-fearing ones**.[20]

Conclusion and Reflection

I have argued in this paper that the *Aleinu* prayer contrasts between pagans and those who accept God as the Creator of the universe, Jews and non-Jews. Hence, it is not a contrast between any small group and others, but an approach that encompasses a large section of humankind. It is thus a prayer that has broad universal potential. Anyone who believes in the Creator of the universe is part of "us," in contrast to the pagans, about whom it says, "For they bow to vanity and emptiness and pray to a God which helps not."

The prayer and its continued repetition over two thousand years invites us to consider who might be included in this "us" today. During Temple times there were no other monotheistic religions. Hence, the "us" could only relate to God fearers.[21] With the advent of other monotheistic faiths, it would seem the "us" could be extended to include these as well. Recognizing God as Creator of the universe and of all mankind can serve as the basis of affirming different religions and of bringing them into the

---

20 *Mekhilta De-Rabbi Ishmael*, trans. J. Z. Lauterbach (Philadelphia: JPS, 1993), v. 3, 141.
21 Its recitation at the Temple also provided an institutional context that is no longer available and is no longer needed. It is striking that the Western Wall functions de-facto as a coming together of Jews and non-Jews in prayer, in an institutional setting that harks back to the *Aleynu's* original context, on the one hand, and that provides a foretaste of the biblical prophecy of a House of Prayer for All Peoples. The recitation of *Aleynu* and the context of the *ma'amadot* provide suggestive possibilities for faith-based liturgies that could be appropriate to such a setting.

circle of commonality referenced by the *Aleinu* prayer. Perhaps that circle of commonality may include or be extended to ethical commonality, and not only faith commonality, and thereby draw one possible circle of sharing that is relevant to the contemporary situation.[22]

That faith, rather than ethnicity, stands at the core of some fundamental texts is a thesis that is important not only for understanding the past but also for our worldview today. The recovery of multiple strands—biblical, rabbinic and liturgical, that draw different lines between "us" and "them" than the commonly perceived borderline that identifies ethnicity and religion, is of great significance for religious thought. If others share that sense of the core, the faith, the gift, the "us," this significantly reduces a sense of uniqueness and superiority, highlighting instead faith in the one God and his guiding word.

---

[22] Such extension may require further theoretical support than the more religiously oriented sources presented here. One likely source for such support may be Rabbi Menachem Hameiri. On the possibility of extending his approach to non-religious humanists, see David Berger, Jews, gentiles, and the modern egalitarian ethos: some tentative thoughts, Marc Stern ed., *Formulating Responses in an Egalitarian Age* (Lanham, MD: Rowman and Littlefield Publishers, 2005), 83–108.

Stanislaw Krajewski

Two Dimensions of Jewish Identity

Introduction and Summary

Our perception of other religions depends on the type of group identity assumed as our religious identity. The issue of identity is too broad to be discussed here in a comprehensive way. Only one aspect of group identity is explored here—the one relating to positive and negative dimensions of identity. It is illuminated on the basis of Jewish texts and from the perspective of social psychology. Its consequences for attitudes to other religions are emphasized.

Generally speaking, negative identity is established by way of contrast: *I am me because I am not you*. It functions naturally, by turning against the enemies of one's own group, especially if identification is formed by the threat. On the other hand, positive identity is established by focusing on the values to be cultivated within the group, by belief in the internal values of one's own group: *I am me because I like being me*. In the context of inter-human (as well as interreligious) encounters, the difference between the two dimensions is beautifully expressed by the famous dictum of the Kotzker Rebbe:

> If I am me because I am me, and you are you because you are you, then I am me and you are you. But if I am me because you are you and you are you because I am me, then I am not me and you are not you.[1]

---

[1] Menachem Mendel was a notable nineteenth-century hasidic master in the Polish town Kock.

The Kotzker's wisdom indicates that the positive identity, emerging from within, is better than the negative one, imposed from outside. The dictum is general, it refers to many, perhaps all, kinds of identity. While originally articulated in the framework of personal identity, its extension to issues of identity between groups, as well as of religions, seems appropriate.

According to social psychology (Zimbardo's experiments, Tajfel's experiments, see below), negative identification can be very strong even if the line of division is invented *ad hoc* and the alienation from the "other" is stimulated artificially. This means that the mere presence of a strong negative identity, against "others," is not by itself a guarantee of its depth or value. Group identification can be accidental, without a real threat or any other genuine source. Of course, there has been no shortage of real dangers in the history of Jews. The sense of forming a "camp," a proverbial besieged fortress, remains one of the essential determinants of the actual Jewish identity. It has rather negative consequences for attitudes to other religions: they are seen as a threat.

Yet the core of Jewish identity, or at least the religious identity, has always been positive—"for" something. It is the identity of the Covenant, the community of witnesses who bear witness to the Creator of this world. Contemporary Judaism is composed of different currents but all of them are united by a sense of faithfulness to the Covenant. If this is to constitute the basis for the attitudes towards other religions there is no reason to be negative about them, even if they are not appropriate for Jews. If the positive identity, i.e. rootedness in one's own tradition, is strong enough, other religions need not be seen as posing any threats.

Two Dimensions of Identity

Our attitude to other religions and their adherents is an instance of intergroup relations. According to social scientists, "Whenever individuals belonging to one group interact, collectively or individually, with another group or its members *in terms of their group identification*, we have an instance of intergroup behavior."[2] Henri Tajfel explains that 'identification,' in contradistinction to sheer belonging to a group defined from outside (for example, hospital patients), involves two necessary components: "a

---

2   M. Sherif, *In Common Predicament: Social Psychology of Intergroup Conflict and Cooperation* (Boston: Houghton Mifflin, 1966), 12; quoted after Henri Tajfel, "Social Psychology of Intergroup Relations," *Annual Reviews in Psychology* 33 (1982), 1–2.

cognitive one, in the sense of awareness of membership; and an evaluative one, in the sense that this awareness is related to some value connotations."[3] Simply put, one has to know about the membership and treat it as valuable. In addition, often "an emotional investment in the awareness" is present.

Negative and positive identity

Ways of describing the opposition between two dimensions of identity

In the Jewish experience, both the negative and the positive aspects of identity are present. The problem is what is the relationship between them and whether one is, in some sense, preferable to the other. Negative identity can be seen in the many situations in which being Jewish means principally the necessity to share the Jewish fate, independently of one's beliefs. The story in the book of Esther is a good example, whether it is historically precise or not.

> And Haman said unto king Ahasuerus, There is a certain people scattered abroad and dispersed among the people in all the provinces of thy kingdom; and their laws *are* diverse from all people; neither keep them the king's laws: therefore it is not for the king's profit to suffer them. If it please the king, let it be written that they may be destroyed. (Esther 3:8–9)

The Jewish people are identified in contrast to others around them. To express Jewish identity, however, much more must be reflected, notably the mission contained in the values and concepts of Judaism. This is a vast issue, but even one quote suffices to see what is meant by the positive character of identity: the people of Israel are called to holiness:

> Ye shall be holy: for I the LORD your God am holy. (Leviticus 19:2)

We see here the basis for positive Jewish identity, based on a particular mission and not reliant on the existence of an "other."

Another way of referring to negative and positive identities is by distinguishing between Jewish fate and Jewish faith. In the Talmud and in *Yoreh De'ah* both elements are mentioned while discussing conversion to Judaism.

> Our Rabbis taught: If at the present time a man desires to become a proselyte, he is to be addressed as follows: 'What reason have you for desiring to become

---

3   Ibidem.

a proselyte; do you not know that Israel at the present time are persecuted and oppressed, despised, harassed and overcome by afflictions'? If he replies, 'I know and yet am unworthy,' he is accepted forthwith, and is given instruction in some of the minor and some of the major commandments. He is informed of the sin Gleanings, the Forgotten Sheaf, the Corner and the Poor Man's Tithe. He is also told of the punishment for the transgression of the commandments. ...

And as he is informed of the punishment for the transgression of the commandments, so is he informed of the reward granted for their fulfillment. He is told, 'Be it known to you that the world to come was made only for the righteous, and that Israel at the present time are unable to bear either too much prosperity or too much suffering.' He is not, however, to be persuaded or dissuaded too much. If he accepted, he is circumcised forthwith. Should any shreds which render the circumcision invalid remain, he is to be circumcised a second time. As soon as he is healed arrangements are made for his immediate ablution, when two learned men must stand by his side and acquaint him with some of the minor commandments and with some of the major ones. When he comes up after his ablution he is deemed to be an Israelite in all respects. (Yevamoth 47a–b)

Almost the same formulations are repeated by Rabbi Joseph Karo (Yoreh De'ah 268:2) as part of legal direction for conversion. In our context, it is of interest that both fate and faith are mentioned, and that fate is mentioned first (Israel is persecuted) even though it has no necessary connection to belief or observance of the Torah, which would seem the main point of conversion. For someone who wants to become a Jew, loyalty to the Torah should be more important than just external belonging, even if becoming a Jew also means sharing the fate of the Jewish people. Why, then, is fate mentioned first and faith second? Is it accidental and unimportant? Does this indicate the primacy of negative identity over positive? Was this the result of historical experience or does it suggest that Jewish identity is predicated on the threat from the outside? To what extent do the Jewish people exist only in relationship to "others"?

Rav Soloveitchik has added two more pairs of terms. The contrast is between a camp, *machaneh*, and a congregation, *edah*, of witnesses (*edim*). The second formulation mentions the contrast between an encampment and a congregation.

The Torah relates that the Holy One concluded two Covenants with Israel. One Covenant was made in Egypt. "And I shall take you unto Me for a people, and I will be to you a God" (Exodus 6:7). The second Covenant was at Mt Sinai. "And he [Moses] took the book of the covenant ... and he said: 'Behold the blood of the covenant which the Lord made with you in agreement with all these words'" (Exodus 24:7–8) ... Just as Judaism distinguished fate from destiny in the realm of personal individuality, so it also differentiated between these two concepts in the sphere of our national-historical existence. The individual is tethered to his nation with bonds of fate and chains of destiny. In accordance with this postulate, one can say that the Covenant of Egypt was a Covenant of Fate, and the Covenant of Sinai was one of destiny....

Fate signifies in the life of the nation, as it does in the life of an individual, an existence of compulsion. A strange force merges all individuals into one unit. The individual is subject and subjugated against his will to the national fate/ existence, and it is impossible for him to avoid it and be absorbed into a different reality...

In the life of a people (as in the life of an individual), destiny signifies an existence that it has chosen of its own free will and in which it finds the full realization of its historical existence. Instead of a passive, inexorable existence into which a nation is thrust, an Existence of Destiny manifests itself as an active experience full of purposeful movement, ascension, aspirations, and fulfillment. The nation is enmeshed in its destiny because of its longing for an enhanced state of being, an existence replete with substance and direction. Destiny is the font out of which flow the unique self-elevation of the nation and the unending stream of Divine inspiration that will not run dry so long as the path of the People is demarcated by the laws of God. The life of destiny is a directed life, the result of conscious direction and free will.

While the covenant of Egypt was concluded without the consent of the people of Israel... the Covenant of Sinai was offered to them before it was promulgated....

Acts of loving-kindness and fraternity, which are integrated into the framework of the Covenant of Sinai, are motivated not by the strange sense of loneliness of the Jew, but by the sense of unity experienced by a nation forever betrothed to the one God. The absolute oneness of God is mirrored in the unity of the nation that is eternally bound to Him. ...

In order to explain the difference between a People of Fate and a People of Destiny it is appropriate to deal with a different contrast—that between an Encampment and a Congregation. The Torah uses both of these concepts with respect to Israel. (Numbers 10:2).

Encampment and Congregation constitute two different sociological experiences, two separate groups that have nothing in common and do not support one another. An Encampment is created out of a desire for self-defense and thrives on fear. A Congregation is fashioned out of a longing for the realization of an exalted moral idea and thrives on love. In the Encampment, fate's rule is unlimited, whereas destiny rules in the Congregation. The Encampment represents a phase in the development of the nation's history. The continued survival of a people is identified with the existence of the Congregation.

... A Congregation is a holy nation that does not fear fate and does not live against its will. It believes in its destiny and of its free will sanctifies itself for its realization. The Covenant of Egypt was made with a people that was born in the Encampment, the Covenant of Sinai was concluded with a holy people.[4]

According to Rav Soloveitchik, there are two ways in which people become a group: one is a camp, formed when they face a common enemy and the other is a congregation of witnesses, co-participants in a shared project. Jews are a people in both these ways. The first, a camp, results from what Rabbi Soloveitchik calls the covenant of fate (*brit goral*) or the covenant of Egypt. The second, a congregation, is called by him the covenant of destiny (*brit ye'ud*) or the covenant of Sinai. It is a call. The presence of this dimension depends not on external factors but on Jews themselves. Both dimensions exist but, we argue, one is higher than the other.

Rav Soloveitchik has applied the categories he introduced to describe the task of the present-day State of Israel. He describes a process that is supposed to raise Jews from being a people to being a holy nation.

> The Jewish community is obliged to utilize its free will in all areas of life in general, but in particular on behalf of the welfare of the State of Israel. ... Our historic obligation, today, is to raise ourselves from a people to a holy nation, from the covenant of Egypt to the covenant at Sinai, from an existence of necessity to an authentic way of life suffused with eternal ethical and religious values, from a camp to a congregation. The task confronting

---

4   Joseph Soloveitchik, *Kol Dodi Dofek*, trans. David Z Gordon (New York:Yeshiva University, 2006), 51–71.

> the religious *shivat ziyyon* movement is to achieve that great union of the two covenants—Egypt and Sinai, fate and destiny, aloneness and loneliness. This task embraces utilizing our afflictions to improve ourselves, and it involves spinning a web of *chesed* that will bind together all the parts of the people and blend them into one congregation, "one nation in the land"; and the readiness to pray for one's fellow, and empathy with his joy and grief. As the end result of this self-improvement we will achieve the holiness conferred by an existence of destiny and will ascend the mountain of the Lord.[5]

These are, Rabbi Jonathan Sacks comments,

> not just two types of groups, but in the most profound sense, two different ways of existing and relating to the world. A camp is brought into being by what happens to it from the outside. A congregation comes into existence by internal decision.[6]

He reinforces the idea that identity can be internally motivated and directed. The Sinaitic covenant is more than just an event, it is a call. The presence of the dimension of destiny depends not on external factors but on Jews themselves. It directs us to the future, it sets a purpose, a task to be fulfilled.

To sum up, four pairs of concepts have been identified: (i) the negative and positive identification, (ii) fate and faith, (iii) camp (*machaneh*) and congregation (*edah*), (iv) the covenant of fate *(brit goral)* and the covenant of destiny *(brit ye'ud)*. The pairs are closely related but not identical. For example, fate and camp are on the same, negative, side, but a camp is clearly made for defense against an external threat, and the Jewish fate encompasses more than potential and actual dangers: after all, it is not necessarily dominated by persecution and negative experiences.

The value of positive identity

Let us come back to the problem of why fate is mentioned first, before faith, in the sources about conversion. Perhaps it is due to historical experience. On so many occasions, fate has dominated all other aspects of Jewish identity. Or, at least, this is our experience, most dramatically felt in the time of

---

5   Joseph Soloveitchik, "The Voice of My Beloved Knocketh," trans. L. Kaplan, in *Theological and Halakhic Responses to the Holocaust*, eds. B. Rosenberg and F. Heuman (Hoboken, NJ, 1993), 104.
6   "Degrees of Prophecy," www.ou.org/torah/article/camp_and_congregation.

the Shoah: then, for the leaders of Nazi Germany and all who worked with them, Jewish origin alone, independently of one's beliefs or identification with the Jewish tradition, meant death punishment. So Jewish fate can be seen as a common denominator. At the same time, we know that there is something more important in Jewish identity than the fate imposed from outside. While both the negative and positive dimensions have occurred in Jewish existence, for Rav Soloveitchik one is obviously higher than the other. Few, it seems, would object. This means that we should stress the positive dimension. It is better to stress affirmation, the mission to bear witness, the internal resources rather than the fate, that is the bond created by common dangers. This should be clear for anyone who appreciates the religious or spiritual dimension of being Jewish, and it also emerges from the quotations given here. The positive identification, unlike the negative one, evokes the future, the Jewish messianic mission. Rav Soloveitchik interprets the distinction between the *brit goral*, "covenant of Egypt" and *brit ye'ud*, "covenant of Sinai," as a task: to go from the (mere) fate to the covenantal community. He applies this also to the State of Israel. "The mission of the State of Israel is neither the termination of the unique isolation of the Jewish people nor the abrogation of its unique fate—in this it will not succeed!—but the elevation of a camp-people to the rank of a holy congregation-nation and the transformation of shared fate to shared destiny."

Soloveitchik's suggestion responds to new realities in Jewish life. However, more general challenges of modernity began much earlier. In a sense different from those considered above, modernity has brought the appreciation of a positive identity. While being Jewish had been largely imposed by the power of one's community and in this sense it was of a negative character, with the advent of modernity it became much more a matter of choice and in this sense it has become positive. This change was positively evaluated by the Abraham Joshua Heschel, the Apter Rebbe, one of the early hasidic masters and an ancestor of the twentieth-century philosopher of the same name. When one is free to choose then the voluntary belonging is more meaningful. In the language used by him, it can impact the work of redemption

> Now we have the best opportunity to achieve redemption. Until the present time a Jew did not have complete freedom of action, insomuch as formerly the leaders of the Jewish community had authority to punish transgressors against Jewish customs and communal regulations. Now, however, anyone

may commit any offense against Judaism with impunity. Hence, he who chooses not to sin through self-control and reverence for his faith is worthier in the eyes of God than the law-abiding Jew of former generations.[7]

Freedom of choice has expanded so much in modern society that many people may have problems with identifications. This situation has been described as an emergence of "liquid" identity. One of the main proponents of the term was Zygmunt Bauman.[8] He noted that nowadays it is as easy to join a group as to quit. As a result, identities are now "market forces." While the dream of identity is a result of the need for security, liquidity makes it impossible. He described at length this rather extreme vision.[9] The problems indicated by him may seem rather abstract to traditional Jews. Equally strange, from a traditional point of view, is the earlier opinion of the famous French (non-Jewish) philosopher Jean Paul Sartre. In his 1946 article "Anti-Semite and Jew," analyzing the self-perception of his Jewish friends, he concluded that it was the antisemitic regard of others that defined the Jewishness of Jews. This concept is contrary to Judaism, but it describes well the extreme form of negative identity. The distinction between positive and negative Jewish identities occurs, as we have seen, within traditional thinking. The already quoted saying by Kotzker remains the best statement on the two types of identity.

The Insight Provided by Social Psychology

We must not underestimate the importance of negative identity. It may seem that not just the Shoah but much of the history of Jews has confirmed the permanence of dangers that shape negative identity. This is well expressed in the familiar *Vehi sheamdah* paragraph of the Haggadah.

> This promise has sustained our fathers and us. For not only one enemy has risen against us; in every generation men rise against us to destroy us, but the Holy One saves us from their hand.

The perception expressed in these verses remains an essential determinant of actual Jewish identity. In addition to hope and belief in the protection

---

7   After Louis Newman, *Hassidic Anthology*, 128–9.
8   Bauman was a sociologist who began his career in Poland, was forced to emigrate in 1968 and after a short stay in Israel, was living in the United Kingdom until his death in 2017.
9   In *Identity: Conversations with Benedetto Vecchi* (Polity Press, 2004).

of *Ha kadosh baruch hu*, it contains the perception that Jews are always surrounded by mortal enemies. We are victims. This is related to what historian Salo Baron critically named the "lachrymose" view of Jewish history. Adherents of this view refer to various historical facts. Nevertheless, radical opinions that "they" are always and everywhere against us are not valid. The fact that this perception seems very strongly rooted is not a proof of its validity. A powerful indirect evidence against it is provided by modern social science. The most telling are Zimbardo's prison experiment and Tajfel's minimal group experiments. According to them, the negative identification with a group can be very strong even if the line of division is completely artificial and the perceived threat is stimulated artificially. This means that the mere presence of a strong identity defined as being against another group is not by itself a guarantee of its reality, not to mention its value. Let us see how this is possible.

Experiments in the framework of social psychology

The first and most famous piece of evidence is Philip Zimbardo's prison experiment (1971). Slightly later Henri Tajfel and his colleagues (Billig, Bundy and Flament) devised the minimal group paradigm, or experimental methodology to investigate the effect of social categorization alone on behavior.[10]

> 1. Zimbardo's Stanford Prison Experiment
> Twenty-five years ago, a group of psychologically healthy, normal college students (and several presumably mentally sound experimenters) were temporarily but dramatically transformed in the course of six days spent in a prison-like environment, in research that came to be known as the Stanford Prison Experiment... Otherwise emotionally strong college students who were randomly assigned to be mock-prisoners suffered acute psychological trauma and breakdowns. Some of the students begged to be released from the intense pains of less than a week of merely simulated imprisonment, whereas others adapted by becoming blindly obedient to the unjust authority of the guards. The guards, too-who also had been carefully chosen on the basis of their normal—average scores on a variety of personality measures-quickly internalized

---

10 I am grateful to Dr. Michal Bilewicz from Warsaw for bringing to my attention Tajfel's experiments and helping to find the appropriate sources.

their randomly assigned role. Many of these seemingly gentle and caring young men ... soon began mistreating their peers and were indifferent to the obvious suffering that their actions produced. Several of them devised sadistically inventive ways to harass and degrade the prisoners, and none of the less actively cruel mock-guards ever intervened or complained about the abuses they witnessed."

The behavior of prisoners and guards in our simulated environment bore a remarkable similarity to patterns found in actual prisons. As we wrote, "Despite the fact that guards and prisoners were essentially free to engage in any form of interaction ... the characteristic nature of their encounters tended to be negative, hostile, affrontive and dehumanising" ...

The environment we had fashioned in the basement hallway of Stanford University's Department of Psychology became so real for the participants that it completely dominated their day-to-day existence (e.g., 90% of "prisoners" in-cell conversations focused on "prison"-related topics), dramatically affected their moods and emotional states (e.g., prisoners expressed three times as much negative affect as did guards), and at least temporarily undermined their sense of self (e.g., both groups expressed increasingly more deprecating self-evaluations over time).[11]

2. Tajfel's Minimal Group Experiments

British schoolboys, participating in what they believed was a study of decision making, were assigned to one of two groups completely randomly, but allegedly on the basis of their expressed preference for paintings by the artists Vassily Kandinsky or Paul Klee. The children knew only which group they themselves were in (Kandisky group or Klee group), with the identity of outgroup and fellow ingroup members concealed by the use of code numbers. The children then individually distributed money between pairs of recipients identified only by code number and group membership. ... The results showed that against the background of some fairness, the children strongly favored their own group.

... Subsequent experiments were even more minimal. For example, Billig and Tajfel (1973) explicitly randomly categorized their participants as X- or Y-group members, thereby eliminating any possibility that they might infer that people in the same group were interpersonally similar to one another because they ostensibly preferred the same artist.

---

11 Craig Haney and Philip Zimbardo, *American Psychologist* 53, no. 7 (July 1998): 709–27.

> ... The robust finding from hundreds of minimal group experiments conducted with a wide range of participants is that the mere fact of being categorized as a group member seems to be necessary and sufficient to produce ethnocentrism and competitive intergroup behavior.[12]

We see that group identification can be accidental or contrived, without a serious source of origin, without any meaning, let alone any real threat. When identification with the group is experienced, it is perceived as being "mine," just because I happen to be in it rather than in another one, the group identity is purely negative. Even if the resulting identification is strong, it can be surprisingly meaningless. The resulting attitudes to other groups are not based on firm grounds. Of course, Jewish identity is not of that shallow kind. Can we, however, be sure that we have never been influenced by some shallow, because fundamentally negative, aspects of identity?

Identity and Relations with the Other

The need for genuine encounter

The Kotzker's dictum, quoted above, is so general that it refers to many, perhaps all, kinds of identity, not just to Jewish identity. If negative identities are at work, there is no real encounter between me and you, because I am not really me and you are not really you; only, if we have positive identities we can meet—I as me and you as you. The issue of genuine interfaith dialogue has been discussed by philosophers including Martin Buber, A. J. Heschel, E. Levinas.[13]

The forming of a camp (*machaneh*), the proverbial besieged fortress, has rather negative consequences for attitudes to those outside one's camp, be they other nations, other religions, or the world at large. All are easily seen as a threat. Whatever is located outside the camp is automatically suspicious, seen as threatening, and as a result rejected, treated without respect. Rejection extends beyond the need to maintain boundaries and prevent unwanted influence by other cultures. "Rejection" casts the other in a negative light. It runs the risk of generating an attitude of disrespect and belittling the value of the other, be it person, society or religion. Such

---

12   Quoted from Michael A. Hogg and Graham M. Vaughan, *Social Psychology* (Pearson Education Limited, 2008), 405.
13   For an account see S. Krajewski, *What I Owe to Interreligious Dialogue and Christianity* (Cracow: The Judaica Foundation, 2017), 71–127.

attitudinal consequences will not follow if one's own approach is not that of camp-identity.

The core of Jewish identity, or at least the religious identity, is fundamentally positive, despite our noticing elements of negative identity even in the conversion ceremony. We are Jews "for" something. We are supposed to be the community of witnesses (*edim*) who bear witness to the Creator of this world. Even though contemporary Judaism is composed of different streams, almost all of them are united by a sense of faithfulness to the special covenant Jews have with God.[14] The nature of the covenant can be disputed as can be the details and more generally the role of *halakhah*. Still, the resulting identity has a positive core. Everything depends on our faithfulness. While it involves being different from others, the contrast itself is not the source of identity. Consequently, identity needs to not necessarily mandate belittling the value of other cultures, societies and faiths. I wish to illustrate this claim in a homiletical manner based on the following commentary on a Talmudic passage.

> Whoever sets a particular place for himself to pray [in the synagogue—this follows from the context], the God of Abraham comes to his aid, and when he dies, people say of him, "What a humble [*anav*] and pious [*hasid*] person he was, of the students of Avraham Avinu." (Berakhot 6b)

Although this Talmudic dictum does not directly deal with identity, it can be interpreted in a way that throws additional light on our distinction between the two dimensions of identity. It presents a rather surprising opinion: What is so praiseworthy about establishing a particular, regular place for worship? And what has it to do with Abraham and "the God of Abraham"? On the face of it, it is just a reference to the supposed initiation of morning prayer in a regular place by Abraham, and the suggestion that if someone imitates Abraham in this respect, he would follow in his footsteps and be similarly humble and pious. Later, the custom of having a regular place in the synagogue is recommended in *Shulchan Arukh*. Still, the praise for following this custom seems to need further justification.

A modern student of *Mussar* gives one: "fixing yourself to one spot you free up all the other space for others to use."[15] This is indeed a striking explanation. It can be interpreted as a praise of a positive identity, attachment

---

14 Reconstructionist Judaism may constitute an exception since it redefines traditional understandings of God.
15 Alan Morinis, *Everyday Holiness*, ch. 7 "Humility," 49.

to one's place, that does not denigrate other places. This applies to different expressions of identity. If we take religious identity as one example, we would be led to read it as follows. If each of our religions has a set place in the world "synagogue" of religions, then the rest of the space is left for others. We have a place, but it is only one among many. Our tradition prevails in our place, but in other places there are other religious traditions.

Rabbi Jonathan Sacks, the former Chief Rabbi of the British Commonwealth, finds in the way Torah describes how Jacob became Israel a teaching that is relevant to positive identity construction. He talks about "being secure in one's own identity," which can be interpreted as a reference to positive identity. And he adds that, similar to the encounter of Israel-Jacob and Esau,

> when brothers, religions, faiths, are secure in their own identity, they can meet as equals and part as friends... Something of the deepest possible consequence is being intimated in the story of Esau. The choice of one does not mean the rejection of the other. Esau is not chosen, but he is also not rejected. He too will have his blessing, his heritage, his land. ... To be chosen does not mean that others are unchosen. To be secure in one's relationship with G-d does not depend on negating the possibility that others too may have a (different) relationship with Him. Jacob was loved by his mother, Esau by his father; but what of G-d who is neither father nor mother but both and more than both? In truth, we can only know our own relationship with our parents. We can never know another's. Am I loved more than my brothers or sisters? Less? Once asked, the question cannot but lead to sibling rivalry (one of the central themes of Bereshit). But the question is an invalid question. It should not be asked. A good parent loves all his or her children and never thinks of more or less. Love is not quantifiable. It rejects comparisons. Jacob is Jacob, heir to the covenant. Esau is Esau, doing what he does, being what he is, enjoying his own heritage and blessing. What a simple truth and how beautifully, subtly, it is conveyed.[16]

---

16 Commentary on Toledot, Jonathan Sacks, *Covenant and Conversation: Bereshit* (Maggid Books, 2009), 146.

Or Rose

Images of the Non-Jew in the *Kedushat Levi*: A Textual and Theological Exploration*

Introduction

The teachings of Hasidism have been an essential part of my religious life since childhood. Raised in the nascent Jewish Renewal community, I was introduced to the sermons, stories, and spiritual practices of the hasidic masters by my parents and their mentors and peers. As a young adult I continued to explore the riches of Hasidism in my personal life and through my graduate studies at the Hebrew University of Jerusalem and Brandeis University. Today, as a rabbi and educator, I regularly study, teach, and write on hasidic thought and practice. After decades of active engagement with it, the language, ideas, and symbols of this great religious and social movement, and of its neo-hasidic interpreters, have become integral to my identity.

    Among the elements of hasidic teaching that I find most meaningful is the call of the Eastern European mystics to recognize the unity of and sacred potential in all life: "God's glory fills the whole earth" (Isa. 6:3). The hasidic imperative to search for the holy within the mundane is a teaching I carry with me daily, knowing that its full realization is always aspirational.

---

* This essay is based, in part, on my earlier article, "Hasidism and the Religious Other: A Textual Exploration and Theological Response," in *A New Hasidism: Branches*, vol. 2, eds. Arthur Green and Ariel Evan Mayse (Philadelphia, PA Jewish Publication Society, 2019), 105–128.

Unfortunately, while these mystical masters plant the seeds of an inclusive spiritual worldview—pointing to the divinity that inheres in all things—when they speak of non-Jews, the *rebbes* (hasidic masters) often do so in strongly negative terms. This includes statements about the ontological superiority of the Jew to the non-Jew and God's exclusive love for Israel. Of course, I am aware of the fact that I live in a very different time and place than many of the *rebbes* whose works I read most carefully and whose insights have shaped my life most profoundly. Still, because these teachings continue to play a significant role in my life and in the lives of countless other Jews—both hasidic and non-hasidic—I think it is crucial to explore these troubling sources critically rather than ignore or apologize for them. This is not only a matter of intellectual honesty but a necessary step in countering voices in our community who might use such texts to inspire or justify chauvinistic views and behaviors.

In this essay, I examine several sources on the non-Jew from the famed early hasidic master, Rabbi Levi Yitzhak of Berditchev (1740–1809). In presenting these materials, I attempt to situate the Berditchever (as he is widely referred to among hasidim) within the historical context in which he lived and the intellectual lineage from which he emerged. Following these reflections, I offer a contemporary response to the Berditchever, making use of hasidic and other resources to do so. It is my hope that in carrying out this reflective exercise, I can contribute in some small measure to the ongoing renewal of this rich and evolving tradition that has provided me, my family, and so many other seekers with vital spiritual nourishment over the generations.

Kedushat Levi: A Case Study

I have chosen the *Kedushat Levi*, Rabbi Levi Yitzhak's (hereafter RLY) major homiletical collection, as my case study for two reasons, one historical, the other personal: First, it is widely considered a foundational text in the hasidic tradition; the book has been reprinted many times since its original publication in (the first full edition) and it is quoted by many other hasidic preachers and writers. RLY is also a particularly beloved figure in the Jewish folk imagination, both within Hasidism and beyond it. Second, I find this book to be deeply insightful and inspiring in many ways, including the master's impassioned call to treat all members of the Jewish community—rich and poor, learned and untutored—with dignity and care. In fact, RLY is known in hasidic circles as the archetype of the compassionate hasidic master. A leader who possessed great intellectual acumen and scholarly erudition, the Berditchever is remembered above all else as an *ohev Yisrael* and a *melitz yosher*, a lover and defender of the people of Israel. This is illustrated in the many legends about him, including tales of his kindness to strangers, his outreach to sinners, and his bold challenges of God for injustices visited upon the Jewish people.¹ RLY's love for his people, so prevalent in the legends, is also reflected in his *derashot* (sermons). One striking example can be found in the following comment on the biblical figure of Abraham:

> Our Father Abraham, a man of compassion (*ish hesed*) ... would always find merit in Israel. It is for this reason that he gave food to the angels when they came to visit him, though he knew that angels do not eat. [He did so] to teach them about human needs, that they might understand our situation and not be harsh with Israel.²

In this imaginative reflection, RLY envisions Abraham as such a caring and thoughtful advocate of the (future) community of Israel that he took it upon himself to teach the angels about the challenges human beings face in their attempts to serve God as embodied creatures with fleshly needs. The importance of a religious leader's care for and protection of his flock is a central theme in the *Kedushat Levi*.³

---

1 See, for example, Samuel Dresner, *Levi Yitzhak of Berditchev: Portrait of a Hasidic Master* (New York, NY: Hartmore House, 1974); Elie Weisel, "Rabbi Levi-Yitzhak of Beditchev," *Souls on Fire: Portraits and Legends of Hasidic Masters* (New York: Simon & Schuster, 1982), 89–112; and more recently, Zalman Schachter-Shalomi and Netanel Miles-Yepez, *A Merciful God: Stories and Teachings of the Holy Rebbe, Levi Yitzhak of Berditchev* (CreateSpace Independent Publishing Platform, 2010). The first scholarly anthology on the life and work of Rabbi Levi Yitzhak is the Hebrew text *Rabbi Levi Yitzhak of Berditchev: History, Thought, Literature, and Song*, ed. Tzvi Mark and Roee Horen (Rishon LeZion, Israel: Yedioth Achronoth & Chemed Books, 2017).

2 R. Levi Yitzhak of Berditchev, *Kedushat Levi*, ed., Michael Aryeh Rand (Ashdod, Israel: Mahon Hadrat Hen, 2005), vol. 2, *Pinhas*, 73–74. All translations are my own unless otherwise noted.

3 In one fascinating text on the subject, RLY teaches (based on Zohar 1:77b and other Jewish mystical sources) that Moses healed Noah's soul by serving as a strong advocate for the Children of Israel, whereas Noah failed to plead before God to stop the flood and save the people of his generation. Among the wordplays the Berditchever uses to support his claim is that when the Israelites sinned by fashioning the Golden Calf, Moses demanded that God forgive them (Exodus 32:32), saying: "... if not, please blot me out (*meheni*) from Your book...." The word *meheni* contains the same letters as *mei*

One might assume, therefore, that RLY compassion for his community, especially those on the margins, might lead him to adopt a similar attitude towards non-Jews (or some segment of this very broad category of human beings). Unfortunately, this is not the case. The vast majority of his teachings on the subject are quite negative. This includes various laudatory and defensive statements about Israel that also include sharp criticism of gentiles. In selecting textual examples to share in this essay, I have organized them using the classical Jewish themes of creation, revelation and redemption. I do so because the *Kedushat Levi* is not designed as a systematic theological or ethical treatise, but rather as a collection of sermons on the weekly Torah readings, Jewish calendar cycle, and other sacred matters. Utilizing this thematic approach, we can see how RLY's scattered comments about the non-Jew form a more coherent (not wholly consistent) religious worldview. As I discuss later in this essay, RLY is not unique among hasidic (or kabbalistic) thinkers in articulating negative sentiments about gentiles and their religious and cultural traditions.[4] However, I focus on his teachings because of his prominence within hasidic and modern Jewish culture, and because of my personal desire to remain in ongoing dialogue with this great spiritual teacher.

Creation: "For the Sake of Israel"

Among the earliest hasidic texts published was *Maggid Devarav le-Ya'akov* (1784), a collection of teachings of Rabbi Dov Baer, the Maggid of Mezeritch (d. 1772), RLY's spiritual mentor.[5] The book opens with the following statement: "God's first thought in creation was to create Israel.... For the Holy Blessed One, past and future are the same, and thus the Holy One derived pleasure from the deeds of the righteous (*tzaddiqim*) even before

---

Noah, "the waters of Noah," thus alluding to a connection between these two figures and the leadership challenges they each faced. See ibid., vol. 1, *Noah*, 29.

4   A detailed comparative study of the views of RLY and other early hasidic masters, especially those in the circle of the Maggid of Mezeritch, on the non-Jew and non-Jewish religious traditions remains a desideratum in the scholarly study of this movement.

5   To learn more about the Maggid and his disciples, see Arthur Green's introduction to *Speaking Torah: Spiritual Teachings from around the Maggid's Table*, vol. 1, ed., Arthur Green, with Ebn Leader, Ariel Evan Mayse, and Or N. Rose (Woodstock, VT: Jewish Lights, 2013), 1–73. See also, Ariel Evan Mayse, "Beyond the Letters: The Question of Language in the Teachings of Rabbi Dov Baer of Mezritch," (PhD thesis, Harvard University, 2015).

creation..."⁶ The assertion that God created the world for the sake of Israel, or for the sake of righteous Jews specifically, is a common trope in hasidic literature. Building on earlier rabbinic and kabbalistic sources, the Eastern European mystical masters imagine God emerging from His pre-creation state of "all-in-all" because of the pleasure (*ta'anug*) He experiences from future *tzaddiqim*.⁷ It is this emotional surge that leads the Divine to bring all of life into being. The ultimate purpose of creation is the emergence of the Jewish people, led by "the righteous of the generation," who satisfy the Creator's deepest desire by entering a covenantal relationship with Him and by freely and lovingly fulfilling the teachings of the Torah. RLY affirms this position in various ways throughout his teachings. The key textual source for him is the midrashic statement, "*Bereshit*—for Israel (*bishvil Yisrael*), who are called *reshit* (first)."⁸ In one such teaching, the Berditchever expresses this idea in harsh comparative terms: "The general principle is as follows: the bounty (*shefa*) that emerged [from the Divine] into the worlds is fundamentally for Israel, while the vitality (*hiyut*) of the nations is the excess (*motariut*), as is well known."⁹

RLY carries this idea further in a reflection on a talmudic discussion about the biblical term "*adam*" (BT Yevamot 61a) based on a brief quotation from Ezekiel 34:31. He approvingly quotes the rabbinic statement that only Israel is called *adam*, but "not the nations of the world." Paraphrasing earlier mystical sources, RLY goes onto say that the word *adam* can be read as *aleph-dam* (joining the letter *aleph* to the Hebrew word for "blood").¹⁰ The message of this wordplay is that the souls of Israel issue from the most sublime region within the Godhead (as represented by the *aleph*, the first letter of the Hebrew alphabet), illuminating their physical beings (represented by the Hebrew word *dam* or "blood").

---

6   R. Dov Baer of Mezritch, *Maggid Devarav le-Ya'akov*, ed., Rivka Schatz-Uffenheimer (Jerusalem, Israel: Magnes Press, 1990), 1.

7   As is common among hasidic preachers, there are instances in which RLY uses this term to refer to the righteous in general, while in other cases he does so to refer specifically to the hasidic masters. Here it is intended as a broad statement.

8   Bereshit Rabbah 1:1, Va-Yikra Rabbah 36:4.

9   *Kedushat Levi*, vol. 1, *Va-Yiggash*, 183. He makes this comment as part of a laudatory statement about Joseph, who "lived in holiness" even while dwelling "among the excess (*motariut*)," in his many years in Egypt. As I discuss below, RLY often blurs the lines between ancient biblical foes such as the Egyptians and the "nations of the world."

10 See Tikkunei Zohar, no. 70, 135a.

> The souls of Israel were hewn within the Upper Mind, as in the saying (Genesis Rabbah 1:4), "Israel arose in thought," and as it says (Deuteronomy 32:9), "For the Lord's portion is His people." Therefore, the *aleph* of *adam* shines on them specifically... This is not true of the nations of the world...[11]

Not only does RLY consider Israel to be God's true joy—His motivation for creation and the central actor in the unfolding of human history—but in this teaching, he claims that there is an ontological difference between Jews and non-Jews; while they might share the same physical bodies, their spiritual makeup is different: Jews possess a light that shines on them from the heights of heaven. It is not surprising, therefore, that elsewhere the Berditchever uses the terms (consciously or not) "Jew" (*Yisrael*) and "human being" (*adam*) interchangeably: "Behold, it is known that all of the worlds were created only for *Yisrael* and for the lower world upon which *adam* serves his Maker."[12] Reading such texts, one wonders if RLY considers non-Jews fully human.

Revelation: What Did God Disclose at Sinai?

Moving from creation to revelation, from Eden to Sinai, the Berditchever writes the following in one of his final comments on the Book of Deuteronomy:

> At first glance it is difficult to understand the meaning of the *midrash* [BT Avodah Zarah 2b] that the Holy Blessed One offered the Torah to every [other] nation, that they did not want to accept it, and that only then did He come to our people. It is hard to imagine that it was possible for God to give the non-Jews the Torah. In truth, the Holy Blessed One did this to [deepen His] love [for] Israel. By approaching every nation, having them decline acceptance [of the Torah], and having the seed of Israel accept it, His love for them [Israel] increased. And so, by making these rounds [added] love came to Israel and added hatred came to the nations of the world. It is for this reason that our sages of blessed memory said (BT Shabbat 89b) that "It [the mountain] is called Sinai, because hatred (*sinah*)

---

11 *Kedushat Levi*, vol. 1, *Pesah*, 414–16.
12 Ibid., vol. 1, *Bereshit*, 7–8. See the Maggid's use of this same wordplay in *Maggid Devarav le-Ya'akov*, no. 24, 38–40; see, also, R. Menahem Nahum of Chernobyl, *Me'or Eynayim*, *Bereshit*, cited in Arthur Green, ed., *Upright Practices, The Light of the Eyes* (New York, NY: Paulist Press, 1981), 72.

descended upon the nations of the world [from it]." This hatred existed only after the giving of the Torah, before it there was no hatred for the nations of the world.[13]

Here RLY designates Sinai (and not creation, as above) as the key moment in which God expresses His love for the Children of Israel and His hatred for the nations of the world. While this may have been God's intention all along, it is only after Israel accepts the Torah that these opposing divine emotions are made manifest in the world. However, it is clear from both the Talmudic text itself, and from RLY's interpretation of it, that God never intended to give the Torah to anyone other than the Israelites. God's tour of the ancient Near East is a sort of ruse, a means by which to strengthen (and/or justify) His opposing emotions for His beloved people and for their detested neighbors. It should also be noted that RLY often uses the terms "*mitzrim*" (Egyptians), "*resha'im*" (evil doers), and "*umot ha-olam*" (the nations of the world) interchangeably, thus lumping together ancient Israelite foes, sinners, and all non-Jews. Throughout the *Kedushat Levi*, he often speaks of a world sharply divided between Israel and the nations—a world in which God has great affection for *Yiddin* (Jews) and animosity for *goyim* (non-Jews).

But if that is the case, RLY asks rhetorically, why do *both* experience divine favor? He answers as follows:

> The Blessed Creator bestows bounty and gives His goodness to His people Israel, but bounty also comes upon the nations. The difference between them is that the goodness that He gives to His people Israel is for the good, but the goodness that comes upon the nations follows the saying "He requites His enemies immediately to be rid of them" (Deuteronomy 7:10).[14]

In a similar text from the end of Genesis, RLY is more explicit about what he means by God ridding Himself of the nations of the world:

> When God bestows goodness upon the gentiles it is to give them all their goodness and reward in this world and to cut them off from the world to come. With Israel, it is just the opposite: it is to increase their reward in the world to come [BT Eruvin 22a].[15]

---

13 Ibid., vol. 2, *Ve-Zot ha-Berakhah*, 182.
14 Ibid., vol. 1, *Va-Yishlakh*, 130.
15 Ibid., vol. 1, *Va-Yehi*, 174–75.

As these texts make clear, while God showers blessing upon Jews *and* non-Jews, His intention in doing so is entirely different in each situation. As in so many other hasidic texts, one's *kavvanah* (intention) is essential to the task at hand.[16]

Redemption: Uplifting Holy Sparks

The hasidic masters often ask about the true purpose of the Israelites' extensive journey through the wilderness after their redemption from Egyptian bondage. Why did they stop at specific places and camp in these locations for longer or shorter periods of time? What message does God wish to transmit to us through the detailed descriptions of these travels? RLY offers the following explanation:

> It is known that all of Israel's travels in the great an awesome wilderness were devised by God ... for the purpose of bringing forth holy sparks that had fallen into the shells there... This is why Israel camped in some places for a long time, while in others for shorter time. Their encampments were in accord with the sparks that needed to be redeemed there.[17]

Like their kabbalistic forebears, the hasidic masters insist that all of God's creations possess holy sparks (*nitzotzot*)—invisible but very real nuggets of divine energy that are hidden within the physical universe.[18] This is true of animate and inanimate objects alike.[19] The task of the Jewish mystical devotee is to free the sparks trapped within or concealed beneath the *kelipot* (shells or husks of materiality) and to return them to their primordial source, where they are purified and "sweetened in their roots."[20] This, in

---

16 One could still ask why God chooses to bestow goodness upon the nations of the world at all if He views them in such negative terms. On more than one occasion RLY argues that this is God's most basic way of interacting with His creations. While God may "garb" Himself in various *middot* (attributes), *hesed* (loving-kindness) is essential to the divine personality. See, for example, ibid., vol. 1, *Va-Yetze*, 109. Elsewhere, RLY teaches that God does not wish to punish people at all—Jews and non-Jews alike—because He fundamentally "desires *hesed*" (Micah 7:18). See, for example, vol. 1, *Bo*, 235–436.
17 Ibid., vol. 2, *Mas'ei*, 78–80.
18 See, Lawrence Fine, *Physician of the Soul, Healer of the Cosmos: Isaac Luria and His Kabbalistic Fellowship* (Stanford, CA: Stanford University Press, 2003), ch. 4.
19 See, for example, *Tzava'at ha-RIVaSH*, no. 109, trans. and ed. Jacob Immanuel Schochet (Brooklyn, NY: Kehot Publishing, 1975), 38.
20 See Louis Jacobs, "The Uplifting of Sparks in Later Jewish Mysticism," in *Jewish Spirituality: From the Sixteenth-Century to the Present*, vol. 2, ed. Arthur Green (New York, NY: Crossroad, 1989), 99–126.

turn, leads to the showering of renewed blessing upon the earthly world. Eventually, when all the holy sparks are unearthed and purified, say the hasidim, the world will be healed, and the messianic era will commence.[21]

In this context, RLY speaks about uplifting the spiritual vitality from within the sullied domain of the gentile world, including bits of divine energy, fragments of wisdom, as well as displaced Jewish souls who reside among the nations.[22] Ruth the Moabite is a particularly important figure in this discussion, as RLY views her as the quintessential lost "spark"—the model convert—among the gentile "husks," who becomes the progenitor of the Davidic line (see Ruth 4:18–22) and of the Messiah. This is why it is so important to read her story on the festival of *Shavuot*—the celebration of the giving of the Torah—as it serves to inspire the Jewish people to persist in its dedication to God and Torah, knowing that there are still many more *nitzotzot* to be gathered up before the age of the eschaton. RLY seeks to communicate to his followers that like their ancient ancestors, their exilic wonderings are purposeful and ultimately redemptive. Interestingly, in speaking about the messianic age, the Berditchever does state on a few occasions that the nations will come to accept God as the one true King and Israel as His faithful companion.[23] Exactly how these people will come to this realization, serve God, and interact with Israel, he does not explain in detail.

Text & Context: The Berditchever's World

The first step, as I see it, in engaging RLY's teachings on the non-Jew is to explore the historical context in which he lived. Doing so allows us to understand better some of the factors that contributed to the development of his worldview. It also provides us with the necessary critical distance to avoid idealizing the Berditchever, realizing that like all of us, he existed in a specific time and place. RLY and his community lived as a vulnerable

---

21 *Kedushat Levi*, vol. 2, *Megilat Eikhah ve-Tisha be-Av*, 91–92. Scholars disagree about the nature of messianic thought in early Hasidism. See, for example, the differing views of Gershom Scholem, "The Neutralization of the Messianic Element in Early Hasidism," in his *The Messianic Idea in Judaism* (New York, NY: Schocken Books, (1971), 176–202, 359–363; and Moshe Idel, "Hasidism: Mystical Messianism and Mystical Redemption," in his *Messianic Mystics* (New Haven, CT: Yale University Press, (1998), 212–247, 401–412.
22 See, for example, *Kedushat Levi*, vol. 2, *Korah*, 45 and *Ha'azinu*, 181–82.
23 Ibid., vol. 1, *Be-Shalah*, 274.

minority with limited rights and freedoms within the Polish-Lithuanian Commonwealth and the Russian Empire (after 1793), occupying a precarious position within the socio-economic landscape of Ukrainian life. Further, leaders in both the Catholic and Ukrainian Orthodox Churches continued to preach older messages of Christian supersessionism and contempt for Jews that were not only spiritually demeaning, but also inspired sporadic outbursts of violence.[24] As one of the leading rabbinic figures of his day—the "Lover" and "Advocate" of Israel—the Berditchever clearly felt a responsibility to help bolster his people's morale, reminding them of their human dignity and spiritual worth.[25] This led him to proclaim fiercely that despite all the evidence to the contrary, the Jewish people remained God's chosen people; they had not been abandoned nor replaced, but were living through a painful (but purposeful) phase of history from which the Divine would eventually redeem them.[26] Not surprisingly, in making his case to his followers, RLY employed sharp polemical and chauvinistic rhetoric (not unlike his Christian counterparts) to make his point.

In examining the many classical Jewish textual sources cited in the *Kedushat Levi*, one can readily see that he drew on a variety of earlier Jewish

---

24 See David Biale et al., *Hasidism: A New History with an Introduction by Arthur Green* (Princeton, NJ: Princeton University Press, 2018). As the editors of this expansive volume point out, while the gentile was often presented as a "monolithic, threatening character" in theoretical texts like the *Kedushat Levi*, Jews and non-Jews actually had more complicated and nuanced relationships. As Biale and his colleagues write, "... real Gentiles came from a variety of social categories and were encountered in numerous contexts. In some, they were feared and hated; in others, they were dealt with matter-of-factly, learned from, and even liked and trusted" ("The Gentile World," 30–32).

25 RLY was, in fact, engaged in various political matters on behalf of the Jewish community, both locally and regionally. See, for example, Yohanan Petrovsky-Shtern, "The Drama of Berditchev: Levi Yitshak and His Town," *Polin* 17 (2004), 83–95.

26 I think this was one of the reasons why RLY chose to publish a selection of his teachings on Hanukkah and Purim several years before his larger collection of sermons appeared posthumously in 1811. Like other Jewish thinkers before him, RLY viewed these minor holidays as examples of the subtle ways in which God can work to sustain and redeem the Jewish people. He contrasted this with the Passover drama, in which the Almighty freed the Israelites with great "signs and wonders." Hanukkah and Purim thus served as important models for how Eastern European Jewry might understand their own communal situation; helping them remain faithful to God, recognizing the power of the *tzaddiqim*—modern, mystical versions of Mattathias, Judah, Mordechai, and Esther—and their own role in this redemptive process. I explore this subject at length in my essay, "Protest or Discernment?: Divine Limitation and Human Agency in the *Kedushat Levi*," in *Be-Ron Yahad: Studies in Honor of Nehemia Polen*, ed., Ariel Evan Mayse and Arthur Green (Boston, MA: Academic Studies Press, 2019), 155–176.

teachings that depict non-Jews and non-Jewish religions negatively. Take, for example, the *Zohar*, perhaps the most influential books on all later Jewish mystics, and a text from which the Berditchever quotes and paraphrases many times. As Arthur Green writes,

> The *Zohar* is filled with disdain and sometimes even outright hatred for the gentile world. Continuing in the old Midrashic tradition of repainting the subtle shadings of Biblical narrative in moralistic black and white, the *Zohar* pours endless heaps of wrath and malediction on Israel's enemies. In the context of Biblical commentary these are always such ancient figures as Esau, Pharaoh, Amalek, Balaam, and the mixed multitude of runaway slaves who left Egypt with Israel... All of these were rather safe objects for attack, but it does not take much imagination to realize that the true address of this resentment was the oppressor in whose midst the authors lived.[27]

One could easily substitute the word "*Zohar*" in this passage with that of "*Kedushat Levi*" without undermining the validity of Green's comments. And in the intervening centuries between the appearance of the *Zohar* in the late thirteenth century and the birth of RLY in the mid-eighteenth century, many other influential Jewish thinkers reiterated similarly negative ideas.[28] This was a significant part of the intellectual/spiritual legacy inherited by RLY and his colleagues.

While it is crucial to understand the historical situation of the hasidic masters and the influence of earlier Jewish traditions upon them, I cannot end the discussion here. As I stated above, because these men have had a significant influence on me, and I continue to turn to their teachings for

---

27   Arthur Green, *A Guide to the Zohar* (Stanford, CA: Stanford University Press, 2003), 88–89. See also Elliot Wolfson, *Venturing Beyond: Law and Morality in Kabbalistic Mysticism* (New York, NY: Oxford University, 2006). Moving beyond the Jewish mystical tradition, see David Novak, *The Image of the Non-Jew in Judaism: An Historical and Constructive Study of the Noahide Laws* (Lewiston, NY: Edwin Mellon Press, 1983), and Alan Brill, *Judaism and Other Religions: Models of Understanding* (New York, NY: Palgrave Macmillan, 2010).

28   See, for example, the comments of Rabbi Judah Loew of Prague cited in *Present at Sinai: The Giving of the Law*, ed. Shmuel Yosef Agnon, trans. Michael Swirsky (Philadelphia, PA: Jewish Publication Society, 1994), 19–20. On the intellectual influence of the Maharal on the early hasidic masters, see Bezalel Safran, "Maharal and Early Hasidism," in *Hasidism: Continuity or Innovation*, ed. B. Safran (Cambridge, MA: Harvard University Press, 1988), 47–144. See also Shahar Rahmani, "Israel's Advocate: The Intellectual Foundation for Levi Yitzhak's Advocacy of Israel in the Writings of the MaHaRaL of Prague," in *Rabbi Levi Yitzhak of Berditchev: History, Thought, Literature, and Song*, 229–61.

inspiration and guidance, I feel compelled to engage them theologically on this and other thorny issues. Further, if I cut off the conversation at this point, without first grappling with the substance of these troubling texts, I risk ceding the discussion to others who would use these sources to legitimize attitudes and behaviors I regard as unethical and dangerous.[29] If a great master like RLY taught that *goyim* are lesser beings than Jews, why should any later Hasid, or any other inspired reader of the *Kedushat Levi*, treat his non-Jewish neighbors with respect and care, let alone consider the wisdom and beauty of their religious or cultural traditions? This is particularly important in a time when violent religious intolerance is thriving in various parts of the world, and Jews have far more power than ever before in our history.

Light and Darkness: A Reading Strategy

In engaging RLY's teaching, I want to explore whether there are hasidic ideas, texts, or symbols that might help me address the disturbing materials under review. While it is certainly possible to articulate my criticism in an exclusively contemporary idiom, I feel that using hasidic terminology is crucial to the renewal of this mystical tradition in which language and symbol are so important. In this context, I turn back to the image of the holy sparks and the husks or shells. I do not wish to use these terms as the Berditchever often did, to separate Jews from non-Jews categorically, but rather to tease apart the hasidic sources themselves. Just as every human being is an admixture of light and darkness, so too are the teachings of these mystical masters. They had moments of great insight to be sure, but they also suffered from instances of spiritual constriction, when their fear, anger, pain, or pride clouded their vision. Using hasidic terms, I would say that the masters moved between states of *gadlut* (expanded consciousness) and *katnut* (limited consciousness). It is the task of the contemporary reader to undertake a thoughtful process of *berur* (discernment), of sifting, sorting, and clarifying which of these materials to embrace, which to reinterpret,

---

29 See, for example, Allan Nadler's report on Rabbi Sa'adya Grama'a book, *Romemut Yisra'el u-farashat ha-galut* (self-published, 2003), *Forward*, December 19, 2003. Grama uses a slew of classical Jewish texts, including hasidic materials, to argue for the racial superiority of Jews over non-Jews. As Nadler notes, several leading Orthodox authorities denounced the book publicly. See, also, Don Seeman, "The Anxiety of Ethics," in *A New Hasidism*, 73–103 (specifically Seeman's discussion of the writings of Rabbi Yitzchak Ginsburgh).

and which to leave aside. This interpretative work is necessarily situational, as each reader (or community of readers) must carefully analyze the texts before her and evaluate their place in contemporary life.

The early hasidic masters are themselves important role models for such an undertaking. As religious revivalists they did not accept the ideas of earlier thinkers—biblical, rabbinic, or mystical—whole cloth, but skillfully selected and reinterpreted those teachings that best represented their spiritual commitments.[30] We, too, need to glean from the hasidic tradition wisely, culling materials that are most helpful to us in our quest for meaning and responsible living. This does *not* mean, however, that one should ignore, excise, or apologize for objectionable teachings,[31] but it does require the reader to privilege some texts over others and to develop new interpretations of older teachings.[32] In our case, this includes drawing on sources that portray non-Jews in a more nuanced and/or positive manner,[33] and reading sources that address only Jews in a more inclusive fashion. Below, I explore a few texts from the *Kedushat Levi* that might contribute to this creative undertaking.

---

30 While Levi Yitzhak and his companions often speak of the importance of *hiddush* (innovation), they tend to be much more daring in their psycho-spiritual readings of classical texts than in their approach to *halakhah* (Jewish law). Still, the hasidim did introduce certain behavioral changes, mostly in the realm of *minhag*, "custom," that challenged established local convention and raised the ire of rabbinic authorities. See Ariel Evan Mayse and Maoz Kahana, "Hasidic *Halakhah*: Reappraising the Interface of Spirit and Law," *AJS Review* 41, no. 2. See also Arthur Green's introduction to *Speaking Torah*, 44–49; and Mordecai Wilensky, "Hasidic-Mitnaggedic Polemics in the Jewish Communities of Eastern Europe: The Hostile Phase," in *Essential Papers on Hasidism: Origins to the Present*, ed. Gershon D. Hundert (New York, NY: NYU Press..., 1991), 244–71.

31 I write this comment as a person who has been involved in editing two popular anthologies of hasidic teachings. The question of how best to introduce readers to materials that I find troubling is one with which I continue to grapple. See Or N. Rose and Ebn D. Leader eds., *God in all Moments: Mystical and Practical Spiritual Wisdom from Hasidic Masters* (Woodstock, VT: Jewish Lights, 2003) and Arthur Green, Ebn Leader, Ariel Evan Mayse, and Or N. Rose eds., *Speaking Torah*.

32 It should be noted that RLY specifies that it is the *tzaddiqim* in each generation that have the power to innovate, while I am inviting a much wider group of readers to participate in this process both individually and communally.

33 See, for example, Shaul Magid, "Ethics Disentangled from the Law: Incarnation, the Universal, and Hasidic Ethics," *Kabbalah: A Journal for the Study of Jewish Mystical Texts* 15 (2006), 31–75. See also the short essay by Yitzhak Melamed, "Hasidic-Muslim Relations in Ottoman Palestine," published on the website TheTorah.com.

Humility, Disagreement, and Compassion in the *Kedushat Levi*

In a commentary on Moses' first encounter with the Divine at the Burning Bush (Exodus 3), RLY focuses on the prophet's response to God's instruction that he should return to Egypt and liberate the Children of Israel. In response to this command, Moses answers: "Who am I that I should go to Pharaoh and bring the Israelites out of Egypt" (3:11)? For RLY, this response is itself proof of why Moses is the right person to play this sacred role: it is Moses' humility that makes him a fitting leader. In explicating this teaching, the Berditchever adds the following comment on Psalm 27:4 in the name of Rabbi Yehiel Mikhel, the Maggid of Zlotchev (d. 1786):

> "One thing I have asked of YHWH… to behold the beauty of YHWH, this I will ask." I will continuously ask that I recognize that there is still a greater rung of understanding above the current one, and that I might behold God's beauty at this more elevated level. And when I reach this higher plane that I continue to inquire, knowing that there is no end to this process.[34]

For RLY, epistemological humility is a key virtue of the spiritual seeker—whether it be Moses, the Psalmist, or the contemporary Hasid. One must know that his knowledge of God is always partial, always limited by the current "rung" on which a person finds herself. And this process is ongoing because God is, according to the very same text in Exodus, *Eheyeh asher Eheyeh*, "I Will Be what I Will Be" (3:14), the mysterious One, whose infinite nature can never be fully known by any human being.

What if we were to apply this teaching in the interreligious realm? If God is truly infinite (*Ein Sof*) and beyond all reckoning (*Ayin*), then how might this shape our understanding of Jews, non-Jews, and our pursuit of truth and goodness? It would require an acknowledgement that none of us—individually or collectively—has a hold of absolute truth ("No thought can grasp Him at all," Tiqqunei Zohar, introduction, 17a). We would need to view ourselves as seekers in perpetual motion, always "on the way" in our spiritual search. If this is the case, what might we learn from others who are involved in similar quests from other religious and ethical communities? Might they possess knowledge or insight that is underdeveloped, peripheral, or even absent from Judaism? This does not mean that we must accept every truth claim as equally valid or that we should stop arguing for what we believe is right and just, but it does mean that we understand that God's

---

34 Ibid., vol. 1, *Shemot*, 202–4.

truth is always greater than ours, and that there is great value in engaging with thoughtful and caring dialogue partners from non-Jewish traditions.[35]

On the issue of dialogue and principled disagreement, RLY offers a relevant comment based on his reading of the ancient rabbinic notion of *teyku*, "let it stand."[36] In this context, the Berditchever explains that it is natural for people to disagree about matters of substance because (drawing once again on earlier kabbalistic teachings) they originate from different realms of the Godhead. This is why, for example, the great sages Hillel and Shammai disagreed about so many important matters. Hillel emanated from the realm of *hesed* (mercy or loving-kindness) and Shammai from the realm of *gevurah* (judgement or rigor); this led them to frequent debate, with each intuitively leaning in the opposite direction.[37] RLY also reminds us that the Talmud teaches (BT Eruvin 13b) that both schools of thought possess elements of truth in their arguments, both are "words of the living God." It is also crucial for the Berditchever—the great "Lover of Israel"—however, that it is Hillel who carries the day in terms of normative practice, because in its pre-messianic state the world needs more *hesed* than *gevurah*.[38] And as the Talmud itself testifies, Hillel and his students embodied this commitment to loving-kindness (and not simply legislative leniency) in their interactions with their rabbinic interlocutors.[39]

---

[35] For a contemporary set of reflections on this subject, see the essays in *Sharing Wisdom: Benefits and Boundaries of Interreligious Learning*, ed. Alon Goshen-Gottstein (Lanham, MD: Lexington Books, 2017).

[36] *Kedushat Levi*, vol. 2, *Liqqutim*, 254–55. See also 410–11.

[37] In drawing on this imagery, I do so heuristically, recognizing that questions of personality formation require much more extensive discussion. I also wish to add that RLY does not discuss the practice of *makhloket* (debate) often in the *Kedushat Levi*. For a broader exploration of this subject in early Hasidism, see Shaul Magid, "The Intolerance of Tolerance: *Makhloket* (Controversy), Exile, and Redemption in Early Hasidism," *Jewish Studies Quarterly*, December (2001) 8.4, 326–68.

[38] RLY is also alluding here to the mystical teaching that in the messianic era the stricter rulings of *Beit Shammai* will be enacted. See, for example, R. Shalom Buzaglo comments in Mikdash Melekh on Zohar 17b. See Zalman Schachter-Shalomi's translation of and commentary on this teaching, "*Teyku*—Because Elijah Lives On!," in *Jewish Mysticism and the Spiritual Life: Classical Texts, Contemporary Reflections*, ed. Lawrence Fine, Eitan Fishbane, and Or N. Rose (Woodstock, VT: Jewish Lights, 2011), 217–20.

[39] In explaining why the law was fixed according to the House of Hillel if the words of each were of "the living God," the Talmud states: "It is because the students of Hillel were kind and gracious. They taught their own ideas and those of the students of Shammai. Further, they went so far as to teach Shammai's opinions first." See BT Eruvin 13b.

However, to engage in such deliberation requires us to view our non-Jewish dialogue partners as our equals, as fellow human seekers with whom we can engage in a reciprocal process of teaching and learning, as well as shared discovery. We cannot maintain a triumphalist spiritual vision in which Jews are considered innately superior to non-Jews. This is where it is important to remember the teaching of another ancient sage, Simeon Ben Azzai. When challenged to articulate the foundational principal upon which all of Judaism rests, he stated: "This is the book of the chronicles of *adam*: On the day that God created the human, He made him in the image of God" (Genesis 5:1). In the context of the original rabbinic discussion, Ben Azzai was offering an alternative to Rabbi Akiva's statement that "Love your neighbor as yourself" (Leviticus 19:18) is the most basic of all Jewish teachings.[40] Ben Azzai is teaching us that we must treat all people—not just those we love or regard as our neighbor—as beings created in the image of the Divine. This seems like a particularly important message to include in a discussion of a figure like RLY—an early modern "Akiva"—whose passionate love for Eastern European Jewry and anger and resentment towards his non-Jewish neighbors—some of which is certainly understandable given their mistreatment of Jews—led him to make sweeping negative statements about gentiles and their cultures.

A Closing Reflection

In concluding this essay, I turn one final time to the *Kedushat Levi*. In the Torah portion of *Terumah* God instructs Moses to build the Tabernacle, saying, "Like all that I show you—the structure of the Tabernacle and the structure of all its vessels—thus shall you do (Exodus 25:9)." Why, classical Jewish commentators want to know, does this command include the seemingly superfluous clause "thus shall you do?" The great French exegete Rashi (d. 1105) understood it as an instruction to use the Tabernacle as the blueprint for the Temple in Jerusalem. A century later, the leading Spanish sage Nahmanides (d. 1270) questioned this reading pointing out that the altar in the Tabernacle and the one in Solomon's Temple were clearly different from each other. In offering his own response to this question, the Berditchever harmonizes the two medieval positions: Rashi was correct to assert that God's command was "for all generations," but this should *not*

---

40   See, Jerusalem Talmud, Nedarim 9:4 and Genesis Rabbah 24:7.

be understood literally. Rather, the message of this biblical teaching is that "in every generation, when you want to build the Temple, the structure should be in accord with the prophecy that is then attained. That should determine the form of Temple and vessels."[41] In other words, the expression "in every generation" is an abiding call to live in the present, based on our understanding (always imperfect) of what God desires of us in the here and now. In engaging RLY critically on his presentation of the non-Jew, I am attempting to live into his teaching. Inspired by the *rebbe*'s instruction, let us continue to search humbly for God's light, actively seeking it out both near and far, sharing in this quest with all those willing to do so with respect, honesty, and compassion.

---

41 *Kedushat Levi*, vol. 1, *Terumah*, 220.

Gershon Greenberg

Israel's Election and the Suffering of the Holocaust

Orthodox Jewish thinkers through the war, whether Torah-centered (Agudat Yisrael), religious nationalist (Mizrahi) or kabbalistic, absorbed the events into religious thought. A central explanation was Israel's election. For some, election necessarily involved suffering. For others, election required separation of Israel from the rest of the nations, so that when Jews violated this separation, disaster ensued. And for one other, Israel's status as elected and separated brought catastrophe at the apocalyptic onset of redemption.

Election Means Suffering

For thinkers of this stream, election carried suffering along with it—not as a matter of punishment under God, but as hatred on the part of others alone.

In response to Kristallnacht, two religious Zionists in Jerusalem, Yeshayahu Volfsberg and Shelomoh Zalman Shragai, evoked Isaiah's "Suffering Servant" (Isaiah 52:13–53:1–10):

> Behold My servant shall prosper.... He was despised, and forsaken of men. A man of pains, and acquainted with disease.... Surely our diseases he did bear, and our pains he carried; whereas we did esteem him stricken, smitten of God, and afflicted. But he was wounded because of our transgressions, he was crushed because of our iniquities: The chastisement of our welfare was upon him, and with his stripes we were healed.... Yet it pleased the Lord to crush him by disease; to see if his soul would offer itself in restitution, that he might see his seed, prolong his days, and that the purpose of the Lord might

> prosper by his hand. Of the travail of his soul he shall see to the full, even My servant.... Because he bared his soul unto death. And was numbered with the transgressors; yet he bore the sin of many, and made intercession for the transgressors.

They held that the people of Israel absorbed not the sin (as in Christianity), but the suffering of others—as the elected servant of God. The troubles in Germany and Austria belonged to Israel's servant-relationship to God. In this relationship, the Jewish people absorbed the world's suffering which resulted from its sins—lest the suffering spread until the world itself was destroyed. By contrast, while the people of Israel absorbed the suffering of others, in Christianity the sins of others were absorbed by Christ.[1]

In Spring 1940, Shelomoh Halevi Faynzilber, the head of the religious court in Kedainiai and president of Lithuania's rabbinical organization, wrote to offer consolation to his fellow sufferers (Faynzilber and his family were killed by Lithuanians in 1941). He drew from Maimonides' Epistle to Yemen (1172), which identified the consequences to God's election of Israel ("Only the Lord had a delight in thy fathers to love them, and He chose their seed after them, even you, above all peoples, as it is this day." Deuteronomy 10:15). The first was enmity and violence which ran from Amalek to Nebuchadnezzar to Abd al-Nabi ibn Mahdi. The second were attempts to destroy Israel through arguments and controversies over its laws (Syrians, Persians, Greeks). The third combined violence and controversy. Its proponents claimed their own prophecy and new law from God, contrary to Judaism's, to stoke destructive confusion: "A remarkable plan, continued by the type of personality who is envious and malicious, and who will strive to kill his enemy and save his own life. And if he cannot achieve this, he will devise a scheme whereby they will both be slain." In his effort to explain the great pain, he cited Maimonides' predictions of the prophet, that the people would be victims of contempt and assault:

---

[1] On Christian uses of Isaiah 53 see Bernd Janowsky and Peter Stuhlmacher ed., *The Suffering Servant: Isaiah 53 in Jewish and Christian Sources* (Grand Rapids: Wm. B. Eerdmans Publishing Co., 2004) and William H. Bellinger, Jr. and William R. Farmer ed., *Jesus the Suffering Servant: Isaiah 53 and Christian Origins* (Harrisburg: Trinity Press International, 1990). Wolfsberg-Aviad, "Penei ha'dor: Eved hashem," *Ha'tsofeh* 3, no. 342 (February 1939): 6. Shragai, "Be'aspeklariah shelanu: Yesurei yisrael," *Ha'tsofeh* 3, no. 360 (March 1939): 6–7.

"O Lord God, cease, I beseech Thee; How shall Jacob stand? For he is small" [Amos 7:5] "My heart is bewildered, terror hath overwhelmed me" [Isaiah 21:4].

Maimonides attributed the animosity to the fact that Israel alone had the Torah. This selective status led to antagonism and persecution. However, Faynzilber explained, the suffering served to test and purify the people (on this see Yehudah Halevi, *Kuzari* 2:44). The people were not out to be dismayed over the enemy's domination, for the process was for the sake of refining Israel. Moreover, God remained with them ("Yet even then, when they are in the land of their enemies, I will not reject or spurn them so as to destroy them, annulling My covenant with them: for I am the Lord and their God." [Leviticus 20:44]); and God would ultimately terminate the persecution ("Since my youth they have often assailed me, but they have never overcome me." [Psalms 129:1]). He cited the Epistle:

> The divine assurance was given to Jacob our father, that his descendants would survive the people who degraded and discomfited them. As it is written, "And thy seed shall be like the dust of the earth" (Genesis 28:14). Although the descendants of Jacob will be abased like the dust that is trodden underfoot, they will ultimately emerge triumphant and victorious. As the simile implies, just as the dust settles finely upon him who tramples upon it and remains after him, so will Israel outlive its oppressors.... As it is impossible for God to cease to exist, so is our destruction and disappearance from the world unthinkable. He declares "For I am the Lord. I have not changed; and you are the children of Jacob—you have not ceased to be" (Malachi 3:6).

Israel's persecutors, however, would eventually cease to exist (see Babylon, Greece). The very dust into which Israel was trampled would rise up to descend upon persecutors in their graves.[2]

Bentsiyon Firer, a religious Zionist who headed the She'erit Yisrael yeshiva in the Ulm D.P. camp outside Munich, believed that Israel's bloody history followed inevitably from its status as chosen and unique. Upon Israel's birth, he wrote in November 1948, God removed it from the realm

---

2 Abraham Halkin, trans., *Maimonides, "The Epistle to Yemen," in Crisis and Leadership: Epistles of Maimonides* (Philadelphia: Jewish Publication Society of America, 1985), 91–146; and Abraham Halkin ed., Boaz Cohen trans., *Moses Maimonides' Epistle to Yemen* (New York: American Academy for Jewish Research, 1952): i–xx. Shelomoh Halevi Faynzilber, *Ma'amar hisna'ari mi'afar* (Kedainiai, 1940).

of history to which all other peoples belonged, and assured Israel of endless eternity, and that it would never be conquered. The divine law was exclusive to the Jews—as stated in Maimonides' Epistle to Yemen:

> Not because of numbers will Abraham be famed or celebrated, but by the noted and illustrious scions of Israel. The phrase "shall be called" simply means, shall be renowned, as it does in the verse, "Let thy name be called in them, and the name of my fathers Abraham and Isaac" [Genesis 45:16] ... The Divine covenant made with Abraham to grant the sublime Law to his descendants referred exclusively to those who belonged to the stock of both Isaac and Jacob.

This exclusivity extended to Israel's endurance. Again, citing Maimonides' Epistle: "As it is impossible for God to cease to exist, so is our destruction and disappearance from the world unthinkable." Firer pointed out that:

> In the history of every other nation there are ascents and descents, eras and epochs of blossoming and periods of decay, decline and misfortune. The history of the Jewish people for the last thousand years is different. Despite the relentless persecution, the Jewish people have not been doomed. The pyres and the crematoria [of the Holocaust] have shaken the nation of Israel and torn away large sections of the Jewish-national organism. But they have not completely destroyed Israel. The Jewish people live on.

Chosen by God, unique, Jews have also had a tragic history. Faynzilber wrote:

> The history of Israel has a monotone character, that of grievous tragedy. A cry of pain of the powerless and unfortunate people, is sounded from every page and line of our history. Collectively, the chapters of Israel's history make up a lengthy, continuously blood narrative. The terrifying tragedy freezes the blood in our veins. There is no real spark of light in our history, no bright star in the cloudy Jewish heaven. Only a black, leaden cloud over the Jewish horizon. This has been so for 2,000 years of exile.

Amalek wanted Israel to be absolutely obliterated; the battle between Israel and Amalek was one of life and death. The tragedy was a consequence of Israel's uniqueness; an eternal hatred for the eternal nation (*Sinat olam le'am olam*). In the Epistle, Maimonides had spoken of the "hatred" of the world toward the eternal nation. He explained:

> The Gentiles are not angry with us because we have a religion which is different than any [one] of theirs. After all, there are many different religions in the universe of the Gentiles; and there is no overwhelming hatred of any particular one towards the other; nothing like the collective hatred of the Gentile religions against the religion of Israel in particular. Their collective anger is due solely to the fact that our religion is totally different, in form and substance, from all other religions in the world. All other religions in the world are essentially idolatrous—idols which are all sensibly, visibly perceptible to the Gentiles. No matter whether the idol is Buddha, Mohammad or the Christian one.[3]

In 1946 Simhah Elberg, who escaped Warsaw for Shanghai in 1941, set down in his *Akedat treblinka*, that as the nation chosen by God for His law, thereby unique and also eternal, Israel was hated—he cited Maimonides' formula, "hatred of the world toward the eternal nation" (Epistle to Yemen). The Jews, Elberg wrote, were mistaken to think that this hatred expressed itself in jealousy and in competition. Rather, hatred meant Treblinka and Auschwitz. At the same time, the suffering was inescapable, for it belonged to Israel's very identity. Israel was the *Akedah* nation, with *Akedah* passing from binding to sacrifice. God showed Abraham that His great nation would pass through history upon the fires of the altar, ever sanctified by the flames. The *Akedah* of Mt. Moriah moved ultimately to Treblinka. There, it atoned for the sins of the generations. Isaac, Elberg wrote, was never taken down from the altar. Rather, Mt. Moriah was transferred from one land to another, from Spain to France, from France to Germany, to Poland. Although the torturer this time was different. Hitler, who spoke in the name of God, brought out a new demonic, trans-natural and trans-rational power.

> Hitler came up with a new creation, one of the murder of an entire nation of millions. That demonic power of mass murder took its destruction further, by placing its stamp upon God's creation. For the first time in world history, creation became completely stained and polluted. Can humankind ever be mended? Cleansed of the sin of murdering creation? I think not. The world has descended into the deepest void, into the abyss of holocaust (*Umkum*)

---

3   Bentsiyon Firer, "Netsah yisrael," *Di yidishe shtime* 3, no. 4 (November 1948): 4; "Parashat Zakhor," "Purim," in *Yisrael vehazemanim* (Tel Aviv, 1956/57), 79–82, 87–89.

and chaos (*Tohu va'vohu*). There has to be a new creation (*Yetzirah*), a new beginning of six days.[4]

To the extent that God's revelation of Torah at Sinai was bound up with the people's election, the suffering which resulted from Sinai belonged to the theme that suffering was implied by election. Yehudah Leb Gerst was working as a writer and teacher in the Beit Ya'akov girls school in Lodz, Poland, when he was forced to move into the ghetto on April 30, 1940. In August 1944, when the ghetto was liquidated, he was transported to Auschwitz. He remained for less than a month, then to Kaufering, Landshut, and finally Dachau. From there he made his way to Bergen-Belsen, from where he immigrated in 1947 to the Land of Israel. There, he wrote that Sinai was the creation point that established absolute rejection of idolatry. Whenever the Jews denied the realm other than Torah's, other nations sought to destroy them. Jews were hated because of Sinai:

> The Nazis could not avoid letting out what was in their hearts and the hearts of other Israel-haters. Namely, the truly mysterious animosity for the nation which dared ever since ancient times to promulgate in the true God's name such incendiary declarations as "Thou shalt have no other gods.... Thou shalt not murder.... Thou shalt not steal.... Thou shalt not commit adultery."

A few years later (1951) Gerst spoke of Israel as being located at the outer of the sphere of history, and the rest of the world at the periphery. Israel's potential was set at Sinai and became actualized, as a matter of course, upon redemption. Specifically, God demonstrated at Sinai that man was to exist as His moral image (Leviticus 11:44), and this heteronymous moral authority served as the basis with which to control the evil inclination. The Nazis set out to obliterate morality; Hitler wanted to explode the tablets delivered at Mt. Sinai. The Holocaust was the culmination of the metahistorical even ontic-level battle between the Jewish people or the nation chosen by God to be His collective image, the expression of written and oral Torah, and the bearer of a heteronymous morality; and the idolatry of satanic Nazism. The life of one meant the death of the other. The Holocaust brought this metaphysical confrontation into history. As Torah was a source of being, and

---

4 Simhah Elberg, *Akedat Treblinka* (Shanghai: Chow Si-Tsing, 1946). See also Nahum Sokolov, *Sinat olam le'am olam* (Warsaw, 1882).

by following Torah the people of Israel necessarily survived. In turn, the Jewish response of Torah during the Holocaust kept Sinai alive.[5]

Violating Election Means Suffering

Another stream of thought, rather than speaking of the suffering of the Holocaust as an unavoidable correlation to the hatred and jealousy which came with election and separateness, assumed that Israel was to blame for the hatred. Israel's election required separation from the rest of the world. As long as antagonism existed, it could be contained if a distance was kept. Once Israel crossed the line, the other side attacked.

Agudat Yisrael

Aleksander Zishar Frydman, the General Secretary of Polish Agudat Yisrael, was incarcerated in the Warsaw ghetto, and then deported to Maidanek—where he was killed in 1943. The historian Mendl Piekaz suggests that his perception of the separation drew from Judah Loew, the Maharal of Prague. According to the Maharal, the people of Israel possessed a sublime soul fit for divine activity—while idolaters possessed diminished souls which were not. That explained why, when God went around to the many nations offering the Torah with its Mitsvot, the idolatrous nations declined while the people of Israel were ready to accept (*Midrash shemot rabbah*, *Parashah 5*, *Siman 9*; *Parashah 27*, *Siman 9*). Because the idolaters (which included Esau, Ishmael and their descendants) had diminished souls, they tended towards evil. At the same time, if any idolater converted it meant that he/she indeed possessed a sublime soul, like any soul of the nation of Israel.

In the late 1930's Frydman spoke of an eternal tension between the realm of Israel and the realm of (Esau) Amalek; between the voice of Torah and prayer and that of murder and theft. Amalek's legacy was one of the inexhaustible hatred of Israel. Israel's faith meant that the Jewish people could not be conquered, even if it meant death in sanctification of God's name. With redemption, Amalek would be annihilated. In the meantime the hatred could only be contained. Israel was "fire" to the nations' "water," and to preserve the flame Israel needed a "pot" to protect itself. Jews erected

---

5   See Gershon Greenberg, "Yehudah Leb Gerst's Religious 'Ascent' Through the Holocaust," *Holocaust and Genocide Studies* 13, no. 1 (1999): 62–89.

such a barrier, until they assimilated—and then the waters flooded down upon the people. In turn, however, the flood was directed by God (there was no human explanation for what the Nazis were doing) and measure for measure (e.g., Jews wanted to intermarry, so Germany declared that mixed marriages were illegal).[6]

Elhanan Wasserman, Rosh Yeshivah of the Baranowicz, Poland yeshiva—who was also a victim, murdered in the seventh Fort outside Kaunas in summer 1941—echoed Frydman's view about the hatred of Israel which came with its unique position as the people of God. Beginning with Esau and then Amalek, the Gentiles were filled with hatred for Israel. That is, they were at war against God, but attacked (and hated) Israel because God Himself could not be reached (*Midrash shemot rabbah, Parashah* 51, *Siman* 5; *Midrash eykhlah rabbah, Parashah* 3, *Siman* 5). But the antagonism remained contained, unless the people of Israel upset the *status quo*. They did so when they diminished their own religiosity, setting off a corresponding destruction from the outside. Wasserman cited the *Sefer Hasidim* (*Siman* 209) which pointed out that any time the Gentiles desecrated something holy for the Jews, it turned out that the Jews had already desecrated it themselves; inner and outer destruction were of one source. For example, when radical Jewish nationalists destroyed from within, antisemitic Nazi nationalists did so from without; when Jews violated the Sabbath, the enemy decreed against Sunday hours. God, Wasserman contended, had the German Amalek transform the very nationalism and socialism which

---

6 Aleksander Zishar Frydman, "Ha'sinah li'yehudim," and "Shirtutim ve'nitsotsot," in *Ketavim nivharim* (Jerusalem, 1959/60), 51–55, 156–57. Maharal (Judah Loew) of Prague, *Kitvei maharal mi'prag: Mivhar*, vol. 1, 197–98; vol. 2, 158. (Firer also cited Maharal.) Shalom Rosenberg writes:

> ...The approach of the Maharal of Prague teaches us the doctrine of estrangement. The Jewish people needs to be in this world, despite the fact that it belongs to another world.... This incompatibility carries in its wake alienation and suffering. This is the meaning of exile. Of course, the redemption will take place, but it will be the result of catastrophe and apocalyptic change. The Maharal thinks that there is a kind of ontological necessity in the existence of the Jewish people in the world. It is a divine mission, but one involving suffering and pain.

Shalom Rosenberg, "The Holocaust: Lesson, Explanation and Meaning," in *The Impact of the Holocaust on Jewish Theology*, ed. Steven J. Katz (New York: NYU Press, 2005), 104. On Frydman and Maharal see Mendel Piekaz, *Hasidut polin bein shetei milhamot ha'olam* (Jerusalem, 1970).

infatuated the Jews, into national socialism. He had the very theaters which enticed them away from Torah closed to them.[7]

Like Frydman and Wasserman, Jerusalem Agudat Yisrael leader and Gur Hasid Yitshak Meir Levin held that the hatred of the nations against Israel—he traced its beginning to Mt. Sinai (see *Ein ya'akov ad Shabbat* 89^b)—could at best only be contained; there had to be a partition and distance between Israel and the Gentiles. When Enlightenment Jews and secular Zionists voided the distance they provoked divine response through Germany.[8]

In his sermons between summer 1941 and winter 1942, Shelomoh Zalman Unsdorfer, a graduate of the Bratislava yeshiva who served as the leading rabbinical figure in war torn Bratislava (He too was killed in Auschwitz in 1944) traced Israel's election to the battle between Jacob and Esau in the womb of their mother (*Midrash bereshit rabbah, Parashah* 63, *Siman* 6). Their individual rivalry, with the selection of Jacob, generated into an ethical dualism for the ages. Jacob symbolized piety, grace (*Hesed*) and compassion, over-against murder and robbery. As a result, while (as the Scriptural story of Joseph conveyed) the people of Israel identified themselves as chosen and they dreamed of greatness, they were humiliated and hated by their antagonists. In the language of the Scriptural story of Joseph, Jews were cast into pits of scorpions (i.e., ghettos), robbed (of their earnings and sold into slavery)—hated because God loved them, raised them above all others, and blessed them with commandments. How could the people of Israel defend themselves from the attacks which came with their election? By holding onto Torah. When they did not, God entered history through a ruler as cruel as Haman (Sanhedrin 97^b), i.e., Hitler, to restore order. Like Frydman, Wasserman and Levin, Unsdorfer spoke of God's direction, and measure-for-measure response to Israel's self-destruction; inner and outer activity corresponded with each other. For example, as Jews abandoned their traditional garb and *Tsitsit*, they were forced to wear Jewish stars; they kept their stores open on Sabbath, and so were forced to identify their stores as Jewish.[9]

---

7   See Gershon Greenberg, "Elhanan Wasserman's Response of the Growing Catastrophe in Europe: The Role of Ha'gra and Hofets Hayim Upon His Thought," *Journal of Jewish Thought and Philosophy* 8, no. 1 (2000): 1–31.
8   See Gershon Greenberg, "Ontic Division and Religious Survival: Wartime Palestinian Orthodoxy and the Holocaust," *Modern Judaism* 14 (1994): 21–61.
9   See Gershon Grenberg, "Shelomoh Zalman Unsdorfer, Disciple of the Hatam Sofer, With God through the Holocaust," *Yad Vashem Studies* 31 (2003): 61–94.

Shelomoh Zalman Ehrenreich, like Unsdorfer a graduate of the Bratislava yeshiva (as well was s killed in Auschwitz, July 1944) spoke of Israel's election as a matter of the Israel of Torah being the very purpose of creation. He held that the evil attackers of Israel were also good; God was using them as a means to beat Israel away from assimilation and back to itself, and God was good. There were potentially positive consequences to the attacks themselves. They could result in Israel's *Teshuvah*. Moreover, Amalek would inevitably fall—for the world was under God—and then the nations would recognize the power of God. Amalek's defeat enhanced the very sacred purpose of the world—for Israel-of-Torah was the sacred purpose of the world. Ehrenreich shared the measure-for-measure dynamic discerned by the others. He asserted that Jews passing through Simleul-Silvaniei from Grosswardein (Oradea), with their fingers mutilated and swastikas branded on their heads, suffered because there were Jews who intermarried; or who envied the riches of the nations and wanted to emulate their fashion. But this dynamic belonged to Amalek's service in the name of preserving elected Israel.[10]

Mizrahi

Mosheh Avigdor Amiel, a Mizrahi leader who was the chief rabbi of Tel Aviv, attributed Israel's Holocaust suffering to Israel's undermining its chosen, separate status, through assimilation and secular Zionism. Amiel maintained that Judaism's intention was originally internationalist. Israel's history began, not with the patriarchs but with the first human being. Thus God went to each and every nation with His offer of Torah, before He revealed Himself and Torah to the people of Israel. Indeed, even after all the other nations turned down the offer, He delivered the Torah in seventy different languages. But with Sinai, the people of Israel's intention turned nationalist. They were chosen by God: "Ye shall be Mine own treasure from among all peoples" (Exodus 19:5)—a grounding principle articulated every time the blessing over wine was recited, on the Sabbath and at festivals: "You have chosen us from among all peoples." As Amiel formulated it, the laws of Mt. Sinai were issued long before the Nuremburg laws; and before *Deutschland, Deutschland über alles*, God's words contained in Scripture

---

10 See Gershon Greenberg, "The Religious Response of Shelomoh Zalman Ehrenreich (Simleul-Silvaniei, Transylvania) to the Holocaust (1940–1943)," *Studia Judaica* 9 (Fall 2000): 65–93.

read "And to make thee high above all nations that He hath made, in praise, and in name and in glory" (Deuteronomy 26:19)—"And thou shalt be above only, and thou shalt not be beneath" (Deuteronomy 28:13). The theme of separation and superiority was brought forward by the rabbinic sages. God established one realm for Israel, the other for the nations: "Israel had her side, the world had its side" (*Midrash bereshit rabbah, Parashah* 41, *Siman* 6. *Pesikta rabbati* 33:3). Israel's racial culture (*Geza*) was unique;[11] indeed exclusively truly human: "You are called a human being and the foreigners of the world are not called human beings" (Baba metsia 114[b]). Over the generations, the principle was applied to mean that Gentiles did not have the right to own land in the Land of Israel (Gittin 47[a]); Jews were not permitted to use their bread, oil or wine.

While the nations of the world hated Israel ever since Sinai (Shabbat 89[b], Ein ya'akov commentary), the hatred could and should have been contained. It was not; there were Jews who abandoned Torah land and racial culture for the realm of impurity. The worse incursions happened with Moses Mendelssohn's *Haskalah*-generated Jewish violation of Torah and racial culture; and Herzl's secular nationalism. The urge to be as, and integrate into, the nations was never as powerful as it was in the decades preceding the catastrophe. So there was never such an outpouring of God's fury, an "As I live" response (Ezekiel 20:33). Hitler, whom Amiel identified with Amalek, rose against Israel on account of assimilation. Assimilation set Hitler against Israel: "For over a hundred years our brethren in Germany did everything possible to push Israel into the other side. What did this bring about? Hitler."[12]

Compromising Election does not Bring Suffering

Shelomoh Zalman Shragai disassociated election from persecution in response to Torah-failure. He maintained that the failure of Israel to keep

---

11   The rabbinic sages used the term Geza to refer to the trunk of a tree (Baba Metsia 118[b]–19[a]; Sanhedrin 105[b]) and to the common origin of a people (Moed Katan 25[b]). It did not refer to blood identity. See Jacques J. Rozenberg, "From Antisemitism and Racism to Ethics: An Epistemological Reflection on the Nuremberg Trials and Code," in *Bioethical and Ethical Issues Surrounding the Trials and Code of Nuremberg*, ed. Jacques Rozenberg (Lewiston, NY, 2003), 1–21.
12   Mosheh Avigdor Amiel, *Am segulah: Ha'leumiut veha'enoshut be'hashkafot olamah shel ha'yahadut* (Tel Aviv, 1942/43). Amiel, *Li'nevukhei ha'tekufah Perek histaklut be'mahut ha'yahadut* (Jerusalem, 1943).

itself separate was an internal matter of Israel's relationship to God, and thus was disconnected from attacks from outside; and he rejected the notion that the nations were punishing Israel on God's behalf so they would atone. Hitler was evil, pure and simple, and without him there would have been no Holocaust. Shragai went further, to reject calls for penitent return as a means to stop the persecution. There was no cause-effect relationship between Israel's behavior and outer events.[13]

Election and the Apocalypse

Ya'akov Mosheh Harlap, the successor to Rav Kook as *Rosh Yeshivah* of Merkaz Ha'rav in Jerusalem, echoed the dualism of such thinkers as Yehudah Halevi, Samuel Uceda and Shneor Zalman of Lyady. Yehudah Halevi wrote:

> Only the sons of Jacob were chosen to inherit the perfect soul and intellect of Adam and transmit it by birth, and this divided them off from all other nations.... / The first man received from the deity a vital soul in all its completeness, and an intellect of the highest possible level for a human being. [Of his children, only Abel received Adam's complete soul and highest intellect.] The sons of Jacob were all chosen [to receive the soul]. All of them together were worthy of the divine message.... Though there were among them sinners who were hated by the deity, there can be no doubt that they were still chosen in a recognizable sense and their roots and nature were "chosen" and they were to beget children who would be "chosen" (*Ha'kuzari* 1:95).

According to Samuel Uceda, a student of Yitshak Luria and Hayim Vital in Safed, the people of Israel possessed a divine image of holiness which was not available to the rest of humanity. All humankind was created in the image of God ("Beloved is man for he was created in the image of God." *Pirkei Avot* 3:14). But this applied only to the pious, namely the holy nation of Israel—as over-against the image of all others which was profane.[14] According to Shneor Zalman of Lyady, founder of Habad (1745-1812), each Jew had two souls, one drawn from the light within the *Kelippot*, the

---

13   Shelomoh Zalman Shragai, *Tehumim* (Jerusalem: Mossad Harav Kook, 1951/52), 81–88, 263–69; *Tahalikhei ha'temurah veha'geulah* (Jerusalem: Mossad Harav Kook, 1958/59), 174–98; *Zemanim* (Jerusalem: Mossad Harav Kook, 1969), 213–15.
14   Shemuel Uceda, *Midrash shemuel: Vehu beur nehmad veyakar al pirkei avot* (New York, 1988), ad perek 3:18.

other from the negative dimension of the *Kelippot* (*Sitra ahra*). The souls of the nations were drawn only from the *Kelippot*. It followed that the nations of *Sitra ahra* (Amalek) and Israel were at war. Also, the people of Israel alone were created in the holy image of God, divinely chosen and by nature receptive to Torah. They had nothing in common with the profane nations, and any contact between them was bound to be destructive.[15]

Harlap held that God selected Israel ("For the Lord hath chosen Jacob for Himself and Israel for His own treasure." Psalms 135:4) and that Israel's selected status was forever ("For I the Lord change not; and ye, O sons of Jacob, are not consumed." Malachi 3:6). Through all of their descents in history the people of Israel remained worthy of their holy name as His chosen children of Jacob. The *Shekhinah* (God's illuminating presence) contracted, even seemed to disappear from Israel, but nevertheless remained enclosed in the innermost recesses, in the essence of the people: "The chosen ones of God, there is a holy fire; a very flame of the Lord within them" (Song of Songs 8:6).

For Harlap the Holocaust was an apocalyptic drama, evoked by redemption, and included two stages. At the point of history's end, the Messiah ben Joseph entered the world, enclosed in a dark vessel—for Israel could not withstand the sudden appearance of pure light; the light of the messiah combined with the darkness of judgment and sorrow. Then Elijah heralded the advent of Messiah ben David, and he removed the shadow and bring the light (Ezekiel 37). The messianic light which was sheathed in the darkness was the collective soul of Israel. Harlap cited Ramban (ad Genesis 1:1), that Israel was rooted collectively in the secret realm where creation and history began. Israel was a sacred seed, which shared a secret, pre-historical source with Torah (Zohar, *Helek* 1, 15^b). Ontically pure, Israel never sinned, even in the slightest (*Zohar ve'tosafot* 3, 42^b). Israel's soul, intrinsically holy, was tied eternally to God and the reality of Israel alone, was of metaphysical character. Further, Israel (alone) was transferred by Torah from a mere people into the holy reality of divine emanation. Altogether, as the messianic light, Israel was objectively holy. In its holiness, Israel remained rooted in eternity.

The darkness of the era of the Messiah son of Joseph was the *Sitra ahra*, forever blemished, with nothing in common with Israel (*Tanhuma*

---

15 Shneor Zalman of Lyady (1745–1813), *Likutei amarim*, Helek 1, Perek 1, 5; and Perek 6, 11^a.

(ed. Buber) Ki tisa 17 [note] 20). While Israel's race was holy, the seed of the nations was as the "issue of horses" (Ezekiel 23:20). Israel was rooted above in holiness, and branched down towards the realm of pollution (*Tumah*); nations remained rooted in the pollution.

Harlap understood the suffering endured by Israel in this context. The nations could have drawn sacred reality through the channel of Israel, but once the apocalyptic drama unfolded, it was no longer possible. Turning to anthropological vocabulary, Harlap offered that the nations, sensing that redemption was imminent and realizing it meant their end, they sought to sabotage the process by destroying its vessel Israel. The nations of the world were driven insane over their imminent demise and targeted the perceived source of their misery for destruction. Filled with a destructive, jealous rage over the prospect of their enemy's survival after them, they attacked.

For Harlap, those killed in the Holocaust were all individuals, who broke the bonds of the world of history (and finitude) which had become identified with the *Sitra ahra*, to burst forth into eternity. Each was a new *Akedah*, bound and then killed. In the era of the imminence of the messiah, Isaac's experience became actualized for collective Israel and all were "souls from before creation" (*Neshamot shel olam ha'tohu*)—souls of infinite yearnings, despaired by finitude: "Their souls were of the realm of *Tohu*, and they were very great. The bounds of the world could not enclose them; their souls ascended to the above." In turn, the destruction of the body testified to the holiness of the soul. They were as the sons of Aaron, who were annihilated in order to see the king ("Through them that are nigh unto Me I will be sanctified." Leviticus 10:3). Each soul which broke forth from the body in love for God, shared in the light of the Messiah son of Joseph—the light which would grow into the light of redemption: "Each and every one of these accepted the yoke of the kingdom of heaven in the final moments [of life] and sanctified himself in love for God. All were of the root of the soul of Messiah son of Joseph."[16]

---

16 The evil's assault at the prospect of its demise, see Zadok Rabinowitz (Zadok Ha'kohen of Lublin), *Sefer yisrael kedoshim* (Benei Berak, 1966/67), 48[a/b]. See Gershon Greenberg, "The Holocaust Apocalypse of Ya'akov Mosheh Harlap," *Jewish Studies* 41 (2002): 5–18.

Reuven Kimelman

Israel's Election and the Moral Dilemma of Amalek and the Seven Nations of Canaan

Introduction

Central to the biblical understanding of revelation is the election of Israel. Concomitant to Israel's election is the idea of ethical nationhood whose goal is the bringing of other nations into God's orbit. The election of Israel is to lead to the universal acceptance of the God of Israel. Nothing is thus more jarring than the notion that Israel is to destroy nations that reject God's moral rule. This essay explores what is it that makes for Israel's election, and what is it that makes for the elimination of its worse opponents? The issue is, as we shall see, multi-dimensional even in the Bible itself.

The major question is whether the axis of election is primarily ethnic or primarily moral. The issue is biblically framed in terms of the holiness of Israel. Leviticus 19 holds that Israel is potentially Holy, as it says: "You shall be holy, for I Lord your God am holy" (19:2). It is thus followed by a whole slew of rules against idolatry while promoting sabbath observance and the ethical life culminating in "Love your neighbor as yourself" (19:17). Deuteronomy holds that Israel is intrinsically holy, as it says not once but twice: "For you are a people holy to the Lord your God: of all the peoples on earth the Lord your God chose you to be His treasured people" (7:6, 14:2). Leviticus emphasizes the moral mandate; Deuteronomy underscores the unconditional status of Israel's chosenness. According to the former, Israel's moral failure could call into question the validity of the election. According to the latter, Israel's holiness is unconditional, intrinsic to its being. Thus, Deuteronomy's prophet-disciple, Jeremiah, can declare: "Israel is holy to the Lord, the first fruits of His harvest. All who eat of it shall be held guilty; disaster shall befall them" (2:3).

If Israel is intrinsically holy, then if follows, as Jeremiah says, that all who seek to consume it are to be destroyed. This type of thinking was applied to Amalek who first sought to destroy Israel after the Exodus, and to the nations of Canaan whose existence in the Land of Israel could undermine Israel's exclusive commitment to the God of Israel.

The question is how does the ethically-conditioned view of Israel's election deal with the commandment for the destruction of others. Is the commandment for their destruction itself ethically-conditioned, that is a factor of their behavior, or is it intrinsic to their being. Just as the election of Israel can be grasped intrinsically and extrinsically, so can the evil of their enemies be grasped intrinsically and extrinsically.

The combination of how Israel is appreciated in terms of a moral calling and how others are rejected in terms of moral failure raises important theological and educational challenges. Does the doctrine of election allow ethnicity to trump morality or morality to trump ethnicity? This dilemma has haunted Jewish ethical reflection throughout the generations.

The dilemma will be dealt with by clarifying three issues: justice and the election of Israel, the command to eliminate Amalek, and the alleged destruction of the ancient Canaanites.

Justice and the Election of Israel

This section seeks to show the link between the ideal of justice and the election of Israel. The thesis is that they are interdependent. The analysis moves from Abraham to the prophets, and then to Deuteronomy. It focuses on Israel's mandate of ethical nationhood.

The project of linking the election of Israel with the ideal of justice starts with Abraham in Genesis18. It goes as follows:

> (17) The Lord said, "Shall I hide from Abraham what I am about to do, (18) seeing that Abraham shall surely become a great and mighty nation, and all the nations of the earth shall be blessed by him? (19) For I have singled him out, that he may instruct his children and his household after him to keep the way of the Lord by doing what is just and right, so that the Lord may

bring about for Abraham what He has promised him." (20) Then the Lord said, "Because the outcry against Sodom and Gomorrah is great and their sin is very grave, (21) I will go down to see whether they have done altogether according to the outcry that has come to Me. And if not, I will know [what to do]."

As the story famously continues, Abraham challenges Divine justice, seeking to save Sodom by the merit of varying numbers of innocent individuals who may, so goes his argument, be found in it. Abraham's challenge of Divine justice is introduced by God's question, "Shall I hide from Abraham what I am about to do?" (Genesis 18:17). The question assumes a degree of intimacy between God and Abraham as if God, in the words of Amos, "does nothing without having revealed His purpose to His servants the prophets" (3:7). If Abraham is normally briefed, then the question is whether this should be the exception. Alternatively, it is testing whether Abraham is worthy of the role of intercessory prophet that he is dubbed subsequently at Genesis 20:7.

In any case, pondering whether He should divulge His plan to Abraham, God, in verses 18–19, considers three factors: Abraham will one day become a great and populous nation; he is to serve as a medium of blessing to all the nations; and he is to instruct his children and his household after him to keep the way of the Lord by doing what is just and right. The first two iterate elements mentioned in Abraham's original mandate in Genesis 12:2–3, the second is also mentioned with regard to Abraham's posterity in Genesis 22:18 and 28:14. The last is unique. It is also the sole explanation in Genesis of the election of Abraham. Indeed, it makes God's promises contingent on Abraham's ability to get over to his posterity the keeping of the way of the Lord, defined as doing what is just and right.[1]

The pair of words for just and right, or justice and righteousness, *tsedakah* and *mishpat*, turn out to be the biblical signature terms of Israel's relationship to God. Abraham's election is thus key to Israel's election. According to the psalmist: "He loves *righteousness* and *justice*; the earth is full of the goodness of the LORD" (33:5), for "*Righteousness* and *justice* are the foundation of Your throne; mercy and truth will precede You" (89:15, see 97:2). According to Isaiah, they are the ways of emulating God who is

---

[1] For the meaning of the unit as whole, see Reuven Kimelman, "Prophecy as Arguing with God and the Ideal of Justice," *Interpretation, A Journal of Bible and Theology* 68 (2014): 17–27.

characterized by the two terms: "The LORD of hosts is exalted in *justice*, and the Holy God shows himself holy in *righteousness*" (5:16). For him, they are God's measuring rods: "And I will make *justice* the line and *righteousness* the plummet" (28:17). Thus, his hope is that God will "fill Zion with *justice* and *righteousness*" (33:5). According to Jeremiah, they are the path for those who seek to know God: "let him who boasts boast in this, that he understands and knows me, that I am the LORD who practices steadfast love, *justice*, and *righteousness* in the earth. For in these things I delight, declares the LORD" (9:23). Jeremiah even makes them the basis of his application of the blessing of Abraham: "and if you swear, 'as the LORD lives,' in truth, in *justice*, and in *righteousness*, then nations shall bless themselves by H/him [God/Israel]" (4:2).

The absence of these qualities among those responsible for the well-being of the polity was especially condemnable. Jeremiah repeatedly lambasts Jehoiakim for not going in the ways of justice and righteousness. Jeremiah's program states:

> Thus, says the LORD: Do *justice* and *righteousness*, and deliver from the hand of the oppressor him who has been robbed. And do no wrong or violence to the stranger, the orphan, and the widow, nor shed innocent blood in this place (22:3).

Thus,

> Woe to him who builds his house by *unrighteousness*, and his upper rooms by *injustice*, who makes his neighbor serve him for nothing and does not give him his wages (22:13).

The model was Jehoiakim's father Josiah, as Jeremiah reminds Jehoiakim:

> Do you think you are a king because you compete in cedar? Did not your father eat and drink and do *justice* and *righteousness* then it was well with him. He judged the cause of the poor and needy; then it was well with him. Is not this to know Me?" says the LORD (22:15–16).

Taking up the same cudgels, Ezekiel inveighs against the oppression of those in political authority:

> The LORD God proclaims: "Enough, princes of Israel! Turn aside from violence and oppression. Establish *justice* and *righteousness*. Cease your evictions of my people (45:9).

For Ezekiel, as for his prophetic predecessors, "A man is righteous if he does *justice* and *righteousness*" (18:5). Isaiah connects the two qualities to redemption: "Zion shall be redeemed with *justice*, and her penitents with *righteousness*" (1:27). Second Isaiah seconds this connection with salvation, saying: "Keep *justice*, and do *righteousness*, for soon My salvation will come, and My righteousness be revealed" (56:1). For Isaiah, "the seekers of God are pursuers of *justice*" (51:1). So consequential are justice and righteousness that Hosea sees them as cementing the covenant: "I will betroth you to Me forever; I will betroth you with *righteousness* and *justice*, with love and compassion" (2:21).

Most significant is the formulation of Second Isaiah:

> Yet they seek Me daily, and delight to know My ways, as a nation that did *righteousness* (*tsedakah*) and did not forsake the rule (*mishpat*) of their God. They ask of Me the *rules of justice* (*mishpetei tsedek*); they take delight in coming near to God (58:2).

By combining references to "nation," "rules of justice," and "nearness to God," Second Isaiah creates a link to the formulation of Israel's national mission as an exemplary nation in chapter of four of Deuteronomy.[2] There as here, the moral terms *tsedakah* and *mishpat* are conflated into the virtually identical legal terms, *mishpetei tsedek* ("rules of justice") and *mishpatim tsadikim* ("just rules"):

> (5) See, I have taught you laws and rules, as the Lord my God commanded me, to abide by in the land you are about to enter and occupy. (6) Observe them faithfully, for that will be proof of your wisdom and discernment to other nations, who on hearing of all these laws will say, "Surely that great nation is a wise and discerning people." (7) For what other nation is so great as to have a god so near as the Lord our God whenever we call upon Him? (8) Or what other nation is so great as to have such *just laws and rules* as this Teaching that I set before you this day?

By deploying the unique form *mishpatim tsadikim* and the expression "great nation," of Abraham's mandate in Genesis 18:18, Deuteronomy expands Abraham's mandate to all of Israel. It thus extends the second half of Genesis 18:18, "And all the nations of the earth shall bless themselves by

---

2   See Shalom Paul, *Isaiah 40–66, A Commentary* [Hebrew], 2 vols. (Mikra Leyisra'el, Jerusalem: Magnes Press, 2008), 2:439, verse 2.

him," to Israel. Israel is the people of Abraham morally, not just biologically. Israel hence becomes a great nation not through numbers or power, but by implementing a legal system so just that it induces the nations of the world to correlate Israel's just laws with its nearness to God. The lesson being that were they to come close to God they could also construct a just society. What a blessing to confer upon the nations.

Connecting the mission statement of Deuteronomy with the specifics of justice and righteousness of the prophets entails a polity of just and righteous laws that would "deliver from the hand of the oppressor him who has been robbed. And do no wrong or violence to the stranger, the orphan, and the widow, nor shed innocent blood in this place" (Jeremiah 22:3). It would also defend the "the cause of the poor and needy" (Jeremiah 22:16), "pay his wages" (Jeremiah 22:13), and call a halt to his "evictions" (Ezekiel 45:9).

The type of understanding reflected in Deuteronomy's emphasis on the justice of the legal system to account for Israel's mandate explains the outrage of Amos at judicial bribery. Whereas the nations roundabout are condemned for international crimes, Israel is condemned for having "sold the innocent for silver, and the needy for a pair of shoes" thereby "trampling the head of the poor into the dust of the earth and pushing the afflicted out of the way" (2:6-7). Perversion of the judicial system undermines Israel's raison d'être.

Amos makes his point about the vulnerability of Israel's election by evoking the language of the election of Abraham. Recall that in Genesis 18:19, God

> *singled out* Abraham that he may instruct his children and his household after him to keep the way of the Lord by doing what is just and right, so that the Lord may bring about for Abraham what He has promised him.

Since God's commitment to Abraham is contingent upon his posterity's commitment to justice and righteousness, Amos says: "You alone have *I singled out* from all the families of the earth. That is why I shall call you to account for all your iniquities" (3:2). The key word is "all." Israel's judicial-social crimes are in the light of its mandate to be judged as the atrocities and barbarism of the other nations. Its uniqueness among the nations entails a unique standard of judgment. Amos thus becomes the father of the double standard regarding judging Israel. Amos's use of the "families of the earth" also evokes the "families of the earth" of Abraham's original blessing of Genesis 12:3 and of his posterity of Genesis 28:14, if not "all the nations of the earth shall be blessed by him" of Genesis 18:18 and 22:18.

The price of being singled out by God is being judged by the standards of God.

Amalek

How does the vendetta against Amalek make sense in the light of the correlation between Israel's election and Israel's commitment to justice? The question is whether the Bible commands the extermination of Amalek, providing a precedent for "ethnic cleansing."[3] Those who answer in the positive filter the data through the prism of the story of Saul's battle against Amalek. Those who answer in the negative view that story as the exception, not the norm. To resolve the issue a systematic analysis of all the Amalek material in the Bible is in order.

The first biblical reference to Amalek appears in Exodus 17. The issue is whether it should be taken literally or metaphorically. It goes as follows:

> (7) The place was named Massah and Meribah, because the Israelites quarreled and because they tried the Lord, saying, "Is the Lord present among us or not?" (8) Amalek came and fought with Israel at Rephidim. (9) Moses said to Joshua, "Pick some men for us, and go out and do battle with Amalek. Tomorrow I will station myself on the top of the hill, with the rod of God in my hand." (10) Joshua did as Moses told him and fought with Amalek, while Moses, Aaron, and Hur went up to the top of the hill. (11) Then, whenever Moses held up his hand, Israel prevailed; but whenever he let down his hand, Amalek prevailed. (12) But Moses' hands grew heavy; so, they took a stone and put it under him and he sat on it, while Aaron and Hur, one on each side, supported his hands; thus, his hands were steadfast/faithful until the sun set. (13) And Joshua overwhelmed the people of Amalek with the sword. (14) Then the Lord said to Moses, "Inscribe this in a document as a reminder, and recite in the ears of Joshua:[4] 'I will utterly blot out the

---

3 On the practice of genocide in antiquity, see Louis Feldman, *"Remember Amalek!": Vengeance, Zealotry, and Group Destruction in the Bible according to Philo, Pseudo-Philo, and Josephus* (Cincinnati: Hebrew Union College Press, 2004), 2-6.

4 For taking *kee* as introducing direct speech see *The Hebrew and Aramaic Lexicon of the Old Testament*, eds. L. Koehler, W. Baumgartner, et al. (3 vols., Leiden: Brill, 1994-1996), 2:471a; and Amos Ḥakham, *Sefer Shmot* (2 vols., Jerusalem: Mossad Harav Kook, 1991), 1:329a.

memory of Amalek from under heaven.'" (15) And Moses built an altar and named it Adonai-nissi. He said, "It means, 'Hand upon the thro[ne] of the Lo[rd]!' The Lord will be at war with Amalek throughout the ages."

Among the many questions raised against a literal reading are the following:

(1) Why could Moses not keep his hands up aware that if raised Israel would prevail?
(2) Why is the term used to describe Moses's hands as steadfast identical with the Hebrew for faithful?
(3) Why was it inscribed in a document and Joshua told that God—not he—is to blot out Amalek?
(4) Why is it God—not Israel—who will be at war with Amalek?
(5) Why then does God not finish them off as was done with the Egyptians at the Sea rather than extending the conflict throughout the ages?[5]
(6) Why do the terms for God and throne appear in the Hebrew orthographically truncated?

The inability to account for these in literal terms has allowed for the possibility that the battle between Amalek and God is a metaphor for the conflict between human evil and divine authority where human evil truncates, as if were, the divine presence and authority.

The metaphorical reading solves many interpretive cruxes that elude the alleged literal reading. It accounts for locating the war with Amalek in Exodus after a crisis of faith—"Is the Lord present among us or not?" (17:7)[6] and why the hands of Moses are described as faithful, i. e., faith-generating. It also accounts for its second location in Deuteronomy after a warning against dishonest business practices ending with "For everyone who does those things, everyone who deals dishonestly, is abhorrent to the Lord your God" (25:16).[7] The appearance of Amalek is thus correlated with the

---

5   As Josephus simply says: "He [Moses] predicted that the Amalekites would perish with utter annihilation and that not one of them would be left hereafter" (*Antiquities* 3.60).
6   Which is how the Midrash takes it; see *Midrash Tanḥuma, Be-Shalaḥ* 25, 92; and *Pesikta de-Rav Kahana* 3.8, ed. Mandelbaum, 1:47 with parallels in n5.
7   So *Pesikta de Rav-Kahana* 3.4, 1:42–43:

> R. Banai, citing R. Huna, began his discourse [on remembering Amalek] with the verse "A false balance is an abomination to the Lord ..." (Proverbs 11:1). And R. Banai, citing R. Huna, proceeded: When you see a generation whose measures

absence of faith and morality. Its presence signifies their absence. The position is epitomized in the rabbinic statement: "As long as the seed of Amalek is in the world neither God's name nor his throne is whole. Were the seed of Amalek to perish from the world the Name would be whole, and the throne would be whole." In fact, an alternative version explicitly states "the wicked" instead of Amalek. Thus the war against Amalek is not against a specific ethnicity, but the machinations of human evil. Such a battle ultimately can only be waged by God, not Joshua. In sum, the more Amalek comes to embody moral evil, the more it moves from ethnicity to ethics.

The metamorphosis of Amalek from the ethnic to the ethical is thought to be a product of post-biblical exegesis, absent in the Bible itself. The possibility that the Exodus text was already understood metaphorically may be gathered from the other references to the actual nation of Amalek in the Bible that either lack reference to the Exodus text or cohere with the suggested reading here. Thus, in the next reference to Amalek, in Numbers 13:29 and 14:25, they are designated by their location only. Numbers 14:43–45 warns Israel:

> (42) Do not go up, lest you be routed by your enemies, for the Lord is not in your midst. (43) For the Amalekites and the Canaanites will be there to face you, and you will fall by the sword, inasmuch as you have turned from following the Lord· and the Lord will not be with you." (44) Yet defiantly they marched toward the crest of the hill country, though neither the Ark of the Covenant nor Moses stirred from the camp. (45) And the Amalekites and the Canaanites who dwelt in that hill country came down and pummeled them to/at Hormah.

There is no allusion to the Exodus episode unless it is in the metaphorical explanation that Israel meets defeat because they turn away from God. In any case, there is no command to do away with them nor any special comment about them. In Numbers 24:20, it is predicted that Amalek will be gone or perish forever without any mention that Israel will destroy them. This lines up with the reading of the Exodus story that the removal

---

and balances are false, you may be certain that a wicked kingdom will come to wage war against such a generation. And the proof? The verse "A false balance is an abomination to the Lord" ... which is immediately followed by a verse that says, "The insolent kingdom will come and bring humiliation [to Israel]" (Prov. 11:2).

See Rashi and Abarbanel to Deuteronomy 25:17 with Tosafot to BT Kiddushin 33b, s. v., *ve-eimah*.

of Amalek is a divine task, not a human one. It correlates well with the last biblical mention of Amalek in 1 Chronicles 4:43 where it is recorded that the last remnant of Amalek was done away with as part of its conflict with the tribe of Simeon, not because of any mandated war against them.

It is the discussion of Amalek in 1 Samuel 15 that is fateful, in terms of the present study. It places the responsibility to blot out the memory of Amalek on the king, as opposed to God in Exodus and the people in Deuteronomy, and identifies "the memory" with all the people and livestock. It states:

> Samuel said to Saul, "I am the one the Lord sent to anoint you king over His people Israel. Therefore, listen to the Lord's command! "Thus, said the Lord of Hosts: I am exacting the penalty for what Amalek did to Israel, for the assault he made upon them on the road, on their way up from Egypt. Now go, attack Amalek, and proscribe all that belongs to him. Spare no one, but kill alike men and women, infants and sucklings, oxen and sheep, camels and asses!

This move was perceived as so harsh that the talmudic rabbi, R. Mani, had King Saul himself protest the order objecting that even if the adult males were guilty the children and livestock were not.[8] Since there is no similar objection with regard to the Amalek material in the Torah, Saul must be objecting to Samuel's interpretation that the proscription of Amalek entails the destruction of even those who did not partake in Amalek's dastardly deeds. After all, Exodus faults Amalek for mounting the attack at all, while Deuteronomy focuses on their crude cowardice of attacking the stragglers. Both accusations are limited to those who fought.

The seeking of moral justification is already in the biblical text. When Samuel slays the king of Amalek, Agag, he refers not to crimes of long ago but to recent criminality, saying: "As your sword has bereaved women, so shall your mother be bereaved among women" (1 Samuel 15:33). If Agag as king is taken as representative of the people, then a four-hundred-year vendetta has been transmuted into a quid pro quod judicial execution. This limits the target to those who have wielded the sword, as Maimonides states: "Amalek who hastened to use the sword should be exterminated

---

8   BT Yoma 22b; see *Yalqut Shimoni* 2:121 (*Genesis—Former Prophets* [10 vols., ed. Heyman-Shiloni, Jerusalem: Mossad Harav Kook, 1973-1999], *Former Prophets*, p. 242) with parallels.

by the sword."[9] Lurking behind this understanding is obviously the verse "Fathers shall not be put to death for children, neither shall children be put to death for fathers. A man shall be put to death [only] for his own sin" (Deuteronomy 24:16).[10] A verse which was already used in the Bible (2 Kings 14:6 = 2 Chronicles 25:4) to prevent cross-generational vendettas. A similar understanding of the battle against Amalek as justified retribution appears in the reference to Amalek immediately preceding our story in 1 Samuel 14:48: "He (King Saul) was triumphant, defeating the Amalekites and saving Israel from those who have plundered it." If the Hebrew of "and" is taken, as it sometimes is, as "namely,"[11] then Saul's defeat of the Amalek is in response to Amalek's plundering of Israel.

The reading that Amalek should get as they gave is justified by David's tit-for-tat response to Amalek's plundering. 1 Samuel 30 states what Amalek did to Israel:

> (1) By the time David and his men arrived in Ziklag, on the third day, the Amalekites had made a raid into the Negeb and against Ziklag; they had stormed Ziklag and burned it down. (2) They had taken the women in it captive, low-born and high-born alike; they did not kill any, but carried them off and went their way.

Again, Amalek attacked the weak left behind. What did David do? Not knowing what to do, he inquired of the Lord:

> (7) David said to the priest Abiathar son of Ahimelech, "Bring the ephod up to me." (8) When Abiathar brought up the ephod to David, inquired of the Lord, "Shall I pursue those raiders? Will I overtake them?" And He answered him, "Pursue, for you shall overtake and you shall rescue."

Evidently, there was no recourse to any standing order to kill Amalek. Indeed, nothing is made of the fact that they are Amalekites. They are

---

9   L. Strauss, *Guide for the Perplexed*, Pines ed., 3:41 (Chicago: University of Chicago Press, 1964), 566; see Eugene Korn, "Moralization in Jewish Law: Genocide, Divine Commands and Rabbinic Reasoning," *The Edah Journal* 5:2 (Sivan 5766/2006), 2–11, esp. 9.

10 Accordingly, Avraham Sachatchover rejected the idea that the seed of Amalek could be punished for the sins of their fathers; see *Avnei Nezer*, part 1: *Oraḥ Ḥayyim* (New York: Hevrat Nezer, 1954), 2.508.

11 See L. Koehler, W. Baumgartner ed., *The Hebrew and Aramaic Lexicon of the Old Testament*, et al., 3 vols. (Leiden: Brill, 1994–1996), 1:258a.

simply called raiders. David's counterattack sought only to recoup his own. Amalekites who fled are left alone. Only livestock is taken as spoil.

> (17) David attacked them from before dawn until the evening of the next day; none of them escaped, except four hundred young men who mounted camels and got away. (18) David rescued everything the Amalekites had taken; David also rescued his two wives. (19) Nothing of theirs was missing—young or old, sons or daughters, spoil or anything else that had been carried off—David recovered everything. (20) David took all the flocks and herds, which [the troops] drove ahead of the other livestock; and they declared, "This is David's spoil."

Note that there is no condemnation of David, à la Saul, for not slaying Amalek or for taking the spoil. Similarly, 1 Chronicles 18:11 records that David dedicated to God the spoils of Amalek just as he did to those of Edom, Moab, Ammon, and the Philistines. Again, Amalek is treated as other enemies without a distinctive comment or special treatment.

It follows that Samuel's demand for the wholesale killing of Amalek is the exception not the norm. It does not even coincide with the other biblical data. After all, if Saul had slain all the Amalekites why did they remain so numerous in David's time? Moreover, in Numbers, Judges, and elsewhere in 1 Samuel (14:48, 27:8) Amalek gets the same quid pro quod treatment as other ancient enemies. This is even their lot at the hands of Saul in 1 Samuel 14:48. This even explains why David did not make an issue of the fact that the alleged slayer of Saul, in 2 Samuel 1:13, was a self-proclaimed Amalekite.

The link between the ethnic and the ethical has a special twist in the Book of Esther. It is common to see the conflict between Mordecai and Haman as an episode in the ongoing bout between Israel and Amalek. This is based on the linking of Mordecai with King Saul and Haman with Amalek. Both links are problematic. The identification of Mordecai with Saul is based on his being identified as "the son of Jair, the son of Shimi, the son of Kish, a man of Benjamin" (Esther 2:5). The assumption is that Kish is the Benjaminite Kish, the father of Saul (1 Samuel 9:1), yet no mention is made of the most illustrious and pertinent ancestor—King Saul. Moreover, Jair is not a Benjamite name, rather a son of Manasseh (Numbers 32:41), or a priest of David (2 Samuel 20:26). Finally, Shimi is identified only as a member of the clan of Saul (2 Samuel 16:5), not as a descendant of Saul.

Frustrated by the difficulties of linking Mordecai to Saul, the Talmud takes Jair, Shimi, and Kish to be simply epithets of Mordecai himself.[12] Although Haman is designated an Agagite (Esther 3:1, 10; 5:8; 8:1, 3, 5; 9:10, 24), he is not designated an Amalekite as other Amalekites are.[13] Moreover, the antagonism of Haman for Mordecai is attributed to Mordecai's provocative behavior (Esther 3:2–5), a stance he maintains even after the decree (Esther 5:9), not to Haman's genealogy.

There is no evidence that Haman had it originally in for the Jews. He only subsequently becomes the nefarious model of classical Judeophobia. Ticked off by one Jew he seeks to eliminate all Jews. Still, Haman himself is not executed because of his genealogy, but because of his murderous machinations. He is specifically hanged on the gallows he prepared for Mordecai as an expression of poetic justice, not for any long-standing vendetta. As Samuel justifies Agag's execution by his nefarious acts so does the Book of Esther justify Haman's by his. Neither is punished for the sins of their fathers.

Similarly, the Book of Esther no more concludes with a mandate to remember Amalek than does the story of Saul and Agag. In both cases by doing away with the enemy, in Haman's case also his children, there remains no remnant in the story itself and the case is closed. Even Haman's sons are slain not because of their father but because, as 9:5–10 notes, they joined in the battle against the Jews. Clearly, the moral structure of the book is predicated on a measure for measure system and not on any historical vendetta.

Instructively, if not ironically, Haman's plan "to destroy, massacre, and exterminate all the Jews, young and old, children and women" (Esther 3:13) smacks of Samuel's order to Saul: "kill alike men and women, infants and sucklings" (1 Samuel 15:3). In pointing out the moral absurdity of Haman's designs there is an oblique critique of Samuel's. Josephus indeed states that Haman's hatred of the Jews derives from this incident,[14] as if to say that the Jews are now getting as they gave. The Midrash, however, sees this as a preemptive comeuppance arguing that "God gave Amalek a taste of his own future work."[15] The Midrash is extending Samuel's moral justification for slaying Agag. Just as Samuel justified killing Agag because he killed others,

---

12 BT Megillah 12b; see *Torah Sheleimah, Megillat Ester* (Jerusalem 1994), 60, n. 45.
13 The absence of any mention of Amalek is why *Targum Rishon* must add "Agag son of Amalek," and *Targum Sheini* adds a genealogy all the way to Esau.
14 *Antiquities* 11.212
15 *Pesikta Rabbati* 13 (end), ed. Friedmann, 55b.

so the Midrash justifies the order for wiping out Amalek because Haman's ordered the wiping out of the Jews. Not able to anchor Amalek's extraordinary punishment in any prior behavior, the Midrash perforce extends its moral compass to Amalek's future behavior.

This moral self-criticism extends to comments made about Amalek's mother Timna. According to the Talmud, her efforts to convert were rejected by all three Patriarchs. Wanting to join this people at all cost, she marries Isaac's grandson, through Esau, Eliphaz. The fruit of this relationship is Amalek who goes on to aggrieve Israel for their having aggrieved his mother Timna.[16] The path to moral growth is paved by self-criticism.

The de-demonization or normalization of Amalek is extended in the Talmud, which claims that the descendants of Haman the Amalekite became students of Torah.[17] The application of Amalek to Haman is already part of the move to identify Amalek with a contemporary enemy who seeks to exterminate the Jews since 1 Chronicles 4:43 already noted that the last remnants of actual Amalekites at Mount Seir were done away with during the reign of Hezekiah (715–687 BCE) centuries earlier. This explains why the Greek versions of Esther 3:1 call Haman the Bougaean or the Macedonian and not the Agagite since the last remnants of Amalek were long gone. In a similar vein, the Talmud understood Hamdata in Esther 3:1, 10 as an expression of moral opprobrium.[18]

Maimonides also makes no special provision for Amalek when he argues that all wars must be preceded by overtures of peace indicating that were Amalek to sue for peace they would not be subject to destruction.[19] The ruling that all must be offered peace flows from the following Midrash:

> God commanded Moses to make war on Sihon, as it is said, "Engage him in battle" (Deuteronomy 2:24), but he did not do so. Instead he sent messengers ... to Sihon ... with an offer of peace (Deuteronomy 2:26). God said to him: "I commanded you to make war with him, but instead you began with peace:

---

16 BT Sanhedrin 99b, *Midrash Ha-Gadol*, Genesis, ed. Margulies, 609.
17 BT Sanhedrin 96b, BT *Gittin* 57b.
18 צורר בן צורר, see BT Yevamot 2:5, 4a with *Penei Moshe* ad loc.; and *Agadat Esther* 3.1, ed. Buber, 26, with Louis Ginzberg, *Legends of the Jews* (Philadelphia: The Jewish Publication Society, 1968), 6:462. See ibid. for the tracing of Haman's genealogy to Roman oppressors not biblical antecedents.
19 *Mishneh Torah*, Laws of Kings and Their Wars, 6:1, 4. This became the normative position; see Aviezer Ravitsky, "Prohibited Wars in Jewish Tradition," in ed. Terry Nardin, *The Ethics of War and Peace* (Princeton: Princeton University Press, 1998), 115–27.

by your life, I shall confirm your decision. Every war upon which Israel enters shall begin with an offer of peace."

As it is written, "When you approach a city to attack it, you shall offer it terms of peace" (Deuteronomy 20:10).[20]

Since Joshua is said to have extended such an offer to the Canaanites,[21] and Numbers 27:21 points out Joshua's need for inquiring of the priestly Urim and Tumim to assess the chances of victory, it is evident that also divinely-commanded wars are predicated on overtures of peace as well as on positive assessments of the outcome.[22] Moreover, the cross-generational struggle against Amalek, according to Maimonides, is dependent upon Amalek maintaining the practices of their biblical ancestors of rejecting the Noachide laws which stipulate the norms of human decency for civil society.[23]

The position that the negation of Amalek is ethical not ethnic is also reflected in the following talmudic anecdote about Amalek's ancestor Esau,[24] who was later identified with Rome:

> Antoninus (the Roman Emperor) asked Rabbi (Judah the Prince): Will I enter the world to come?" "Yes," said Rabbi. "But," said Antoninus, "is it not written, 'And there will be no remnant to the house of Esau'" (Obadiah 18). (Rabbi replied:) "The verse refers only to those who act as Esau acted." We have learned elsewhere likewise: "And there will be no remnant of the house of Esau," might have been taken to apply to all (of the house of Esau), therefore Scriptures says specifically—"of the house of Esau," to limit it only to those who act as Esau acted.[25]

---

20   *Deuteronomy Rabbah* 5:13 and *Midrash Tanḥuma*, Ṣav 5.
21   *Leviticus Rabbah* 17:6, ed. Margulies, 386 and parallels.
22   The position that all wars must be preceded by an overture of peace gained widespread acceptance; see Maimonides, *Laws of Kings and Their Wars* 6:1, 5; Nahmanides and Rabbenu Baḥaya to Deuteronomy 20:10; *SeMaG* positive mitzvah no. 118; *Sefer Ha-Ḥinukh* mitzvah no. 527 along with *Minḥat Ḥinukh, ad loc.*; and possibly Sa'adyah Gaon, see Yeruḥam Perla, *Sefer Ha-Mitsvot Le-Rabbenu Sa'adyah* (3 vols., Jerusalem, 1973) 3:251–52. Cf. Tosafot, BT Gittin 46a, s.v. *keivan*. See also Reuven Kimelman, "War," in *Frontiers of Jewish Thought*, ed. Steven Katz (Washington, DC: B'nai Brith Books, 1992), 309–32, 320–21.
23   See *Mishneh Torah*, Laws of Kings and Their Wars, 6:4, with Avraham Sachatchover, *Avnei Nezer*, to *Oraḥ Ḥayyim* 508.
24   See Genesis 36:12, 16; I Chronicles 1:36.
25   BT Avodah Zarah 10b. On Antoninus and his conversion, see Ephraim Urbach, *The Sages: Their Concepts and Beliefs* [Hebrew] (Jerusalem: Magnes Press, 1969), 492, n. 2*.

Based on such statements and the midrashic claim that Haman's descendants became students of Torah, Maimonides ruled: "We accept converts from *all* nations of the world."[26] Radak, ad loc., even entertains the possibility that the Amalekite who refers to himself as a *ger* in 2 Samuel 1:13 meant a convert to Judaism. It follows, that for him and Maimonides, wiping out Amalek implies wiping out Amalekite qualities. Maimonides also underscores: "It is also a positive commandment to remember always his (Amalek) evil deeds."[27] Indeed, he argues that Amalek was initially punished so harshly to deter future Amalek wannabees.[28]

It is clear in the history of interpretation that Amalek becomes more and more a metaphor for human evil thereby shifting the eradication of Amalek from the national-historic plane to the psycho-spiritual plane.[29] The moral relevance of Amalek was also circumscribed by restricting the waging of a war of destruction against Amalek to King Saul.[30] This essay shows how these positions best reflect the total biblical data.

The Seven Nations of Canaan

How does the commandment to destroy the seven nations of Canaan make sense in the light of the correlation between Israel's election and Israel's commitment to justice? The popular conception is that the Bible demands a holy war against them providing a precedent for genocide at most,[31] and for ethnic cleansing at least. The question is whether this is an accurate reading of the biblical evidence and the subsequent Jewish tradition. The response will divide the issue into seven parts.

---

26 *Mishneh Torah*, Laws of Prohibited Relations, 12:17.
27 *Mishneh Torah*, Laws of Kings and Their Wars, 5:5. The subsequent codes, *replace with* "Arh'ah" Turim and the *Shulkhan Arukh,* make no mention of Amalek's elimination.
28 Maimonides, *Guide for the Perplexed*, ed. Pines, 3:41 (Chicago: University of Chicago Press, 1963), 566.
29 See *Zohar* 3:281b with Alan Cooper, "Amalek in Sixteenth Century Jewish Commentary: On the Internalization of the Enemy," in *The Bible in the Light of Its Interpreters: Sarah Kamin Memorial Volume*, ed. Sara Japhet (Jerusalem: Magnes Press, 1994), 491–93. The approach gained currency in hasidic literature and other modern traditional commentaries; see Yaakov Meidan, *Al Derekh Ha-Avot* (Alon Shvut: Tevunot, 2001), 332–35; and Avi Sagi, "The Punishment of Amalek in Jewish Tradition: Coping with the Moral Problem," *The Harvard Theological Review*, 87 (1994): 323–46, esp. 331–36.
30 See *Minhat Hinuk* to *Sefer Ha-Hinukh*, end of mitzvah no. 604; and Avraham Karelitz, *Hazon Ish Al Ha-Rambam* (Bnei Brak, 1959), 842.
31 On the practice of genocide in antiquity, see above, n. 3.

1. What are the different biblical approaches to the native nations of Canaan?
2. According to the Bible, what happened to them?
3. What is the evidence that the Bible is sensitive to the moral issues involved?
4. How has the Jewish tradition removed the category of the seven nations from its ethical agenda?
5. What is the role of the doctrine of repentance?
6. What is the relevance of the "Sennacherib principle"?
7. How relevant is the category "holy war"?

Regarding the extermination of the seven nations of Canaan,[32] sometimes called Canaanites sometimes Amorites, the biblical record is also not of one cloth. The clarification of their status in the Bible requires a systematic treatment of all the data book by book.

Genesis (12:6, 15:16) is aware that the Canaanites were in the land when Abraham arrived and would remain for generations. From Genesis 38 and the end of The Book of Ruth we learn that from the progeny of Abraham's great grandson Judah and the Canaanite Tamar will issue King David. Also, Simeon's son is identified as "Saul the son of a Canaanite women" (Genesis 46:10, Exodus 6:15) without comment.

Exodus (23)'s position on the elimination of the Canaanites (v. 23) is a gradual dispossession by God, not by the Israelites:[33]

> (27) I will send forth My terror before you, and I will throw into panic all the people among whom you come, and I will make all your enemies turn tail before you. (28) I will send a plague ahead of you, and it shall drive out before you the Hivites, the Canaanites, and the Hittites.[34] (29) I will not drive them out before you in a single year, lest the land become desolate and the wild beasts multiply to your hurt. (30) I will drive them out before you little by little, until you have increased and possess the land.

Leviticus (18) refers to God casting out of the nations:

---

32 Sources differ on the number. For seven, see Deuteronomy 7:1, Joshua 3:10, 24:11. For six, see Exodus 3:8, 17; 23:23, 33:2, etc. For five, see Exodus 13:5, 1 Kings 9:20, 2 Chronicles 8:7. For three, see Exodus 23:28. The most comprehensive list is Genesis 15:19–20 with ten.
33 The *Septuagint* and *Pseudo-Jonathan* have, in Exodus 33:2, the angel expelling them.
34 This is apparently behind the historical recollection of Psalm 4:2.

> (24) Do not defile yourselves in any of those ways, for it is by such that the nations that I am casting out before you defiled themselves. (25) Thus, the land became defiled; and I called it to account for its iniquity, and the land spewed out its inhabitants.

Here there is a coordination between God and land. The land spews out its inhabitants for defiling it and God expels them.

Numbers (33) refers to the Israelites deporting the local inhabitants:

> (51) Speak to the Israelite people and say to them: "When you cross the Jordan into the land of Canaan, (52) you shall dispossess all the inhabitants of the land; you shall destroy all their figured objects; you shall destroy all their molten images, and you shall demolish all their cult places. (53) And you shall take possession of the land and settle in it, for I have assigned the land to you to possess."

The issue here is not ethnic but religio-cultural. The fear is that Israel will be ensnared, especially through intermarriage, by local mores and cultic practices.

Exodus 34 emphasizes the religious factor:

> (12b) Beware of making a covenant with the inhabitants of the land against which you are advancing, lest they be a snare in your midst. (13) Rather you must tear down their altars, smash their pillars, and cut down their sacred posts; (14) for you must not worship any other God, because the Lord, whose name is Impassioned, is an impassioned God. (15) You must not make a covenant with the inhabitants of the land, for they will lust after their gods and sacrifice to their gods and invite you, and you will eat of their sacrifices. (16) And when you take wives from among their daughters for your sons, their daughters will lust after their gods and will cause your sons to lust after their gods.[35]

Leviticus 18 emphasizes the moral factor:

> (26) But you must keep My laws and My rules, and you must not do any of those abhorrent things, neither the citizen nor the stranger who resides among you; (27) for all those abhorrent things were done by the people who were in the land before you, and the land became defiled. (28) So let not the land spew you out for defiling it as it spewed out the nation that came before

---

35 See Exodus 23:32, 33:2.

you. (29) All who do any of those abhorrent things—such persons shall be cut off from their people. (30) You shall keep My charge not to engage in any of the abhorrent practices that were carried on before you, and you shall not defile yourselves through them: I the Lord am your God.

Numbers 33 warns Israel against the assimilation of Canaanite norms lest they share the Canaanite fate of expulsion:

(55) But if you do not dispossess the inhabitants of the land, those whom you allow to remain shall be stings in your eyes and thorns in your sides, and they shall harass you in the land in which you live; (56) so that I will do to you what I planned to do to them.

The exception is Deuteronomy 7 with its alleged demand of destruction:

(1) When the Lord your God brings you to the land that you are about to enter and possess, and He dislodges many nations before you—the Hittites, Girgashites, Amorites, Canaanites, Perizzites, Hivites, and Jebusites, seven nations much larger than you—(2) and the Lord your God delivers them to you and you defeat them, you must doom them to destruction: grant them no terms and give them no quarter.

Even according to Deuteronomy, however, the fear is not of their DNA but moral assimilation, for it goes on to say: "Lest they lead you into doing all the abhorrent things that they have done for their gods and you stand guilty before the Lord your God" (20:18). For Deuteronomy (12:31; 18:9–12), the abhorrent things include child sacrifice.

Strangely, Deuteronomy continues with a provision against intermarriage:

(3) You shall not intermarry with them: do not give your daughters to their sons or take their daughters for your sons. (4) For they will turn your children away from Me to worship other gods, and the Lord's anger will blaze forth against you and He will promptly wipe you out. (5) Instead, this is what you shall do to them: you shall tear down their altars, smash their pillars, cut down their sacred posts, and consign their images to the fire.

Apprehension about intermarriage or coming to terms with an eradicated people is strange unless Deuteronomy is aware that its demand to doom them will not be (or was not) implemented. And, in fact, as we shall see the evidence from Judges 3 is that they did intermarry.

Alternatively, ḥerem does not entail the elimination of the Canaanites only their isolation, that is, they are to be quarantined. This understanding follows its Semitic cognates where it means to separate, to set aside.[36] The goal is to exclude any intercourse with them. Thus verse 5 only refers to the elimination of their objects of worship not their persons. This opens the possibility that "What we have is a retention of the ... traditional language of ḥerem, but a shift in the direction of its acquiring significance as a metaphor ... for religious fidelity."[37]

Even stranger is the description of the confrontation with Sihon king of the Amorites. Within the context of Deuteronomy, one would expect an outright attack when God says to Moses: "See, I give into your power Sihon the Amorite, king of Heshbon, and his land. Begin the occupation: engage him in battle" (2:24). Instead, what does Moses do:

> (26) Then I sent messengers from the wilderness of Kedemoth to King Sihon of Heshbon with an offer of peace, as follows, (27) "Let me pass through your country. I will keep strictly to the highway, turning off neither to the right nor to the left. (28) What food I eat you will supply for money, and what water I drink you will furnish for money; just let me pass through."

Sihon rejects the offer and attacks Israel. Sihon is destroyed only in the counterattack.

If there is no evidence for the expulsion of the Canaanites, whence the position of Deuteronomy 7:1–2? It has been speculated that Deuteronomy took "both the expulsion law of Exodus 23:20–33, directed against the inhabitants of Canaan, and the ḥerem (total destruction) law of Exodus 22:19 ("Whoever sacrifices to a God other than the Lord shall be proscribed), directed against the individual Israelite, and fused them into a new law that applies ḥerem to all idolaters, Israelites and non-Israelites alike."[38] In other

---

36   See Baruch Levine, *Numbers 1–20* (AB 4a) (New York: Doubleday, 1993), 446–47, with Leviticus 27:28, and Ezekiel 44:29.
37   R. W. L. Moberly, "Toward an Interpretation of the Shema," in Christopher Seitz and Kathryn Greene-McCreight ed., *Theological Exegesis: Essays in Honor of Brevard S. Childs* (Grand Rapids, MI: W.B. Eerdmans, 1999), 124–44, at 136. For an expansion of this metaphor thesis, see Nathan MacDonald, *Deuteronomy and the Meaning of "Monotheism"* (Tübingen: Mohr Siebeck, 2003), 108–23.
38   Jacob Milgrom, *Numbers, The JPS Torah Commentary* (Philadelphia: Jewish Publication Society, 1990), 429; see idem, *Leviticus* (AB 3) (New York: Doubleday, 1991–2001) 3:2419. Alternatively, see Ziony Zevit, "The Search for Violence in Israelite Culture and in the Bible," in David Bernat and Jonathen Klawans ed., *Religion and Violence: The Biblical Heritage* (Sheffield Phoenix Press, 2007), 16–37, at 25 and 31.

words, the *ḥerem* is not against Canaanites as Canaanites, but idolaters as idolaters. Thus Deuteronomy (13:13-19) imposes the very punishment on Israelite idolaters. The choice of the word *ḥerem* also promotes a sense of quid pro quod, for, according to Numbers 14:45, the Canaanites and the Amalekites pummeled Israel to Hormah a word which could simply designate a place or also serve as a toponym since *ad haḥormah* could be rendered "to utter destruction."[39] The point of the paronomasia is that the Canaanites and the Amalekites got as they gave.

In any case, except for some sources in Joshua (6:21 and chapters 10-11) the later biblical sources follow the earlier biblical books from Exodus to Numbers rather than Deuteronomy. Even the Joshua material raises some questions. According to Joshua 10:33, Joshua destroyed the people of Gezer. Yet Joshua 16:10 (like Judges 1:29) states: "They failed to dispossess the Canaanites who dwelt in Gezer; so, the Canaanites remained in the midst of Ephraim, as is still the case. But they had to perform forced labor." In actuality, they stayed there until the reign of Solomon only to be killed off by Pharaoh as noted in I Kings 9:16. Apparently, once the people were defanged by having its army destroyed, they were given quarter.[40] As a subject nation they apparently present no religious threat. Save for the peculiar case of Judges 3:5, the surrounding nations, not the Canaanites, are blamed for Israelite apostasy.[41] In fact, according to Joshua 8:29 and 10:27, the bodies of Canaanite kings hung by Joshua were buried by nightfall just as Deuteronomy 21:23 enjoins. Apparently, Human dignity is inalienable even for Canaanite kings.

The triumphal picture of Joshua is undermined by the facts on the ground. For example, Joshua 11:12 gives the impression that Joshua wiped out all the cities around Hazor and burned them to the ground. Yet the next verse says: "However, all those towns that are still standing on their mounds were not burned down by Israel; it was Hazor alone that Joshua burned down." In fact, only two other cities were burned—Jericho and Ai.

---

39 Levine, *Numbers 1-20*, 372; see *Targum Jonathan*, ad loc. Similarly, the last word of Numbers 21:3 can be rendered as Hormah or "Destruction"; see Milgrom, ibid., *Numbers*, 172, 456-48. According to Judges 1:17, Hormah was destroyed later; see Jeffrey Tigay, *Deuteronomy*, *The JPS Torah Commentary* (Philadelphia: The Jewish Publication Society, 1996), 348n121.
40 See Yehezkel Kaufmann, *Sefer Yehoshua* (Jerusalem: Kiryat Sefer, 1959), 146-47.
41 See Yehezkel Kaufmann, *The Religion of Israel: From Its Beginnings to the Babylonian Exile* (New York: Schocken, 1960), 248. Regarding Judges 3:5-6, see ibid., n4.

Similarly, Joshua 11:23 claims: "Thus Joshua conquered the whole country, just as the Lord had promised Moses," whereas 13:1 concedes "and very much of the land still remains to be taken possession of." Even where Israel spread out much of the native population could remain in their midst, as it says later in the same chapter: "the Israelites failed to dispossess the Geshurites and the Maacathites, and Geshur and Maacath remain among Israel to this day" (13:13). The sparing of the Canaanite population was common. Regarding southern Israel, Joshua 15:63 says: "But the Judites could not dispossess the Jebusites, the inhabitants of Jerusalem; so, the Judites dwell with the Jebusites in Jerusalem to this day." Regarding central Israel, Joshua 16:10 says: "However, they failed to dispossess the Canaanites who dwelt in Gezer; so, the Canaanites remained in the midst of Ephraim, as is still the case. But they had to perform forced labor." And regarding northern Israel, Joshua 17:12–13 says: "The Manassites could not dispossess [the inhabitants of] these towns, and the Canaanites stubbornly remained in this region. When the Israelites became stronger, they imposed tribute on the Canaanites; but they did not dispossess them."

Judges 1:27–36 follows suit. It begins:

> (27) Manasseh did not dispossess [the inhabitants of] Beth-shean and its dependencies, or [of] Taanach and its dependencies, or the inhabitants of Dor and its dependencies, or the inhabitants of Ibleam and its dependencies, or the inhabitants of Megiddo and its dependencies. The Canaanites persisted in dwelling in this region. (28) And when Israel gained the upper hand, they subjected the Canaanites to forced labor; but they did not dispossess them. (29) Nor did Ephraim dispossess the Canaanites who inhabited Gezer; so, the Canaanites dwelt in their midst at Gezer…

All these sources mention the failure to dispossess the Canaanites, despite the Israelites' power to do so. No mention is made of any extermination.[42] Joshua 24:13 does mention the expulsion of two kings but without resorting to the sword and bow, a point reiterated in Psalm 44:5. Most remarkable is the story in Judges 4. There it is told that God punished the Israelites by handing them over to Yabin the king of Canaan and Sisera his general. In the divinely commanded revolt against Yabin, God promised to deliver his people into the hands of the Israelites, not to wipe them out.

---

42   Judges 11:23, Psalm 44:3, 80:8b, 2 Chronicles 20:7, *Fourth Ezra* 1:21, and *The Testament of Moses* 12:8 mention only dispossession.

Joshua concedes in his farewell address the failure of his policy. The most he can hope is that "The Lord your God Himself will thrust them out on your account and drive them out to make way for you" (Joshua 23:5). In the meantime, they are exhorted to be resolute not "to intermingle with these nations that are left among you. Do not utter the names of their gods or swear by them" (23:7). He them mentions the apprehension of Deuteronomy of intermarriage: "For should you turn away and attach yourselves to the remnant of those nations—to those that are left among you—and intermarry with the you joining them and they joining you, know for certain that the Lord your God will not continue to drive these nations out before you; they shall become a snare and a trap for you" (23:12–13).

In fact, Judges 3 states that they did intermarry: "The Israelites settled among the Canaanites, Hittites, Amorites, Perizzites, Hivites, and Jebusites; they took their daughters to wife and gave their own daughters to their sons, and they worshiped their gods" (5–6). Intermarriage was likely a factor in the absence of biblical or extra biblical evidence for Israel's expulsion of the Canaanites.

The archaeological record confirms that Israel primarily settled in previously unoccupied territory in the central highlands rather than rebuilt towns on destroyed Canaanite cites. In Judges 2, they are threatened with the consequences of not dispossessing them:

> (1) An angel of the Lord came up from Gilgal to Bochim and said, "I brought you up from Egypt and I took you into the land which I had promised on oath to your fathers. And I said, 'I will never break My covenant with you. (2) And you, for your part, must make no covenant with the inhabitants of this land; you must tear down their altars.' But you have not obeyed Me—look what you have done! (3) Therefore, I have resolved not to drive them out before you; they shall become your oppressors, and their gods shall be a snare to you."

The Israelites not only did not drive out the inhabitants, they concluded treaties with them. Their expulsion by God was contingent upon Israel's refusal to conclude a treaty with them. Neither took place.

Even at the height of ancient Israelite power under the reign of Solomon there was no move to do away with them only to subject them to forced labor, as I Kings 9 (= 2 Chronicles 8:7–8) states:

> (20) All the people that were left of the Amorites, Hittites, Perizzites, Hivites, and Jebusites who were not of the Israelite stock—(21) those of their descendants who remained in the land and whom the Israelites were not able to annihilate—of these Solomon made a slave force, as is still the case.[43]

Nonetheless, Uriah the Hittite not only marries Bathsheba but also serves as a trusted officer in David's army.

Psalm 106 laments the total failure of the policy. According to it, everything that Joshua warned against, they did and more. Following Deuteronomy 12:31, it also provides the moral basis by documenting the abhorrent behavior of the Canaanites to their own children:

> (34) They did not destroy the nations as the Lord had commanded them, (35) but mingled with the nations and learned their ways. (36) They worshiped their idols, which became a snare for them. (37) Their own sons and daughters they sacrificed to demons. (38) They shed innocent blood, the blood of their sons and daughters, whom they sacrificed to the idols of Canaan; so, the land was polluted with bloodguilt. (39) Thus, they became defiled by their acts, debauched through their deeds.[44]

Verses 34–35 attest to the non-implementation of the policy of Deuteronomy 20:17–18.

Remarkably, the Rabbis explain the non-implementation of the policy against the Canaanites through their conversion, against which there was objection:

> R. Samuel bar Nahman began his discourse with the verse: "But if you will not drive out the inhabitants of the Land before you, then shall those that remain of them be as thorns in your eyes and as pricks in your sides" (Numbers 33:55). The Holy One reminded Israel: I said to you, "You shall utterly destroy them: the Hittite and the Amorite" (Deuteronomy 20:17). But you did not do so; for "Rahab the harlot, and her father's household, and

---

43 For the presence of Canaanites in King David's administration, see the chapter "King David's Scribe and High Officialdom of the United Monarchy of Israel," in Benjamin Mazar, *The Early Biblical Period: Historical Studies*, eds. Shmuel Ahituv and Baruch A. Levine (Jerusalem: Israel Exploration Society, 1986).

44 The prophetic harangue against Canaanite practices focused on their abhorrent behavior to their children; see Isaiah 57:5; Jeremiah 2:23; 3:24; 7:31-32; 19:5-6, 11; 32:35; Ezekiel 16:20-21; 20:25-26, 30-31; 23:36-39. According to Deuteronomy (12:31; 18:9-12) such practices include child sacrifice. *The Wisdom of Solomon* (12:5-6) extends this to slaughtering children and feasting on human flesh and blood.

all that she had, did Joshua save alive" (Joshua 6:25). Behold, Jeremiah will spring from the children's children of Rahab the harlot and will thrust such words into you as will be thorns in your eyes and pricks in your sides.[45]

Irony of ironies, the thorny and prickly issue is no longer the continuity of pagan practices but the pointed prophetic barbs from the progeny of converts.

The tendency to blunt the impact of the seven-nations policy of Deuteronomy is also furthered by two other comments in rabbinic literature. The first contends that Joshua sent three missives before embarking on the conquest of the Land of Israel. The first said: "whoever wants to leave—may leave"; the second: "whoever wants to make peace—make peace"; and the third: "whoever wants to make war—make war."[46] War was only conducted against those who opted for war.[47] That war was not waged against those who did not opt for war may be supported by the following verse in Joshua:

> When all the kings of the Amorites on the western side of the Jordan, and all the kings of the Canaanites near the Sea, heard how the Lord had dried up the waters of the Jordan for the sake of the Israelites until they crossed over, they lost heart, and no spirit was left in them because of the Israelites (5:1).

No war no killing. Similarly, Joshua 9 mentions that all six nations of Canaan mobilized for war against Israel as opposed to the Gibeonites who made peace with them. Even though the peace was made under false pretenses, Joshua in chapter 10 honored his "treaty to guarantee their lives" (9:15) by rescuing them from the attack of the five Amorite kings. The treaty here entails security arrangements in exchange for submission. Also, in the beginning of chapter 11 Joshua defeats those nations that had mobilized for war against him. None of these accounts attribute their destruction to their religious depravity, only to their initiation of attack on Israel.[48]

---

45 *Pesiqta de-Rav Kahana* 13.5, 1:228f.
46 *Leviticus Rabbah* 17:6; see *Deuteronomy Rabbah* 5:13-14; P. T. Sheviit 6:1, 36c; and Maimonides, "Laws of Kings and Their Wars," 6:5. According to the midrash, the Girgashites took up Joshua's offer and settled in Africa. Accordingly, there is no mention of their defeat in the conquest narratives of Joshua 6–12, albeit they are listed in Joshua 24:11 among the seven nations handed over to Joshua.
47 See *Sifrei Deuteronomy* 200, ed. Louis Finkelstein (Jewish Theological Seminary, 1969), 237, l. 10. This refers to the thirty-one kings of Canaan whose defeat is narrated in Joshua 12.
48 See Lawson Stone, "Ethical and Apologetic Tendencies in the Redaction of the Book of Joshua," *CBQ* 53 (1991), 25–36.

The other rabbinic comment rules that by transplanting and mingling the populations he conquered, the Assyrian king Sennacherib dissolved the national identity of the Canaanite nations in ancient times.[49] Accordingly, Maimonides ruled that all trace of them has vanished.[50] R. Abraham Kook, former chief rabbi, attained the same goal by limiting the commandment to expel the Canaanites to the generation of Joshua. He writes:

> If it were an absolute duty for every Jewish king to conquer all the seven nations, how would David have refrained from doing so? Therefore, in my humble opinion, the original duty rested only on Joshua and his generation. Afterwards, it was only a commandment to realize the inheritance of the land promised to the patriarchs.[51]

Moreover, non-Canaanites captured along with a majority of Canaanites were to be spared just as Canaanites caught with a majority of non-Canaanites were to be spared[52] reducing possibilities of any wholesale slaughter. In fact one commentator contends that the destruction of a city is predicated upon the unanimous opposition to submission to the Israelites for "we cannot impose a death penalty on them (women and children) because of the sin of their fathers and the guilt of their husbands."[53] Finally, the Maimonidean ruling that all war must be preceded by an overture of peace and that only the nations of Canaan that maintained their abhorrent ways are to be doomed reduced the possibility of any war of total destruction.[54] His position is rooted in the repeated classical rabbinic comment to the verse "Lest they lead you into doing all the abhorrent things that they have done for their gods and you stand guilty before the Lord your God" (20:18)—"This

---

49   See *M. Yadayim* 4:4, *T. Yadayim* 2:17, ed. Zuckermandel, 683, T. Qiddushin 5:4 BT Berakhot 28a, BT Yoma 54a, with *Oṣar Ha-Posqim, Even Ha-Ezer* 4.

50   *Mishneh Torah*, Laws of Kings and Their Wars, 5:4; Laws of Prohibited Relations, 12:25. See idem, *The Book of Commandments* no. 187: "They [Amalek(?) and the seven nations] were finished off and destroyed in the days of David. Those that survived were dispersed and assimilated into the nations so that no root of them remained."

51   Abraham Kook, *Tov Ro'i* (Jerusalem, 5760), 22.

52   See *Sifrei Deuteronomy* 200, 237, with n10; and Joseph Babad, *Minḥat Ḥinukh* to *Sefer Ha Ḥinukh*, mitzvah no. 527,

53   Yaakov Zvi Mecklenburg, *Ha-Ktav Ve-Ha-Kabbalah* (New York: Om Publishing Co., 1946), 52a, to Deuteronomy 20:16.

54   Laws of Kings and Their Wars, 6:1, 4; see *Leḥem Mishnah* ad loc.; Shlomoh Goren, *Meishiv Milḥamah*, 3 vols. (Jerusalem: Ha-Idrah Rabbah, 1986), 3:361–66; and Reuven Kimelman, "War," in *Frontiers of Jewish Thought*, ed. Steven Katz (Washington, D. C.: B'nai Brith Books, 1992), 309–32, 321.

teaches that if they repent they are not killed."⁵⁵ Similarly, *The Wisdom of Solomon* notes that the Israelites did not wipe out the Canaanites "at once, but judging them gradually You gave them space for repentance" (12:10). In any case, according to classical Midrash, the Canaanites were singled out not only because of their geography, but also because "they were the most idolatrous of all nations, the most immoral of all nations… immersed in idolatry, sexual debauchery, and murder."⁵⁶

The best biblical example of judging Canaanites by their behavior, not by their genes, is the case of Rahab of Jericho. Since she acknowledged the God of Israel as "the God of heaven and earth" (Joshua 2:12) and threw her lot in with Israel, she and her household were not only spared but were welcomed "into the midst of Israel" (Joshua 6:25). Rabbinic tradition extended this welcome to marrying Joshua and becoming the progenitor of priests and prophets.⁵⁷ Moreover, based on the fact that "The young men … went in and brought out Rahab … and her brethren … all her kindred also" (Joshua 6:23), it was understood that her immediate relatives, and also their relatives totaling many hundreds were also spared.⁵⁸ The other salutary example is the Canaanite Tamar who trumped Judah morally (see Genesis 38:26). Her reformation marks the Book of Ruth 4:12, which goes out of its way to link Ruth herself with the erstwhile Canaanite Tamar, as if to valorize her as the Tamar of our day. Indeed, Ruth 4:18 traces the lineage of her offspring to Peretz, Tamar's son, as opposed to Judah himself. The result is a genealogy that goes from the Canaanite Tamar to King David.

That behavior or life-style trumps genes explains the permissibility of marrying the captured woman in Deuteronomy 21:10. Having left her previous ways she no longer presents a temptation of apostasy. Rabbinic tradition following suit specifically included a Canaanite as long as she had shed her idolatrous ways.⁵⁹ In the same vein, rabbinic tradition held that

---

55 *Sifrei Deuteronomy* 202, p. 238, lines 14-15; *T. Sotah* 8:7, ed. Lieberman, p. 205, with idem, *Tosefta Kiphshutah* 8:702, lines 78-79, with n. 24; and BT Sotah 35b with Tosafot, s.v., *lerabot*.

56 See *Sifrei Deuteronomy* 60, p. 125, lines 11-12, with n. 12 and *Sifra*, ed. Weiss, 13, 7-8, p. 86a.

57 See *Sifrei Numbers* 78, ed. Horovitz, p. 74; *Sifrei Zutta*, ed. Horovitz, p. 263; *Midrash Ruth Rabbah* 2:1; *Pesikta De-Rav Kahana* 13. 5, 12, 1:228, 237; and *Yalqut Shimoni*, Joshua 9, *Nevi'im Rishonim*, ed. Heyman-Shiloni (Jerusalem: Mossad Harav Kook, 1999), 16f., n. 4f., along with Michael Fishbane, *The JPS Bible Commentary Haftarot* (Philadelphia: The Jewish Publication Society, 2002), 232, n. 11; p. 482, n. 11.

58 See *Ruth Rabbah* 2:1 and parallels.

59 *Sifrei Deuteronomy* 213, p. 246, line 9-10 (R. Akiva); B. *Yevamot* 48b.

the descendants of the Canaanite general Sisera became Torah teachers in Jerusalem,[60] and that Abraham's servant Eliezer was removed from the category of Canaanite due to his loyalty to Abraham,[61] indeed, deemed his peer in piety, worthy of entering Paradise alive.[62] In the light of the biblical doctrine of repentance ("For it is not My desire that anyone shall die—declares the Lord God. Repent, therefore, and live!"—Ezekiel 18:32), it is hard to contemplate an alternative. Such a doctrine does not sit well with the possibility of irredeemable evil.[63] A lesson that Jonah had a hard time learning. According to The Book of Jonah, even Nineveh, the capital of the empire that brought ruin on the lost tribes of Israel and annihilated everything in its path (see Isaiah 37:11), could avert destruction by engaging in repentance. Finally, the evidence that the issue was all along ethical and not ethnic lies in the fact that Abraham was prevented from taking possession of the land in his day because of the moral consideration that "the iniquity of the Amorites was not yet complete" (Genesis 15:16), whereas his descendants were allowed to take possession because of the "wickedness of these nations" (Deuteronomy 9:4–5).

The midrashic tradition followed the biblical categorization of groups through a combination of ethics and ethnicity. With regard to repentance, the Midrash pointed out that the Torah was given in the third month whose Zodiac symbol is twins to make the point that were Jacob's twin Esau to repent and convert and study Torah God would accept him.[64] In fact, God looks forward "to the nations of the world repenting so that He might bring

---

60   BT Gittin 57b, BT Sanhedrin 96b, *Midrash Psalms* 1:18. Sennacherib got a similar comeuppance (ibid.), while the Moabite king Balak became the progenitor of Ruth; see BT Sotah 47a with parallels.

61   See *Genesis Rabbah* 60:7, p. 647; and *Leviticus Rabbah* 17:5, p. 383.

62   *Beit Ha-Midrash*, ed. Jellinek, 6:79; *Derekh Erets Zutta* 1:18, ed. Sperber, p. 20. The position became categorical: "As long as they [Israel] does God's will, God spots a righteous person among the nations of the world such as Jethro, Rahab, and Ruth and such as Antoninus and brings him and joins him with Israel" (*Ecclesiastes Rabbah* 5:11, ed. Hirshman, p. 316, lines 302-304, and parallels).

63   Accordingly, the *Aleinu* prayer looks forward to the day when "all the wicked of the earth will turn to You and all the inhabitants of the world will recognize and know that to You every knee will bend and every tongue vow" which is why the Rosh Hashanah liturgy also prays: "evil [not evildoers] will be silenced and all wickedness [not the wicked] will dissipate like smoke"; see Reuven Kimelman, *The Rhetoric of the Liturgy: A literary and Historical Commentary to the Jewish Prayer Book*, Chapter 7, "The Aleinu," section 8 (forthcoming).

64   *Pesikta De-Rav Kahana* 12.20, 1:218.

them nigh beneath His wings."[65] Kindness is also a criterion for inclusion; its absence a criterion for exclusion. The Canaanite Rahab is allowed in for her act of her kindness.[66] Even Egyptians, according to Deuteronomy 23:8b–9, are accepted after three generations apparently for having initially extended kindness to Israel.[67] The case of the Moabite Ruth is exemplary. According to Deuteronomy 23:4–5, Moabites are not allowed into the Congregation of the Lord because of their lack of human decency and hospitality to Israel after the Exodus. In contrast, Ruth is accepted because of her decency and kindness to her Jewish mother-in-law.[68] Her example led to the wholesale exemption of women from the Deuteronomic prohibition.[69] She, as noted, is a latter-day Tamar. Both Tamar and Ruth are erstwhile barren foreign widows of Israelite men who insinuate themselves into the messianic line through linking up with prominent progenitors of David through a combination of feminine wiles and moral rectitude.

In the same vein, Eliezer's criterion, according to Genesis 24:14, for incorporating a woman into Abraham's family was precisely kindness and hospitality to strangers. In fact, the Midrash lists ten biblical women of Egyptian, Midianite, Canaanite, Moabite, and Kenite origin whose kindness accounts for their acceptance as converts.[70] As noted, kindness qualifies one for inclusion as its absence qualifies one for exclusion, as the Talmud says, "Anyone who has mercy on people, is presumed to be of our father Abraham's seed; and anyone who does not have mercy on people, is presumed not to be of our father Abraham's seed."[71] Maimonides follows suit by defining charitableness as "the sign of the righteous person, the seed of Abraham our Father. Indeed, if someone is cruel and does not show mercy, there are grounds to suspect his or her lineage."[72] Obviously, Abrahamic lineage has also an ethical DNA marker.

In sum, there are basically four strategies for removing the seven-nations ruling from the post-biblical ethical agenda and vitiating it as a precedent for contemporary practice:

---

65 *Song Rabbah* 5.16.5, and *Numbers Rabbah* 1.10 (middle).
66 See Joshua 2:2 with *Pesikta De-Rav Kahana* 13.4, 1:227.
67 See Rashi ad loc., and Philo, *On the Virtues* (Harvard University Press, 1939), 106–8.
68 See Ruth 2:11–12, 3:10. R. Zeira (*Ruth Rabbah* 2:14) attributes the composition of The Book of Ruth to its acts of kindness.
69 BT Yevamot 77a; see M. Yevamot 9:3; *Sifrei Deuteronomy* 249, p. 277, and parallels.
70 See *Yalqut Shimoni*, Joshua 9, *Nevi'im Rishonim*, ed. Heyman-Shiloni (Jerusalem: Mossad Harav Kook, 1999), 17, line 15.
71 BT Besah 32b.
72 *Mishneh Torah*, Gifts to the Needy, 10:1–2.

1. The recognition that the mandate for their extermination was a minority position in the Bible, significantly limited to Deuteronomy 7:1–2, and was only thought to be partially implemented in parts of the Book of Joshua.
2. The realization that since the threat was posed by Canaanite religion and ethics a change in them brings about a change in their status.
3. The limitation of the jurisdiction of the ruling to the conditions of ancient Canaan at the time of Joshua.
4. The application of the "Sennacherib principle" that holds that under the Assyrian empire conquered peoples lost their national identity.

These four strategies of the biblical and post-biblical exegetical tradition mitigate, if not undermine, the ruling regarding the destruction of the Canaanites. In both cases, ethics end up trumping genealogy. This understanding helps account for the absence of any drive to exterminate or dispossess the seven nations even when Israel was at the height of its power under the reigns of David and Solomon.

According to John Yoder's *When War Is Unjust*, holy wars differ from just wars in the following five respects:

1. holy wars are validated by a transcendent cause;
2. the cause is known by revelation;
3. the adversary has no rights;
4. the criterion of last resort need not apply;
5. it need not be "winnable."[73]

This study illustrates how the antidotes to 3–5 were woven into the ethical fabric of the biblical wars of destruction. In most cases, the resort to war even against the Canaanites was only pursuant to overtures of peace or in counterattack, and even the chances of success against Midian were weighed by the Urim and Tumim. It is therefore not surprising that the expression "holy war" is absent not only from the Bible but also from the subsequent Jewish ethical and military lexicon.[74]

---

73 John Howard Yoder, *When War Is Unjust: Being Honest in Just-War Thinking* (Minneapolis: Ausburg Pub. House, 1984), 26f.
74 This point is conceded by Reuven Firestone in the Preface to his book titled *Holy War in Judaism* (New York: Oxford University Press, 2012). The biblical "wars of God" (Numbers 21:14; 1 Samuel 17:47, 18:17, 25:28) are simply battles fought by the

The Challenge of Moral Survival

Regarding Israel's relation to election and to the Canaanite nations, there is a privileging of the ethical over the ethnic. How then ought the demand for justice and righteousness play into our contemporary self-understanding? The problem is increasingly complex at a time when the nations of the world have adopted Amos's double standard of judging modern Israel by a standard not applied to any other nation. A harsher standard by those who love you is not comparable to a harsher standard by those who hate you. Condemnations of hate do not qualify as rebukes of love. Indeed, to tie this to the doctrine of election, it would be worth assessing whether the hatred of Israel is correlated with the illusion of being chosen or with the support of another candidate for election. The goal of destroying Israel can become part of a stratagem for laying a claim to the mantle of election by eliminating the most widely-acknowledged alternative.[75]

Dealing with the tension between the ethnic and the moral in the doctrine of election requires a system of checks and balances. The tension is already in the term "ethical nationhood." It requires enough latitude to allow for nationhood without the excessive latitude that submerges the ethical. The challenge lies in maintaining the proper balance between the requirements of morality and the requirements of survival. Obviously, to be a light unto the nations requires first to be a nation. Nonetheless, as important as it is to sustain nationhood, so is it important to keep the light on.

---

people of God. Although Maimonides ("Laws of Kings and Their Wars," 4:10) does take them as wars fought for God in the sense that they are fought to promote God's unity or to sanctify the Name, he does not categorize them as commanded wars; see Gerald Blidstein, "Holy War in Maimonidean Law," in *Perspectives on Maimonides: Philosophical and Historical Issues*, ed. Joel Kraemer (The Littman Library of Jewish Civilization, 1991), 209–20, esp. 220, n. 33. Nonetheless, there is no case in the Bible of a war for spreading the Israelite religion to foreigners or compelling then to accept it nor is there an example of wars of conquest being dubbed holy even when booty is dedicated to God. For the insinuation of "holy war" into Protestant, primarily German, biblical scholarship based on the model of the Islamic *Jihad*, see Ben Ollenburger's Introduction to Gerhard von Rad, *Holy War in Ancient Israel* (Grand Rapids, MI: William B. Eerdman's Publishing Company, 1991), 1–33; and John Wood, *Perspectives on War in the Bible* (Macon, GA: Mercer University Press, 1998), 16 with note.

75   This helps explain the common denominator of the historical Christian, Muslim, Nazi, and Communist programs for the elimination of either Jewry, Judaism, or Israel.

Menachem Kallus

From Enmity to Unity—Recovering the Ba'al Shem Tov's Teachings on Non-Jews

Introduction

The hasidic movement represents some of the most dedicated individuals, committed to realizing the highest ideals of Torah and Jewish spirituality. In sociological terms, the movement is associated with an inward-facing and withdrawn attitude to many values of the broader world, in the interest of cultivating its spiritual ideals. Even in cases where specific streams embrace aspects of modernity, especially technology, there are still strong boundaries that characterize its sociological and ideological positioning. One of the strongest boundaries, though not one unique to it, is the boundary between Jews and non-Jews. Many, both inside and outside the hasidic movement, consider that authentic kabbalistic teaching assumes an ontological divide between Jews and non-Jews and that the attitudes ensuing from such a viewpoint are negative. One would not naturally turn to hasidic sources as resources for an irenic or ecumenical approach to people outside of Judaism.

While the negative perspective can certainly be supported by many hasidic texts, it is not the only one within the hasidic tradition. Significantly, its founder, Rabbi Yisrael Ba'al Shem Tov, offers several fundamental teachings that amount to a view of gentiles, significantly different from the popular perception of hasidic views. The present essay is an attempt to recover several strands of thought that date to the earlier generations of Hasidism, and that have their source in the teachings of the Ba'al Shem Tov and several of his close disciples. These texts add up to a composite picture that helps offset many other views found within the hasidic movement.

Creation and Humanity

Hasidic authors were heirs to two competing views of non-Jews, in relation to Israel. Many strands of classical Kabbalah put forth dualist-essentialist constructions of Jew/Gentile ontology.[1] Contrast that with the valuation of the gentiles in a positive light in the earliest classical kabbalistic text, the Sefer haBahir, and amongst some early kabbalists influenced by it, where such dualist-essentialist presuppositions are lacking.[2] The place of Israel and non-Jews in the scheme of creation is very different according to each of these perspectives. Thus, one notes with interest the continuation of the Bahir's influence in the earliest hasidic teachings. The influence of the Sefer haBahir's valuation of the gentiles in a positive light, without dualist-essentialist presuppositions, may be found in the work of the chief disciple and amanuensis of the BeShT, R Yaakov Yosef of Polnoye [d. 1783?]. In his introduction to the Toldot Yaakov Yosef,[3] the first hasidic book published, we read:

> ... And the purpose of the creation of humanity is so that matter be transformed into form and thereby there will be one [integrated] unity and not that

---

1 This is the most prevalent trend in Kabbalah. Its origins are traced to the gnostic-dualist school of the thirteenth-century "Cohen Brothers" [contrasting 'Holy Adam,' with *Adam belial* (pointless man)], see G. Scholem, *Madai haYahadut* no. 2 ["*The Kabbalot of R Yaakov and R Yitzhak, Sons of R Yaakov haCohen*": Towards a History of Kabbalah Before the Revelation of the Zohar—(Hebrew), Jerusalem 1928] and is reflected in many Zoharic texts—particularly in the Tiqunei haZohar, and is found in essentialist orientations in Lurianic Kabbalah, and see note 6 for some sources. but see below, note 20 as an example of a "non-essentialist orientation" in Lurianic Kabbalah.
2 In the Bahiric model, the Princes of the Nations are described as [in the Abrams ed., no. 63-65; 94-95 in other editions]: "Holy forms [and Divine Names] engraved upon the Divine Throne of Glory." This ideation has a long and varied history in Heichalot and in Midrashic literature, wherein different degrees of unification are expressed. [I compiled an annotated collection of these and other ecumenical Rabbinic sources, out of which the present article was extracted and re-crafted].
3 [Henceforth, TYY] Koretz 1780, 4a. It was the decisive influence of Nahmanides on the thought of both, RYY and the BeShT [as will be evident in numerous instances in the texts of my forthcoming collection *Essential 'Ba'al Shem Tov on the Torah'*] that enabled this new approach. On the centrality of the Sefer haBahir in the mysticism of Nahmanides, see E.R. Wolfson, "By Way of Truth," *JSOR* 1989.

there remain separate entities. And just as this is the case with regard to the individual, so it is with the totality of the Israelite nation. For the masses, the peoples of the land, because their occupation is in the realm of materiality, they as a whole represent the material realm. Whereas the righteous ones who are occupied with Torah and the service of the Divine, are the "form".[4] And what is of most importance is that one transform "matter" to "form," as is written [Malachi 2:7]: "The lips of the priest shall heed knowledge" ... [ibid. 2:6] "and the masses did he return from transgression." And just as this is so in the particular nation of Israel, so it is with regard to the world as a whole. For there are "Seventy nations grasping onto the branches of the Holy Tree and Israel grasps the root of the Tree."[5] And Israel must draw effluence to all the 70 nations. This is the purpose of the 70 bulls sacrificed on the Sukkot Festival, whereby the 70 Princes receive their effluence mediated by Israel, and thereby they are in control, so as to be within the domain of holiness. Thus, the material realm is controlled by the spiritual realm and all faces are luminous. Then the Israelite Nation cleaves to His Great Name—the Tree of Life, and through this, effluence is drawn to all. Then Israel is on the level that transcends Nature, as Nahmanides wrote in his commentary on the Torah Portion va'eRa regarding [Exodus 6:3] "and by My Name Tetragrammaton I did not reveal Myself." For the Tetragrammaton is beyond nature. Thereby, Israel and the Nations are constituted by the appellation of Oneness, the "Complete Adam."

Given that the cosmic ideal here, is the integral One "complete" or "whole" [Cosmic] Man, we may presume that the universal integration would also include the transcendent element. This ideal Macrocosmic view of humanity is also borne out in the hasidic view of the religious obligations of all Jews, even during the present era of "Exile," as we find in the two following quotes from direct disciples of the BeShT, in his name, on the issue of mutual responsibility:

> "And the Lord God commanded humanity ..." (Gen. 2:16)—The Talmud (BT Sanhedrin, 56a) derives the Seven Noahide Laws (from this verse). And I heard in the name of R. Israel Baal Shem Tov, that regarding these

---

4   And see TYY P. VayaShev, where 'form' is equated with will and intelligence.
5   See from the Sefer haBahir, Abrams ed., no. 67-68; other eds., 98-100. Note that here, we find Israel and the Nations as "One Tree"—not two—holy Adam [as in Lurianic Etz Hayim Gate 42 chapter 3, or Emeq haMelech Gate 11 chapter 10] and pointless Adam, following here, the Nahmanidean model, informed by the Bahir.

Seven Commandments to the Noahides, Israel bears the responsibility of a guarantor (areivut), on the part of the Nations of the world.[6]

> ... For our sages have said [BT Shavu'ot 39a], "All of Israel are mutually responsible [areivim]"—this is because [as the BeShT taught] they are intermixed [me'uravim], and have one common root.[7]

Moreover, regarding the universality of Macrocosm-Microcosm formula we note in the following text that it includes Israel's enemies, and not only neutral non-Jews.

> The human being is a microcosm containing Moshe and Aharon as well as the Egyptians. The wholly developed person is one who has the clear knowledgeable consciousness to be able to connect with all of the levels manifesting in one's generation, raising them and uniting them with their roots, while also uniting oneself with them. Such a one is called "Moshe" who contains in his person the entire generation. And she or he is called Daat—Consciousness, and her generation is called "the conscious generation." By contrast, the evil person is called "immature"—one who does not possess awareness.[8]

Teachings of other disciples of the BeShT also express a recognition of a consciousness of universal solidarity as an essential component of intent in pursuing the fulfillment of the Messianic Age.

> Also, we have a teaching from R. Gedalyah of Lynitz who said this in the name of his teacher, the Mokhiach [Preacher] of Polnoya[9], that the Messiah will advocate on behalf of all of Israel—defending even the wicked, proclaiming that "they were right." And due to the finding of merit on their behalf, they will repent—whereby they will be redeemed and liberated. For [BT Yoma 86b] "we are redeemed by the merit of] our Return." And he used to say that

---

6 Sefer BeShT al haTorah (henceforth BeShT Torah) [Lodz, 1938, Jerusalem 1948; reprinted numerous times] Parshat Bereshit, no. 120, taken from Sefer R. Yeivi (in Brooklyn ed., 1994), 58a; Parshat vaYeshev by R Yaakov Yoseph ben Yehudah [R Yeiv"I 1731-1791]. Such a teaching ought to have greater impact on hasidic rabbinic oversight of weapons sales in their respective countries
7 Divrei Moshe [Bnei Braq, 2002] P. Shemini, by R Moshe of Dolena [1740?-1830?], from BeShT Torah Parshat ki Tissa no. 9.
8 BeShT Torah Parshat Shemot, no. 19; TYY 12b.
9 Rabbi Yehudah Leib of Polnoya, an elder student of the BeShT, who introduced R. Yaakov Yoseph to him; both referred to as "the Mokhiach."

"lesser Tzaddiqim love the 'mildly wicked' whereas great Tzaddiqim love even the very wicked, but the Messiah will be able to find merit in even the completely wicked. And anyone who attempts to come to the defense of all [or—everyone] of creation manifests the Messianic element."[10]

Solidarity and Compassion Through Divine Unity

A related principle that dates to the earlier generations of Hasidism, especially to the disciples of the Maggid of Mezritch (d. 1772), affirms solidarity with non-Jews by making reference to Divine unity. We find the principle of Universal international solidarity based on universal monotheism in one of the teachings of R Levi Yitzhak of Berditchev (1740–1809), a senior disciple of the Maggid of Mezritch, the acknowledged 'successor of the BeShT. In his Qedushat Levi[11] we read:

> [BT Shabbat 31a— ... you may convert me] on the condition that you teach me the entire Torah while I stand on one foot ...' The convert said: 'I want to convert [to Judaism] so that I'd understand that even the civil laws carry this 'taste' and purpose of Divine unity—then I'll convert and serve the One, Unique and Unified, for when I'll realize this, I'll know that secular civil laws do not realize this, and they have no [compelling] reason—for even as for the laws of the land, one must know that one Divine Power create us all. So Hillel told him: 'don't subject your companion to what is hateful to you'—i.e. all civil law is founded on this principle of 'don't subject your companion to what is hateful to you.' And the reason for this is because 'one God created us all',[12] and we were all hewn from the same 'quarry.' Thus, every Israelite feels and senses the struggles of one's companion and feels joy in the joy of one's companion. So we find that the reason for the Torah's civil commandments is based on the unity of the blessed Creator, whereas also regarding the secular civil law of the land one must serve the One God and understand that He is One Unique and Unified. For this reason the

---

10   R. Gedalyah of Lynitz was disciple of the BeShT, of Rabbi Yehudah Leib, of R. Yaakov Yosef, and of the Maggid of Mezritch. This text was originally published in Teshu'ot Chen (Berdichev, 1816; Lvov, 1862; Brooklyn, reprint) in the miscellany at the end of the book, beginning: "biTrey-'Asar. Teachings such as these can serve as resources for Jewish involvement in social justice movements.
11   Slavita, 1798; in the Jerusalem 1993 ed. it's on p. 196–97.
12   Paraphrase of a Shabbat eve hymn written by the twelfth-century Spanish-Jewish poet, R Avraham ibn Ezra "Tzamah Nafshi."

nations of the world need to turn to the Nation of God and thereby will be fulfilled the verse that states [Tzafanya 3:9]: "Then shall I transform unto [the] nations a clear language, to serve [the Divine] with one consent" and then [Isa. 2:3]: "many nations shall go and declare: 'let us all go and proceed in the Light of God and traverse His paths …" Amen Sela! This is the meaning of [Lev. 19:18]: "and you shall love your neighbor as yourself, I am God." In other words, My commanding you to 'love your neighbor as yourself,' is because 'I am God,' and one God created us all. Therefore we are obligated to rejoice in the happiness of one's companion, and so too, to the contrary, Heaven forfend. And this is the meaning of the verse [Lev. 18:4]: "fulfill My laws and keep my statutes, so as to proceed according to them, I am your God" and Rashi explained there, that the civil interpersonal laws ought to be fulfilled, because "I am your God," and one God created us all.

The basis for universal love and its conditions of mutual empathy, is in the understanding that the same God created us all.[13]

From another senior disciple of the Maggid, and colleague of R Levi Yitzhak, R Elimelech of Lizhensk (1717–1787), we read:[14]

[Num. 21:14] 'Et Vahev Sufah' [—as interpreted in the Talmud, BT Qedushin 30b to mean: "mutual love comes at the end of argument"—when conducted for the sake of Heaven]—For in the Future, when the Righteous Messiah arrives, quickly in our time, and all the Nations will flow towards him, for the nations shall have great love for him and will offer him many gifts, as is written [Psalm 76:12]: "they shall offer tribute to the Teacher …" and so too, many verses.[15] Now the Righteous One with his righteousness brings about that also during this bitter exile we may find favor in the eyes of the nations so that they come to love us. This is the meaning of the aforementioned verse—referring to when the nations will love us.

From another of the disciples of the Maggid of Mezritch, R Yaakov Yitzhak, known as the Seer of Lublin (1745–1815), and successor to the Noam Elimelech], we read:

---

13 There is no doubt that there are many vindictive pronouncements about gentiles in the Qedushat Levi. Or Rose's contribution in the present volume struggles with these sources. The present citation is one possible resource for balancing out the views of R. Levi Yitzhak from within his own body of teachings.
14 Noam Elimelech, P. Hukat (Lemberg, 1787), 82d
15 See this optimistic attitude in Breslov, in R Nachman's secret sermon on the Messianic process, "Megillat Setarim"—recently published by Tzvi Mark (Ramat Gan, 2006).

The tribulation of all people should be hard for you to bear [and the Prophets were also perturbed by the suffering of the Nations]—this applies even to those who hate and speak ill of you. Be silent [about it] as is written [Psalm 37:7]: "be silent unto God" so that there be no desecration of the Divine Name, as is written. Rather, be not glad on account of their suffering.[16]

In a similar vein, the Maggid of Kozhnitz (1736–1814), another disciple of the Maggid of Mezritch and a colleague of the Seer of Lublin used to pray:

If You do not yet wish to redeem Israel, then at least redeem the goyim.[17]

These magnanimous attitudes are reflected in the writings of one of the chief disciples of the Seer of Lublin, the great Kabbalist R Tzvi of Zydachov (1753–1831). Although R Hayim ben Attar (d. 1743, Jerusalem), the early eighteenth-century Moroccan kabbalistic sage was held in especially high esteem among the early hasidim, R Tzvi saw it fit to criticize him for his position concerning the [insignificance of the] suffering of gentiles. In his commentary on the Zohar we find the following:[18]

... And I am puzzled by the [statement of R Hayim ben Attar, author of the Or haHayim]—how did he not penetrate this? And—apologizing in advance for belittling his honor—I register a complaint against his assertion that the tribulations of the nations are not genuine tribulations, and therefore Levi had [sexual relations during the famine-years of Egypt]—as some commentators have stated. And I am baffled by this assertion—the Zohar itself refers to those times of [the Egyptian] famine as being "days of tribulation." For were there only wicked idolators in the world? There were wild and domestic animals, and insects ... and those privy to the secrets of the Divine ought to know of God's great compassion—even on plants and fruit—how can we not have pity on all the holy sparks—[potential] souls incarnating in them so as to attain further purification. Scripture openly declares [Gen. 8:1] "And God remembered Noah and all the animals ..."—i.e. they arose in His Memory so as to have compassion on them. How many prayers were we enjoined to pray on behalf of all creatures, so that no ill befall them. For it is only with

---

16   HanHagot haTzaddikim, Satmar 1937, in the section on the "Seer of Lublin."
17   Martin Buber, "Two Foci of the Jewish Soul (1932)" in: *The Martin Buber Reader: Essential Writings*, ed. Asher D. Bierman (New York: Palgrave Macmillan, 2002), 111. I am grateful to my friend Rabbi Bezalel Naor for providing this reference.
18   My thanks to Dr. Avi Segal, who brought that source to my attention, while he was a student of mine in 2005.

regard to those wicked who are clearly not deserving of being saved—but as for all creatures in the world, all of them came to be for His Sake and we must pray on behalf of them all for compassion so that [after Psalm 145:9] "God be good to all and His compassion be upon all His enactments," so that bad days not be in-force in this world—rather, may the grace of God flow from world to world, forever and ever, Amen.

Facing the Enemy[19]

A third set of teachings from the BeShT and his disciples can be appreciated in light of the two thematic strands cited above. It relates to positive approaches to the enemy and to praying for the enemy. Of course, not all references to the enemy need be understood only in relation to non-Jews. However, the texts below can be read in this way, and one text in particular makes the connection between the attitude to the enemy and the attitude to non-Jews explicit. If so, this means that the theoretical and metaphysical foundations encountered above can also be considered as the source for a moral and pietistic approach that breaks down the barriers between Jews and non-Jews, even while recognizing the enemy as the non-Jew. Even so, hasidic metaphysics suggests ways other than negativity and hatred towards that enemy, based on its broader vision of unity. This was stated explicitly by the great hasidic kabbalist, R Isaac of Komarno.[20] Let us consider the witness of the following texts containing teachings of the BeShT:

---

19 Many of the following teachings are taken from my [annotated bi-lingual] collection of early hasidic teachings on contemplative prayer: "Pillar of Prayer" Louisville, KY: Fons Vitae Press, 2011).

20 Upon completion of this piece I was informed by an early reader, Dr. Tzvi Leshem, curator of th Scholem Library section of the National Library of Israel, that a book featuring many of the teachings presented here [in a hasidic-Lurianic context] was published in 2009: *You Are What You Hate: A Spiritually Productive Approach to Enemies*, ed. Sarah Yehudit Schneider (Jerusalem: Still Small Voice Press, 2009). On p. 179 and 182, Schneider quotes the great hasidic kabbalist R Isaac of Komarno, who states that these teachings of the BeShT apply to non-Jewish enemies as well. He based his assessment on an apocryphal story about the late twelfth-century Ashkenazi sage, R Yehudah the Pious. Here however, we argue that based on the previously presented hasidic teachings featuring universalist assessments of the common humanity of Jews and Gentiles, that the sources presented below ought to apply to Gentiles as well.

How Thoughts Create Enemies or Unconscious Tendencies

I heard from my teacher [the BeShT] that the consciousness of an oppressive adversary is created as a result of one's cultivating an ulterior motive, which constitutes a "complete"²¹ structure.²²

How Thoughts Create the Thoughts of Enemies
I heard in the name of the BeShT, who said that when the Talmud states [BT Sotah 49b] that "one's enemies are the people of his household," it refers to the sins that one has committed that created obscuring shells that are enclothed in the consciousness of people, in accordance with the principle "merit is delivered by the meritorious [etc.],"²³ and they dissent²⁴ and do battle with the person.²⁵

The Transformation of One's Enemies
I heard from my Master and grandfather [the BeShT] regarding the verse [Prov. 16:7] "when a man's ways are pleasing to God, He makes even one's enemies to be at peace with him." The BeShT pointed to the phrase "one's enemies," and not simply "enemies," and said there are two types of enemies, those who hate the person as such, and those who hate someone due to his or her shortcomings, so that when one mends one's ways and purifies the holy sparks that are scattered due to one's sins, then the obscuring shells are nullified automatically. This is the meaning of "When a man's ways are pleasing to God ... " i.e., when one mends one's ways and repents, then " ... He makes even one's enemies to be at peace with him"—those due to one's scattered Holy sparks; and then peace can be made.²⁶

Praying for One's Enemies
I heard in the name of my teacher [the BeShT] that one needs to pray for one's enemies, for they are part of the unrectified incarnate spirit of the

---

21 Being coherent thought, it embodies the Divine immanent ontological structure (containing the elements of "event," feeling-emotion, conceptual-mind, and [Divine] presence).
22 BeShT on Prayer P. [henceforth, BP] in BeShT Torah Parshat Noah, no. 62; ZP 18a.
23 And so too, the opposite, that retribution is delivered by the wicked.
24 Because they resent being cast in the role of carrying someone else's deficiency.
25 Meqor Mayim Hayim on BP P. Noah, no. 38; Sefer Teshu'ot Chen Parashat Ki Tetze'; and see below, following no. 156.
26 Meqor Mayim Hayim ibid., no. 38; DME = Degel Mahaneh Efraim by R Moshe Hayim Efrayim of Sudlikov (1742–1800), the oldest grandson of the Ba'al Shem Tov, Parashat Pekudey.

[aspect of the person which is the] Tzaddiq. Through prayer [the Qəlippot and judgments surrounding the soul of the enemy become] sweetened in their roots, and [the aspects of] one's own spirit [that are connected with one's enemy, being "imprisoned" there] are returned. And [the negativity that] remains there disintegrates of its own.[27]

Praying for One's Enemies/ One's Shortcomings
I heard in the name of my teacher [the BeShT], how one ought to pray for one's enemies, and the benefit that accrues from it. For it is written [Prov. 24:16]: "Seven times does a Tzaddiq fall, and yet rises again." This is to say that the [potentials of] one's animating soul, emotive-spirit, and consciousness-soul [Nefesh, Ruach, Nəshamah] transmigrate within the [manifestations of the] seven [lower] Sefirot. One's servants and animals[28] are the [manifestations of the potential of one's] animating soul; the [potential of the Ruach] emotive-spirit of the person is embodied in one's marital relationship—and one's speech is also the manifestation of one's consort.[29] This is as it is said [BT Yevamot 63a], "If a man merits she is a helpmate, if not, she is against him." For if one blemishes one's power of speech by speaking slander or the like, [the energy generated by this act] becomes [manifested by] one's enemies who speak out against him or her.[30] The Neshamah-consciousness-soul is manifested as one's children.[31] A blemish in the realm of thought brings about the pain of child rearing. And a blemish in the Nefesh-animating soul causes one to be disturbed by one's servants and livestock.

Now a person is able [with little relative difficulty] to raise the different levels of his or her soul from within their transmigrations in the seven lower Səfirot, but regarding the seventh, Malkhut [referring to the power of speech and action; it is difficult], for from this level, the "shining [attractive] obscuration" [Kelippat Nogah][32] derives sustenance, and thus it is a great struggle to raise one's' soul from that level.[33] One's adversaries who derive from the blemish of speech are rectified and raised through prayer. But if

---

27 BP, no. 156; Toldot Yaakov Yosef 23b.
28 In modern parlance, one's possessions, work colleagues and subordinates
29 I.e., one's inner relation with oneself and one's companions.
30 See above, BP, texts referred to in notes 22, 25, and 26.
31 As well as in one's intellectual endeavors.
32 The neutral level of existence, which can veer to merit or to obscuration, based on the person's intention.
33 Because, being manifestations of the "outer realm" exemplified in self-interest and self-importance, the person may easily succumb to their attraction.

these are not honestly confronted[34] and are cast aside, then they become even greater adversaries on account of becoming more coarse and materialistic.

For this reason [Prov. 17:26], "when one is punished on account of the Tzaddiq, it is not good" [for the Tzaddiq]—because the wicked person [being punished] is [nonetheless] an aspect of the spirit of the Tzaddiq.[35] Therefore, one needs to pray for one's enemies so as to rectify them and raise them up. And through prayer they are sweetened in their root, so that the spirit of the Tzaddiq can emerge from captivity within them, and the evil that remains disintegrates by itself. May the wise hear and add insight. This was the special quality of Moshe of blessed memory, who raised and rectified his power of speech. At first [the sparks of his potential for communication were tied up in] livestock, and he was a shepherd. Then[36] [the holy sparks] transmigrated and became his disciples to whom he gave the Torah and with whom he studied.[37]

Enemies born of Faulty Speech
The principle that may be derived is that one's enemies who hate the person derive from the blemish of speech, and one needs to pray for them so that they repent and be rectified, as is said in the Talmud [BT Berakhot 10a] regarding R. Me'ir, whose wife Beruriyyah said to him [based on Ps. 104:35]: "may sin—and not [people who happen to be] sinners—cease from the world." If one does not pray for them, the sinners become even more coarse and vulgar, and hate the person even more.[38]

Seeing God in One's Adversary
[on "It is not good than man should be alone, I shall make for him a helpmate to correspond to him" (Gen. 2:18)]: R Moshe Isserlis[39] wrote [Code, 1] that the verse [Psalm 16:8]: "'I place God before me [linegdi] always' is a central principle of the Torah and in the comportment of Tzadiqim." Indeed, one

---

34 I.e., as they appear in the form of one's enemies, or as one's obstructing thoughts that disturb one's concentration, so that rather than raising the obscuring thought to their root, whereby one would derive insight into the areas that one needs to improve oneself, they are ignored, or thoughtlessly followed.
35 ... and is being punished because the Tzaddiq was not successful in rectifying the sinner.
36 Upon completing that phase of his life with conscientiousness.
37 BP, no. 157; TYY 126b.
38 BP, no. 158; TYY 126b.
39 The late sixteenth-century Ashkenazi Halachic decisor recorded in the Code of Jewish Law.

must understand why the verse doesn't use the word 'lifanai'—lit. 'before me' and uses instead, 'linegdi'—meaning literally 'against me,' as in [BT Yevamot 63a][40] 'if one merits, she [one's wife] is a helpmate, if not, '[she is] against him'—though I heard[41] that one ought to regard oneself as being far from the blessed holy One—thus, one ought to place God before [linegdi] me always"—always 'against' me [as demanding more]. But it seems to me, based on what I received from my teachers and colleagues, as to how one must cultivate compassion towards all people, and in addition, when you observe something unseemly in another person, take to heart that also there, the blessed Name abides, for there is no place devoid of Him. Thus this display is for one's own benefit, to indicate that the observer also shares something of the unseemliness observed, and one ought to take heart to return [to God], as I mentioned in the appendix of this work in the name of R Nachman [of Horodenka][42] that if one experiences distraction from learning or prayer, on account of one's companion, the person should take heart that it is for one's own good—perhaps one wasn't doing the service completely properly, or perhaps one ought to use another [creative holy] intention [in one's service] and accept the distraction as being for one's own good. Then, one will realise that this is indeed the case. Thus, "I place God ['s Presence] in what is opposed to me [linegdi]—always."

The Fault I see in the Other is in me

"It is not good than man should be alone, I shall make for him a helpmate to correspond to him" [Gen. 2:18]. I heard an explanation from the renowned veteran saint, Rabbi, R. Nachman [of Horodenka], of the words of our Rabbi [the BeShT] o.b.m., that with each word one ought to contemplate [by means of] the process of subduing-distinguishing-sweetening. For the judgments that emerged from the Attribute of Gevurah are sweetened by not judging the people of the world unfavorably, but rather by consciously entering into the realm of Compassion and cultivating a view of merit with regard to everyone.

Also when you observe something unseemly in your friend, consider that it is for your benefit, and discern that within you there is also a semblance

---

40 Regarding the verse [Gen. 2:18]: " ... I shall make for him a helpmate to correspond to him [kenegdo—lit. to oppose him]."
41 RYY in TYY 22a, BeShT Torah Bereshit, no. 123.
42 Below, in the teaching immediately following. R. Nahman of Horodenka [d.1765] was among the earliest of the disciples of the BeShT, who married his son to the daughter of the BeShT.

of it. Return to God in your thought, on account of this; and this shall be of mutual benefit!⁴³ For if you were the only one in the world, you would think that you were a holy person! But now, you may be aided by your adversary through insightful mirroring. So if a nasty neighbor disturbs your prayer or study, etc., understand that it is for your own good. Your contemplation must not have been entirely whole, and thus you were sent this distraction in order to become sensitized and strengthened—and the wise gain from experience. Essentially, one must take heart to understand that the blessed Name is within all space and in all of one's affairs, and even in idle talk one may sense the Creator, just as in prayer and study.⁴⁴

These later texts obviously have an internal context. Reference to being disturbed while concentrating in prayer would more likely relate to a fellow Jew and how to deal with adversity within. I cite these in order to show how deep the thinking runs and how broad its manifestations. While much of the day to day application of this strand of thoughts relates to one's immediate acquaintances, it is appropriate to also apply it to non-Jews. The testimony of R. Isaac of Komarno, regarding the applicability to this teaching of the BeShT to non-Jews is further corroborated in the following text that ties different strands of our presentation together. The notion of cosmic unity ties in with the approach to the enemies and non-Jews. Thus, a vision of cosmic unity provides the theoretical and experiential foundation for an approach to enemies and to other nations that seeks to elevate and transform.

The final text shared in this essay is an ecstatic teaching from R. Pinchas of Koretz, a direct disciple of the BeShT on the Divine Letters.

> [on Tiqunei haZohar no. 69, 105b]⁴⁵ "... Meanwhile, an old sage who illuminated worlds—R Pinchas ben Yair is his name ... Rabbi Shimeon declared ... [everything was created to be] under the dominion of such a one—even fiery angels and heavenly messengers [pay attention to the words of such a one] ...."—From here it is understood that when a person opens one's mouth in prayer, countless numbers of angels pay attention to these words and bring these prayers before the blessed Name, and all higher and lower worlds—including the Nations of the world, were created only to

---

43   This is because the "enemy" derives a positive cause, by having been the cause of your repentance; opening a path for the enemies' repentance.
44   BeShT Torah, Parashat Bereshit, no. 121; TYY 209b.
45   In the 2003 edition of Imrei Pinchas haShaleim vol. 1, 286–87, no. 3.

attend to such a person. For [Prov. 16:7] "when a man's ways are pleasing to God, He makes even one's enemies to be at peace with him." And we read in the [Lurianic] Writings, in the Gate of Unifications, that every single letter is the Chariot of the Divine Presence and the blessed holy One, and the entire world and [all] the souls are hinged on [every single] letter.[46] Thus when a person speaks and has faith, that in every single letter, all worlds and angels depend, and with it [the letter] s/he unites the blessed holy One with His Divine Presence, with this, one carries all creatures towards the Creator, may His Name be blessed, even the nations of the world—all are being borne [to Him], and anyone with the potency to be raised, is sweetened there; and one who does not have the life-potency to rise, falls below. And by this means one may pray even on behalf of the wicked of the nations—thereby 'he ruled and he died'[47]—and was left without life-substance at all. For as long as one does not pray in this manner, the Messiah won't arrive; and this [manner of prayer] will also be relevant for the resurrection of the dead.[48]

With this we may explain [the verses Deut. 33:2–4]: "... from His right, the eternal fire of the Law—He also is fond of the Nations [all His holy ones, in Your Hands] ... the Congregation of Yaakov ..."—"The eternal fire of the Law"—having been given in the Torah to Israel; "He also is fond of Nations"—for all the attractiveness and life-energies of the Nations, and all the holiness of Israel and all their life-energies, and all the Worlds, all these are in Your Hands, for it all is included in one letter of the Torah [Deut. 33:3]—"and they [all] place themselves at Your feet," to become essential and enter before Your feet [ibid] "bearing Your Words." For by means of Your Word, they [all] rise ....

We began by presenting different exemplars of early hasidic thought in relation to non-Jews that represent an inclusive approach to Gentiles. As we saw in the case of R. Levi Yitzhak of Berdichev, both inclusive as well as dualistic assessments can exist even in the thought of one author, and even an author who engages the negative dimension extensively, can nevertheless also incorporate the positive dimensions of inclusivity for non-Jews. The positive teaching often has a messianic-eschatological dimension and evokes biblical prophecies of future inclusivity. This may be observed in the

---

46 See Etz Hayim Gate 3, chs. 3–7 at length.
47 For this locution, see Genesis 36, and the narrative on the "Kings of Edom," taken [as of the Zohar, 3:128a] as the myth of the primordial origins of the potential for evil; also referred to as the "Cosmic Breaking."
48 The next eschatological stage, where further unification-incorporation [and perhaps also differentiation] would ensue.

teaching of R Pinchas of Koretz, as well as in the eschatological teaching by R Gedalyah of Lynitz. As for the teachings by R Moshe of Dolena and R "Yeivi," both in the name of the BeShT, about the mutual responsibilities shared between Jews and Gentiles; as well as those by R Yaakov Yoseph, regarding integration and ongoing striving towards social and metaphysical ideals and similar ones evinced from the No'am Elimelech, the Seer of Lublin and others, those would apply irrespective of an acute eschatological emphasis.

It appears that thinkers who are more messianically aware, who consider their work self-consciously as part of messianic work, may be more able to transcend historical hostility and to revisit it in light of an ultimate future realization of a fundamental unity of God and creation. Recognition that this awareness is part of a future realization and striving in the present for messianic rectification empowers some of the hasidic thinkers to rise above contemporary tensions and to affirm the deeper cosmic unity and its moral consequences, that are fundamental principles of hasidic thought going back to its founding fathers.

Alon Goshen-Gottstein

Conclusion: Judaism's Challenge—Being Israel in Changing Circumstances

The essays in our collection cover a span of several thousand years, from biblical times till the present day. They are characterized by a diversity that is due both to the depth of time and to the breadth of ideas, concepts and understandings that characterize the view of Israel throughout the different periods. A sense of Israel having a special relationship with God and carrying a special mission is a constant in the sources surveyed. Yet, we have detected shifting emphases throughout, and these have shifted in relation to prevailing historical circumstances. The degree to which Israel is viewed as whole unto itself, with little interest in other nations, is contrasted with more active, missionary understandings of Israel's role in the world. The understandings may reflect different spiritual temperaments. But they certainly also reflect changing historical circumstances. For example, we noted that the ideal of a Kingdom of Priests understood as a teaching vocation becomes central under historical conditions when Jews have the possibility of influencing others, given their independent social standing.

The same is true for how the non-Jew is portrayed. One of the important dimensions of dealing with negative views of non-Jews, such as found in the Zohar and in hasidic works, discussed by Or Rose, is to consider them in historical context. While historical context may not be a sufficient strategy for addressing these texts, it is a necessary one. One might go as far as to say that there is an inbuilt tension between dimensions of spirituality and history, in how Israel conceives of itself and how it views the other. Menachem Kallus' presentation of a school of hasidic teaching that extends love and prayer to the enemy, including the non-Jewish enemy, is a mark of the triumph of spirituality. Other instances, even those involving great masters of Jewish spirituality, are instances in which history and its pressures triumph in shaping consciousness.

History is an important lens by means of which we can analyze the varied data that inform our own religious awareness. But it is more than that. It is also what shapes our awareness at the present moment. The need to undertake the present project is itself an expression of a particular historical moment. The quest of the essays collected here is to consider Israel's election or what it is to be Israel in light of particular contemporary challenges. These not only provide the motivation for the essays but also color their approach and suggest the direction they take, which in most cases is more than historical-descriptive and seeks to offer resources for making sense of being Israel today, within a broader framework. That broader historical framework accounts for the particularity of the present project. It is now time to consider this framework, or rather the different historical dimensions that converge in our project, and to reflect on progress that has been made, especially relating to the one historical context that provided the impetus for our project—the challenge of present-day interreligious relations.

I would like to identify several historical contexts from within which our enquiry has taken place and to which it sought to contribute, beyond the contribution to a topic that has been at the center of Jewish thought for millennia. I can identify three contexts that are reflected in our essays. The common denominator of these different contexts is that they require us to restate the meaning and purpose of being Israel, within the opportunities and challenges of the particular situation.

One contemporary context is spelled out in Or Rose's paper, is referenced in Menachem Katz' paper and it likely informs some of the other contributions. This is the context of a contemporary society in which humanitarian values provide a common denominator for peoples across nationalities and religions. The quest for equality, dignity and morality characterizes this orientation. While it does not strictly speaking contrast with an understanding of election and particularity and there are any of a number of ways of reconciling these perspectives, in terms of orientation, mentalité and approach in general, it is not always easy to reconcile these perspectives. The quest for equality and the fear of chauvinism, two points raised by Rose, characterize a broader mentality that is characteristic of large sections of American Jewry. It seems to me our volume contributes the following to this particular way of framing the challenges:

A. Strategies for reducing the dualistic, hard-edge of what it is to be Israel. Strategies include identifying moral common ground, reading strategies, and identifying alternative voices within the tradition that offset some of the voices that relate Israel to others in an oppositional manner.

B. A profiling of spiritual riches that have been practiced internally and highlighting their value also in relation to those outside the people of Israel. This was seen particularly in Menachem Kallus' paper, where the ideals of hasidic spirituality triumph over negativity born of historical context. The messianic orientation that we have seen throughout provides a further spiritual perspective that can be evoked.

C. Suggestions regarding conceptual categories by means of which Israel's election and being Israel are expressed. Themes such as being a blessing, a Kingdom of Priests and even notions of suffering on behalf of others all give depth to the experience of Israel's particularity that does not compromise the broader mindset that frames this first historical challenge.

A second historical context is the establishment of the State of Israel. The relationship of the People of Israel and the State of Israel is a matter of faith and ideology. Certainly, for those who see a close relationship between them, as expressed by Rabbi Soloveitchik in a passage quoted by Krajewski, the state raises special opportunities and challenges related to being Israel. Framing the matter in terms of positive and negative identity remains a vital concern today, half a century after these ideas were first enunciated. Much of Israeli, and by consequence a related view of Jewish, identity is constructed negatively. The invitation to consider the positive dimensions of identity and how they open up to others is significant. Similarly, some of the moral challenges that our authors grapple with take on greater urgency in the context of the State of Israel. Issues of attitude to the other, seen in light of biblical precedent of the original inhabitants of Canaan surface time and again in the Israeli public sphere. Coupled with negative identity construction it can lead to a shallow and negative application of Jewish identity and being Israel, now translated to both people and state. Affirmation of common moral ground and of common spiritual principles that apply to Jews and non-Jews can help address this negative orientation. But far more significant for present purposes is the grappling with the question of what responsibilities the State of Israel, or perhaps rather the opportunities it provides for Jewish life and vocation, have in furthering the People of Israel's historical mission and vocation. Israeli society continues to be torn between an aspiration for normalization of life for the Jewish people, unrelated to its historical roots and future messianic quest and a view that considers these to be the ultimate raison d'être of the Jewish state. Our collection contributes to this ongoing debate within the Jewish people by visiting the issue of election, in its theoretical sense, and of being Israel, in the existential sense, from multiple perspectives, some of them novel. Such revisiting is an invitation to continue engaging the question, something that occupies less and less of public attention, or when it does, as Eliezer Schweid notes, occurs within a highly politicized context. The essays presented here are one further opportunity for examining the age-old visions and how they might relate to the State of Israel. In particular: might the notion of a Kingdom of Priests find novel significance now that there is a "kingdom"? Can the notion of blessing help orient the attitudes of individuals, communities, and the state, as these interact with others?

The context of the State of Israel is particularly relevant for concerns of boundaries and their crossing. Throughout, we have noted the implications of how we view Israel not only for others but also for those who are associated with it and wish to join it. As we have seen, there are various ways of associating oneself with Israel and its message. Different shades of identification, association and conversion have presented themselves to us throughout our essays. The invitation to join, to share, to convert is fundamental to the project of being Israel, as I see it emerging from our project. The very quest for being Israel and affirming its identity and mission are taken over by political concerns in the framework of the state. Similarly, the invitation to join Israel the people undergoes hardening in the framework of state mechanisms, impacted by political concerns. Beginning with Knohl's problematizing of the biblical heritage of the *ger* and following with various references to Israel's teaching mission to the nations, we struggle with the question of just how much being Israel is also an invitation to others to become Israel, or at least, as Katz suggests, to find that common space of the "us" that joins together Israel and those who have heard its message, without becoming a part of itself. All these dynamics are significantly complicated in the framework of the Jewish state. We are pushed to the recognition that while the state could hold promise for realization of long-term ideals, it also frustrates their appropriate implementation, inasmuch as policies and their application are all too often entrusted to those who have a different perspective on what being Israel is. Differently put, the State of Israel is a kind of battleground for competing views of what Israel is and ought to be. The conversation carried out in this volume is an opportunity to offer a reminder of a particular vision and its possible application within the framework of the state. If only those who needed to be part of the conversation partook of it.

The third context is the one that gave birth to the present project. It relates to the question of election, Israel's status and mission, in the framework of a contemporary theology of religions and of contemporary interfaith relations. At least one author, Or Rose, was explicit about the implications of the view of the non-Jew he discussed in that it inhibits the possibility of sharing spiritually across religions. While the association is by no means a necessary one, Rose does make the association between a certain view of Israel and the other and the view of truth as residing exclusively within one religion. Other authors also frame their contribution in terms of Judaism and other religions. As the essays were initially authored with that perspective in mind, most of the contributors to the project sought to find ways of affirming positive relations with other faiths and their believers while upholding or engaging belief in Israel's chosenness. In the interest of allowing our volume to speak more broadly to contemporary concerns, the explicit engagement of other religions was downplayed in the final version, but it is still mentioned in many of the papers, and is relevant to the overall structure of the book and its thesis. Considering our collective efforts in terms of this contemporary challenge, I would claim we have made a meaningful contribution to considering Israel's particularity also in the context of world religions. Beyond the individual references, I'd like to profile some of the points that I see emerging from our project, and to revisit two contributions in particular.

A. Being Israel is a dynamic process that requires articulation under changing circumstances. In the same way that certain ideas came to the fore under the appropriate historical circumstances, whether these be understandings of election in polemic with other religions or Israel's priestly teaching vocation when it could be realized historically, so the present encounter of Judaism and world religions is a moment of making sense of Israel and its mission. It is a challenging moment, inasmuch as the fight for Israel (the people)'s survival has often eclipsed a sense of mission and purpose. What it is that Judaism, Israel, still has to offer the world is a question that is harder to answer than one might think, unless one holds a position that all religions are false and Israel alone is in possession of the fullness of truth.

B. One cannot enter such a conversation and such an exploration with negativity in one's heart. An oppositional view of Jews and non-Jews renders efforts at dialogue ineffective and insincere. To be clear, going beyond an oppositional view does not imply accepting a particular view of Jewish election or rejecting the concept altogether. However, the new opportunity that has opened up as world religions establish new paradigms for their encounter does affect some long-held attitudes, some of the dimensions of mentalité that define what being Israel is for some, perhaps for many.

C. The key challenge is how to shift the discourse of nations to that of religions. Israel, being a nation, is also the carrier of a particular religion, Judaism. Exploring Israel's particularity and mission is easier to carry out in the conceptual framework of nations. What happens to the idea when it is transposed to the area of religions? Such a shift has already taken place centuries ago. I think of R. Menachem Meiri's reference to Christianity and Islam as "nations that are bound by the ways of religion." Meiri uses language of nations, corresponding to Israel in terms of self-definition, to describe other religions, though they may not be constituted along national or ethnic lines. While in theory we could replicate this move, in fact a conversation on election with reference to other religions involves us in some degree of crossing categories.

If the fundamental framework is one of outreach, it is easier to envision the extension of Israel's message to other people, rather than to other religions. Still, the move is possible. Two possibilities open up. The one would consider other religions as receiving something from Israel, either by its very being or by way of the teachings of Judaism, and undergoing some internal transformation or conversion. The other possibility is to consider some religions as having already internalized fundamental aspects of Judaism's teaching and seeing them as carriers to humanity of Israel's message. This involves us then in more complicated evaluations of Christianity, Islam and some of their offshoots and in the question of whether they have taken up Israel's message correctly and exhaustively. What does Israel have to say to the world given that most of the world follows faiths begotten of Israel, but distinct from it? Does it seek to correct imperfections in these faiths? Is its message only relevant for others? Or perhaps Israel's being radiates to the world something that transcends the teaching vocation that has been partly or successfully undertaken by these religions. The contributions by Eugene

Korn and myself provide valuable gateways for reflecting on the question of Israel's enduring teaching and mission, as source of blessing and as teachers, in the presence of other faiths. The range of options in understanding these themes interacts in rich ways with the challenges of the interreligious reality and holds promise for constructive thinking and theological growth.

D. Krajewski's discussion of positive and negative dimensions of establishing identity draws out an important implication of positive identity construction for views of other religions. Krjaewski associates positive identity building with secure identity, which in turn has room for the other. Applied to the interreligious context, positive identity-construction makes it possible to affirm another religion in its particularity. The view is certainly pluralist and his original contribution included reference to one of the most pluralist moments in the history of Jewish thought, the reference by Rabbi Nethanel Al-Fayumi to the possibility of multiple revelations, all valid, leading to different religions. Krajewski's contribution focuses on negative and positive identity construction, as they impact attitudes of openness and acceptance of the other. Krajewski does not attempt to define what it is that Israel still has to give other religions from such pluralist and self-assured perspective of positive identity affirmation. What Krajewski does model for us is the possibility of openness to other religions as a natural outcome of Israel being true to itself. This is itself a somewhat shocking thought, considering a long oppositional history. But this is precisely what the present moment of interreligious relations enables—a revisiting of age-old attitudes and exploration of new ways of being in relation to others and their implications for being Israel. Surely, it will be a different exploration of what it means to be Israel and of what is Israel's enduring testimony to other faiths when this is conducted on the basis of openness to others, while seeking to articulate Israel's particular message. Perhaps the process might require reciprocity, compared to the one-sided giving that typically characterizes a view of Israel and the nations or other religions. This provides us with an important segue to further expressions of Gellman's understanding of Israel's chosenness.

E. Jerome Gellman's contribution opens with reference to changes in Christian theology and a broader invitation for religions to reformulate their theology of the other. Recognizing the centrality of election for Judaism, he has developed a new proposal for understanding Jewish chosenness that is relevant not only for other nations, but is supposed to also work for other faiths. I would like to reintroduce here elements of his original essay that I suggested not be included, in the interest of letting the volume speak to a broader situation than just that of interreligious relations. Now is the time to revisit some further nuances of the interreligious implications of Gellman's thesis.

Given Gellman's conception of Jewish chosenness, how would he view theistic religions other than Judaism? No other theistic religion carries quite the sense that Judaism has of how God overwhelmed the Jews. Jesus worked no overwhelming of the Jews when he came to preach to them. Quite the contrary—the great majority of the Jews were utterly unconvinced. Islam has a thicket of complexity concerning compulsion and tolerance, including conflicting verses in the Quran in favor of and against compulsion (In favor: "fight until there is no infidelity." Quran, 8:39; Against: "There is no compulsion in religion, for the right way is clear from the wrong way." 2:256). However, this compulsion, if it be, is again not the compulsion of which Gellman speaks. This compulsion involves the human enforcement of Islam on non-believers. It does not involve a sense of God's overbearing presence in the religion's formative experiences. None of the other features of divine embrace exist on a mass scale for Islam or Indian religions as they do in Judaism. On Gellman's Judaic view, world religions other than Judaism are freely given answers to God's non-coercive call, emanating from Sinai and onwards—responses offered within the freedom of varying cultural contexts. These other religions are developing, along with Judaism, toward the time of the Messiah, when there will be one house of prayer for all nations (Isaiah 56:7).

Indeed, at times a freely given response to God can be more pleasing in God's eyes than the response to God's overwhelming love. Gellman expands on the following Midrash that tells how beloved to God are converts to the Jewish religion:

> Rabbi Shimon ben Lakish said: "The convert [to Judaism] is more beloved to God than those who stood at Mount Sinai. Why? Because all those had they not seen the sounds and the torches and lightening and the mountains shaking and the ram horns sounding, they would not have accepted upon themselves the kingdom of heaven. But this one saw none of these and comes and attaches himself to God and accepted on himself the kingdom of heaven, is there anyone more beloved than that? (*Midrash Tanhuma* [Buber] [Jerusalem: Eshkol, 1971/72], 5. Translated by Gellman).

Rabbi Shimon ben Lakish speaks of converts to Judaism. The Israelites experienced frightening events at Sinai (Exodus 20:15–16), which events compromised their freedom in accepting God's Word. Not so converts to Judaism who come to God in full willingness. Converts are for this reason more beloved to God than non-converts.

According to Gellman, we might expand the scope of this Rabbi's saying to possibly include those who sincerely respond to God in freedom and joy, whether Jewish or Greek, man or woman, free or slave. God desires a new acceptance of God by the Jews and a free response by the non-Jews to God's ongoing noncoercive call to them. These responses can be more beloved to God than the previous ones.

Gellman takes God's "call from Sinai" to humanity at large in a metaphorical way. The cashing of the metaphor occurs in the intimations of the divine scattered throughout history and throughout human reality. That includes the wonders of the natural world, great spiritual figures who have opened people to the divine, private or public experiences that people interpret in religious ways, and religions that carry that call forward. To term these intimations a "call" is to affirm the belief that God wishes to have an intimate relationship with humanity, freely given and enjoyed. To dub it a call from "Sinai," is to indicate that the call to the other peoples of the world is an echo of God's overwhelming embrace of the Jewish people. And to speak of it as coming from "Sinai" is to point to God's love of the Jews as a sign of God's desire for all nations and all people.

The rich variation of religions represents, in principle, a manifold of appropriate responses to God, given the complexity of the human psyche and the wide variances in human culture. For that very reason, Judaism should be interested not only in the compliance of other religions with the seven Noahide laws, but with learning the detailed content of those religions, as a response to God's call. This is because each religion issues from a deep place in the human psyche, where there is a fundamental commonality of all humanity. Confronting other religions can thus nurture in me, says Gellman, and in my people an appreciation of how it is to freely respond to God in ways appropriate to each cultural world inhabited by human beings. In this way, religions of the world reciprocate to Judaism by serving as models for Judaism of freely responding to God and of the need for adherents of Judaism to go beyond God's overbearing presence in a freely given and deeply self-determined way. It is precisely this two-way modeling of relationships to God, between Judaism and other religions, that Jews should nurture in inter-religious dialogue.

F. The final point I wish to make flows nicely from Gellman's reference to the convert as someone who freely chooses God, based on the coercive precedent applied previously to Israel. The notion of conversion has appeared repeatedly throughout this collection. If Judaism functions properly, if Israel knows its calling and is true to it, then conversion is a reality to be reckoned with. Conversion may take multiple forms. These can include conversion to Judaism, conversion to Judaism's message to the nations, typically understood as the seven noachide commandments, or conversion to some reality of truth, not specified by religious boundaries, as in the example provided by Menachem Katz. Perhaps as I just alluded, conversion could also take place within another religion, in a manner similar to how the term is used in Christian circles, where conversion also covers the semantic field referred to in Judaism as *teshuva*.

However conversion is understood, it is characterized by receiving a message, an understanding, an insight, a calling, and responding through some meaningful change in one's life, a change oriented towards coming closer to God. If the structure of Jewish election is one of extending love and sharing of a message, then Judaism, in this presentation, emerges as fundamentally missionary. Millennia of avoidance of missionary activity, given Israel's historical reality, have shaped a religion that is much more introvert, often seen as a family affair. Yet, if my reading of what emerges from these essays is correct, the missionary drive, understood as the drive to share a message and a teaching, rather than the drive to become Jewish, is fundamental to Israel's spiritual DNA. We must consider, then, how this drive relates to the interreligious situation.

Typically, interreligious engagement is viewed in opposition to missionary work, inasmuch as the former is based on acceptance of the identity of the other and its validity, while the latter seeks to undermine and replace it. Instances where a religious institution seeks to practice both, such as in the case of the Catholic Church, lead to serious critique of its intentions in the interreligious domain. It may be the case that something of the missionary drive is inherent in any religious tradition. There may be various checks and balances that frustrate it, be they considerations of caste and the inability to convert, in the case of Hinduism, or the difficulties of Jewish history, that have turned Judaism into an inward-looking non-missionary faith. Yet, these considerations are only relevant as far as active proselytizing and an institutional missionary agenda are concerned. Total inwardness means the religion has nothing to say to others, no message to carry, no hope to share and no transformation to offer. In my opinion, a religion that has no vision will die. A Judaism with no vision other than its survival will similarly pass away. Religious vitality requires articulation of a message, and once the message is articulated there is an internal impulse to share it with others. The conundrum of respecting identity while sharing the message is best resolved when we approach conversion not in terms of identity changing strategies but in terms of internal transformations that help orient a religion and its adherents towards their own higher goals or the higher goals that one can envision for them.

In this understanding, Judaism's encounter with other religions is a vital arena for the fulfillment of its ultimate vocation. If Israel's vocation is to share divine love, to spread a message, then today's circumstances of interreligious relations are a vital arena for the exploration of this mandate. The problem Jews have is that they are all too often unable to articulate their message, and what they often imagine as their message for other religions can only be articulated in the absence of the other, inasmuch as it is either disrespectful of the other or represents a false understanding of the other. We have lost the core vocation of sharing and need to regain it. The interreligious situation is one in which we might rediscover it. Rather than compromising or threatening our identity, it may allow us to regain something fundamental to our identity.

There is one difference between how Israel's mission has been classically envisioned and the new paradigm of interreligious sharing. The former is a one way sharing that Israel undertakes for the sake of God and humanity. The latter is a reciprocal process undertaken mostly for the well-being of society and secondarily in the pursuit of wisdom and inspiration. But this significant difference does not make the opportunities for realizing Israel's vocation through engagement with other religions any less important. We have too much to learn about our own voice and message after centuries of near silence. We have too much to rethink concerning where other religions are, after centuries of persecution that have given way to interreligious understanding. Too much has changed and we require the time to discern what being Israel means under these new circumstances and what part of Israel's message, what expression of its vocation, can come to light under present circumstances. The situation calls us in ways that I consider deeply true to the mandate of who we are. If we do not yet know what it will draw from us and what it will bring to us, that is no worry. It will allow us to enter the engagement with the religious other not only from a situation of some humility but also, and more importantly, as part of our own self-exploration and quest for deeper understanding of ourselves and our calling. In fact, it will force us to take up questions we leave aside when we are in the comfort and security of our community. In this it may be a blessing, a blessing that we can share with others and a blessing to our very being, by following the invitation to discover what it is to be Israel in this new situation. Perhaps herein lies one important key to the messianic fulfillment of Israel's vocation and its ultimate sharing with others.

Notes on Contributors

Jerome Yehuda Gellman has written seven books and over 110 articles on the philosophy of religion and Jewish thought. He is a past Fellow at the Harvard Center for the Study of World Religions and past Alvin Plantinga Fellow at the Center for the Philosophy of Religion, Notre Dame University. He was also a Fellow at the Advanced Institute of the Shalom Hartman Institute, Jerusalem. He edits a series for Brill Publishers in philosophy of religion and is an editorial board member of four philosophy journals. His 2019 book *Perfect Goodness and the God of the Jews: A Contemporary Jewish Theology* (Academic Studies Press) is the last in a trilogy on contemporary constructive Jewish theology.

Alon Goshen-Gottstein is the founder and director of the Elijah Interfaith Institute, and lecturer and director of the Center for the Study of Rabbinic Thought, Beit Morasha College, Jerusalem. Ordained a Rabbi in 1977, he holds a PhD from Hebrew University of Jerusalem in the field of rabbinic thought. His fourscore publications are divided between the areas of interreligious dialogue, theology of religions, Jewish spirituality and rabbinic thought. He has published fifteen books in the field of theology of religions and interfaith relations. He is editor of the Interreligious Reflections series, where work of the Elijah Think Tank is featured at Wipf and Stock publishers. His most recent monograph is *Luther the Antisemite: A Contemporary Jewish Perspective* (Fortress Press, 2018).

Gershon Greenberg is Visiting Professor in the Department of Jewish Thought, Hebrew University of Jerusalem, in the fields of religious thought through the Holocaust and history of Jewish thought in America; and Professor of Philosophy and Religion at the American University in Washington, DC in the field of comparative religious thought. His most recent book is, with Yedidyah Assaf, *Mishpateha tehom rabbah: Orthodox Theological Responses Through the Holocaust* (Mossad harav kook, 2016).

Menachem Kallus has been researching and translating hasidic works for over thirty years. In 2011, he published an anthology entitled: *Pillar of Prayer: Guidance in Contemplative Prayer, Sacred Study, and the Spiritual Life, from the Baal Shem Tov and His Circle* (Fons Vitae Spiritual Affinities Series). His bilingual two-volume *Essential Baal Shem Tov on the Torah* will be ready for publication in 2020. He lives in Jerusalem with his wife and son.

Menachem Katz is Academic Director Emeritus of the Friedberg Manuscripts Project in Jerusalem. He is also Head of Department of Rabbinic Studies at Chemdat Hadarom College. Dr. Katz has published widely on the Jerusalem Talmud and Aggadic literature, as well as in the field of Digital Humanities. In 2016, he published a critical edition of Talmud Yerusalem Tractate Qiddushin (Yad Izhak Ben-Zvi & Schechter Institute of Jewish Studies).

Reuven Kimelman serves as rabbi of Beth Abraham, the Sefardic Congregation of New England, and as Professor of Classical Judaica at Brandeis University. He is the author of the Hebrew book *The Mystical Meaning of 'Lekhah Dodi' and Kabbalat Shabbat* (The Hebrew University of Jerusalem) and the forthcoming *The Rhetoric of the Jewish Liturgy: A Historical and Literary Commentary to the Prayer Book*. His audio course books are *The Hidden Poetry of the Jewish Prayer Book* and *The Moral Meaning of the Bible*. He has also been commissioned to produce the *JPS Commentary to the Siddur*.

Israel Knohl is the Yehezkel Kaufmann Professor of Biblical studies at the Hebrew University of Jerusalem and a Senior Fellow at Shalom Hartman Institute in Jerusalem. His books deal with the integration of scientific and archaeological discoveries with biblical accounts, early Israelite beliefs, a survey of Israelite cults, and how and where the Israelites originated. His most recent book is *How the Bible was Born* (Kinneret-Dvir, 2018. Hebrew).

Eugene Korn is a teacher, scholar, and writer living in Jerusalem. He holds a doctorate in moral philosophy from Columbia University and

Orthodox rabbinical ordination from *Pirchei Shoshanim*. Previously the founding editor of *The Edah Journal* and National Director of Interfaith Affairs at the Anti-Defamation League, for the past ten years he has been the Academic Director of The Center for Jewish-Christian Understanding and Cooperation in Israel. Dr. Korn has taught at Columbia and Yeshiva Universities, as well as the Graduate Department of Judeo-Christian Studies of Seton Hall University. He is a contributor and co-editor of six books, including *Jewish Theology and World Religions* (with Alon Goshen-Gottstein), *Plowshares into Swords? Reflections on Religion and Violence*, *Returning to Zion: Christian and Jewish Perspectives*, and *Covenant and Hope: New Frontiers in Jewish and Christian Theology*. His other books include *The Jewish Connection to the Land of Israel—A Brief Introduction for Christians, Two Faiths, One Covenant?*

Stanislaw Krajewski, professor at the Institute of Philosophy of the University of Warsaw, has been involved in research in logic and philosophy of mathematics, as well as in the philosophy of religion and interfaith dialogue. After 1989, he was among the founders of the Polish-Israeli Friendship Society and then of the Polish Council of Christians and Jews, of which he has been the Jewish co-chairman since its inception. A former member of the board of the Union of Jewish Religious Communities in Poland and the International Council of the Auschwitz Camp Museum and Memorial, he also co-authored the postwar section of the core exhibition in POLIN, the Museum of the History of Polish Jews in Warsaw. His most recent book is *What do I Owe to Interreligious Dialogue and Christianity* (The Judaica Foundation, 2017. English and Polish).

Or Rose is the founding Director of the Betty Ann Greenbaum Miller Center for Interreligious Learning & Leadership of Hebrew College. Rabbi Rose is the co-editor of *Speaking Torah: Spiritual Teachings from Around the Maggid's Table* (Jewish Lights), *My Neighbor's Faith: Stories of Interreligious Encounter, Growth, and Transformation*, and *Words to Live By: Sacred Sources for Irreligious Engagement* (both published by Orbis).

Index

Abd al-Nabi ibn Mahdi, 130
Abiathar, 153
Abraham, xvii, xix, xxiv-xxv, 2-7, 9, 12, 23, 25, 50-64, 66, 69-70, 84-85, 92n14, 110, 114, 132-133, 144-146, 148-149, 159, 170-171
Abravanel, Isaac, 15, 59
Adam, 21, 75, 116-117, 127, 140
Agag, 152, 155-156
Agudat Yisrael, 129, 135-138
Aharon (Aaron), 37-38, 91-92, 142, 149, 177
Ahasuerus, 78n9, 100
Ai, 164
Akedah, xxiv, 133, 142
Akedat Treblinka, see Elberg, Simchah
Aleinu prayer, *also Aleinu Leshabeach*, xxi-xxii, 83-97, 170n65
Amalek, xxv-xxvi, 122, 130, 132, 135-136, 138-139, 141, 143-173
Amidah, also Shemoneh Esreh, 83-84, 86, 88
Amiel, Moshe Avigdor, 138-139
Amoraim, 85n3
Amorites, 84, 159, 161-162, 165-167, 170
anti-Semitism, xiii, 69, 71, 106, 136, 139n11, 155
Antonius, 157
Arvit, also Maariv, 84
Ashkenazi, 29, 34, 87, 89, 181n20, 184n39
Ashlag, Yehudah Leib (Rabbi) xix, 38-41, 46, 48
Assyria, 55-56, 130, 168, 172
Assyria, 55-56, 168, 172
Augustine of Hippo, 80
Auschwitz, 133-134, 137-138
Austria, 130

Ba'al Shem Tov, *also BeShT*, xxvi, 174-188
   Sefer BeShT, 177n6
Babylon, 3, 7, 11, 131
Balaam, 122
Baranowicz, 136
Baron, Salo, 107
Bar-On, Shraga, 90
Bathsheba, 166
Bauman, Zygmunt, 106

Bergen-Belsen, 134
Berlin Declaration, 71
Berlin, Naftali (Rabbi), *also* Netziv, 60
Bet Midrash, 88
Bible, xi-xii, xv, xvii-xviii, xxiii, xxv-xxvi, 1-12, 17-19, 25, 50-52, 54-57, 63, 67, 69-70, 74, 76, 87-88, 92-93, 95-97, 114, 116, 122, 124, 128, 137-138, 143, 145, 149, 151-154, 156-159, 163, 165, 169-173, 180, 187, 189, 191-192
   Torah, xxi, 10, 12, 16, 18-19, 26, 32-33, 35-37, 39-40, 48, 52-53, 59-60, 69, 76, 78-79, 81, 86-89, 93-95, 101-103, 111, 115-118, 120, 127, 129, 131, 134-135, 137-139, 141, 152, 156, 158, 170, 174, 176, 178, 184, 187
   Genesis, 2-4, 20-21, 23n27, 25, 50-51, 53-56, 58-63, 66, 69n13, 75, 81, 84-85, 89, 93n16, 111, 118, 127, 131-132, 141, 144, 145, 147-149, 157n24, 159, 169-171, 176, 180, 184-185, 187n47
   Exodus, 8, 13, 15-35, 37, 42-44, 51, 60, 76, 81, 84, 102, 114n3, 125, 127, 138, 149-152, 159-160, 162-163, 176, 197
   Leviticus, 12, 20, 22, 32-33, 92, 95, 100, 127, 131, 134, 142-143, 160-162, 179
   Numbers, 20n15, 22n26, 85, 103, 151, 154, 157, 160-161, 163, 167, 172n74, 179
   Deuteronomy, 6-11, 16-20, 22, 65, 79, 117-118, 130, 139, 143-144, 147-148, 150-153, 156-157, 159n34, 161-163, 165-167, 169-172, 187
Nevi'im
Former Prophets (Nevi'im Rishonim), 169n57, 171n70
   Joshua, 5n1, 159n34, 163-165, 167, 169, 171

Judges, 154, 162-165
1 Samuel, 85, 152-155, 172n76
2 Samuel, 95, 154, 158
1 Kings, 159n34, 163, 166
2 Kings, 153
Latter Prophets (Nevi'im Aharonim)
Isaiah, 17, 19-20, 23, 25, 27, 30, 35, 51, 53, 55, 58, 60-61, 84, 88, 92, 96, 112, 129-131, 146-147, 166n44, 170, 179, 196
Jeremiah, 51n1, 53-55, 144, 146, 148, 166-167
Ezekiel, 51n1, 53-54, 116, 139, 141-142, 146-148, 162n38, 166n44, 170,
Twelve Minor Prophets (Trei 'Asar)
Hosea, 8, 65, 147
Amos, 131, 145, 148-149, 173
Obadiah, 157
Jonah, 170
Zephaniah, 179
Zechariah, 51n1, 53-54, 65n10
Malachi, 26, 131, 141, 176
Ketuvim
Psalms, 15n3, 18-20, 25, 27, 64, 84-85, 91-93, 125, 131, 141, 145-146, 159n34, 164, 166, 179-181, 184
Proverbs, 150n6
Ruth, 120, 159, 169-171
Esther, 78, 100, 154-156
1 Chronicles, 152, 154, 156-157
2 Chronicles, 153, 159n32, 164n42, 166
Bilewicz, Michal, 107n10
Billig, Michael, 107-108
binitarianism, 90
Book of Commandments, see Maimonides, Moses
Brandeis University, 112
Bratislava, 137-138
Buber, Martin, 109
Buddhism, 77, 133
Bundy, R.P., 107

Canaanites, xxvi, 3, 144, 151, 157, 159, 161-173
Catholic Encyclopedia, the, 82

Chabad, 30n37, 44, 140
Chaim ibn Attar (Rabbi), 180 *also Or Hachayim*, 37, 180
Charlap, Yaakov Moshe (Rabbi), xxv, 140-142
chosenness, xvi, xx-xxi, 45, 71-82, 84, 94, 102, 111, 121, 131-134, 137-138, 140-141, 144, 173, 193, 195-196
Christianity, xii, 25, 48n79, 56, 58-59, 69, 71, 73-74, 87, 121, 130, 133, 194-195, 198
Catholic, 71-72, 82, 121, 198
Orthodox, 121
Protestant, 71, 173n74
Cohen, Hermann, 68n12
commandments, xxv-xxvi, 8, 16, 19n14, 22, 27, 32, 38, 58, 63, 76, 95, 101, 135, 137, 144, 158, 168, 177-178
Noahide, xx, 17, 57-58, 157, 176-177, 197-198
Ten Commandments, 76, 78
Congress of Jewish Studies, 83
creation, xxi, xxvii, 18, 21-22, 25, 27, 38-39, 58, 60, 62, 72-73, 75, 81, 87-91, 93, 96, 99, 110, 114-119, 127, 133-134, 138, 140-142, 175, 178-181, 186-188

Da'at (Tree of Life), 177
Dachau, 134
David, 19n14, 85, 120, 153-154, 159, 166, 168-169, 171-172
divine love, xvi-xvii, xix-xx, xxiii-xxviii, 6-8, 22n24, 64-66, 73-74, 76-77, 79-81, 84, 111, 113, 117-118, 130, 137, 140, 146, 196-199
Dov Ber of Mezeritch (Rabbi), *also* the Maggid of Mezeritch, 178
Maggid Devarav leYaakov, 115
Dovber Shneuri, the Middle Rebbe, 43

Eden, 63, 117
Edom, 85, 154, 187n47
Egypt, 7, 15, 55-56, 60, 76, 80-81, 85, 102-105, 116n9, 118-119, 122, 125, 150, 152, 165, 171, 177, 180
Ehrenreich, Shlomo Zalman, 138
Elberg, Simchah
Akedat Treblinka, 133
election, xi-xviii, xix-xxii, xxiv-xxv, xxviii, 1-13, 15, 18, 20-21, 25, 27, 41, 45, 52, 56, 60-61, 115, 129-173, 190-195, 198
Eliezer, 170
Elimelech of Lizhensk (Rabbi), 65-66, 179, 188
Eliphaz, 156

Enlightenment, 68, 137
enmity, xvi, xxvi, 71, 130, 174-188
Esau, 64, 85, 111, 122, 135-137, 155-157, 170
eschatology, 17, 28, 41, 43, 54, 69, 88, 120, 187-188
Esther, 78, 121n26
Evans, C. Stephen, 74, 82
Eve, 75
Exodus, xxi, 20n14, 33, 80-81, 144, 171

Fainzilber, Shlomo, 130-132
Fayumi, Nethanel, al (Rabbi), 195
Firer, Benzion, 131-132, 136n6
Flament, Claude, 107
France, 89, 106, 127, 133
Friedman, Alexander Zusia, 135-137
Friedman, Yaakov (Rabbi), 42-43, 46
    Oholei Yaakov, 42 instead Oholey *galut*, 41

Gaon, Saadia (Rabbi), 86n4, 157n24
Gedalyah of Lynitz (Rabbi), 177-178, 188
Gellman, Jerome, xiin6, xx, xxii, xxiv, 195-198
    God's Kindness Has Overwhelmed Us, xiin6
gentiles, non-Jews, nations, xiii-xvi, xx-xxi, xxiii, xxv-xxvii, 6, 11, 17, 23, 25, 47-48, 51-52, 54-61, 63-71, 78-79, 81-82, 90-91, 93n16, 95-97, 106, 113, 115, 117-128, 133, 136-137, 139, 174-175, 177-181, 186-191, 193-194, 197
ger, xviii, xx, 9-12, 27, 158, 192
Germany, 36, 68n12, 105, 130, 133, 136-137, 139, 173n76
Gerst, Yehudah Leb, 134
Geshurites, 164
Gevurah (emanation), 126, 185
Gezer, 163-164
Gibeonites, 167
Gikatilla, Joseph ben Abraham (Rabbi), 63
Girgashites, 161, 167n48
God's Kindness Has Overwhelmed Us, see Gellman, Jerome
Goliath, 85
Gomorrah, 145
Goshen-Gottstein, Alon, xviii, 51n2, 68n12
Greece, 130-131, 156, 197
Green, Arthur, 122
Guide for the Perplexed, see Maimonides, Moses

Haggadah, 106
Halakhah (Jewish law), 17, 77, 110, 124n30, 184n39
Halevi, Yehudah *Kuzari*, 131, 140

Haman, 100, 137, 154-156
Hameiri (Meiri), Menachem (Rabbi), 97n22, 194
Hanukkah, 121
Haran, 2-4, 58
Haran, 2-4, 58, 60
Hasidism, xiin3, xv, xxiii, xxvi-xxvii, 15-16, 21n19, 30, 37, 41-45, 48-49, 65-66, 76-77, 98n1, 105, 110, 112-116, 119-120, 122-125, 136-137, 158n29, 174-189, 191
Hazor, 164
Hebrew University of Jerusalem, 112
Heinemann, Joseph, 88-90
Hepburn, Ronald, 73
herem, 162-163
Heschel, Abraham Joshua, *also* the Apter Rebbe, 105, 109
Hillel (sage), 126, 178
Hirsch, Samson Raphael (Rabbi), 28-36, 39n60, 44, 68n12, 95
Hirschman, Menachem, 95
Hitler, Adolf, 133-134, 137, 139-140
Hittities, 72, 159, 161, 165-167
Hivites, 159, 161, 165-166
Holocaust, *also* the Shoah, xxiv-xxv, 69, 105-106, 129-142
Hopstein, Yisroel (Rabbi), *also* the Maggid of Kozhnitz, 180
Horeb, see Hirsch, Samson Raphael Horowitz, Yaakov Yitzhak (Rabbi), *also* the Seer of Lublin, 179-180, 188
Hur, 149

Ibn Ezra, Abraham, 18, 178n12
idolatry, ix, 5-6, 26-27, 55, 58, 89, 91, 96, 1 33-135, 143, 163, 166-167, 169, 180
Isaac of Komarno, 181, 186
Isaac, 4, 9, 51, 58, 63-64, 84-85, 92n14, 132-133, 142, 156
Ishmael (Rabbi), 62, 95-96
    Mekhilta de-Arayot, 95
Ishmael, 62, 64, 135
Islam, xii, 6, 56, 58-59, 173n74, 194, 196
Isserlis, Moshe (Rabbi), 184

Jacob ben Asher (Rabbi), *also* Ba'al Haturim, 20-21, 41, 43-44, 46
    Yoreh De'ah, 100-101
Jacob, 9, 17, 25, 27, 35, 51, 58, 64, 84-85, 92n14, 96, 111, 131-132, 137, 140-141, 170
Jebusites, 161, 164-166

Jehoiakim, 146
Jericho, 164, 169
Jerusalem, 35, 65n10, 84, 91, 129, 140, 164, 169, 180
Jesuits, 77
Jesus Christ, xxi, 73, 80, 87, 196
Joshua bin Nun, 89, 149-151, 157, 163-169, 172
Josiah (King), 11, 146
Judah ben Samuel of Regensburg (Rabbi), *also* Yehudah the Pious, 181n20
    Sefer Hasidim, 136
Judah Loew, *also* the Maharal of Prague, 122n28, 135-136
Judah Maccabee, 121n26
Judah the Prince, 157
Judah, 53, 159, 169

Kabbalah, xiin3, 37, 63, 175
Kadesh, 85
Kahana, Menachem, 85-86
Kallus, Menachem, xxvi-xxviii, 48n78, 189, 191
Kandinsky, Vassily, 108
Kara, Avigdor (Rabbi), 41
Karaites, 24-25
Karo, Joseph (Rabbi), 101
    Shulchan Arukh, 110, 158n27
Kasher, Hanna, xi-xii
Katz, Menahem, xxi-xxii, xxvii, 190, 192, 198
Kaufering, 134
Kedushat Levi, see Levi Yitzhak of Berditchev
kelippot, 140-141, 183
Kenites, 171
Keter (emanation), 63
Kiddush Hashem, 43
Kierkegaard, Soren, 73, 76
    Philosophical Fragments, 73
Kimchi, David, *also* Radak, 15, 53-56, 61, 158
Kimelman, Reuven, xxv-xxvii
Klee, Paul, 108
Knohl, Israel, xvii-xix, 192
Kook, Abraham Isaac (Rabbi), *also* Rav Kook, 24n29, 28-37, 42, 44, 46-48, 140, 168
    Midbar Shur, 30n39, 33
Korn, Eugene, xviii-xx, 194-195
Krajewski, Stanislaw, xxii-xxiii, 191, 195
Kristallnacht, 129

Landeshut, 134
Leshem, Tzvi, 181n20

Levi Yitzhak of Berditchev (Rabbi), *also* RLY, the Berditchever and Derbarmdiger, xxiii-xxiv, 38, 112-128, 178-179, 187
    Kedushat Levi, xxiii, 37, 112-128, 178-179
Levin, Yitzhak Meir, 137
Levinas, Emmanuel, 109
Lithuania, 121, 130
Lodz, 134
Luria, Isaac, 140, 175n1

Maacathites, 164
ma'amadot liturgy, xxii, 90, 93, 96n21
    Maggid Devarav leYaakov, see Dov Ber of Mezeritch
Maidanek, 135
Maimonides, Abraham, 16-17, 23-24
Maimonides, Moses, *also* Rambam, 16-17, 40, 58, 61, 130-133, 152, 156-158, 167n48, 168, 171, 173n76
    Book of Commandments, 58, 168n52
    Guide for the Perplexed, 61n6, 152-153, 158n28
    Mishneh Tora, 58-59, 61n6, 156n19, 158n26, 168n50, 171n72
Malkhut (emanation), 63-64, 183
Malkhuyyot, 86
Manasseh, 154, 164
Mani (Rabbi), 152
Mattathias ben Johanan, 121n26
Megiddo, 164
Melchizedek, 93n16
Mendelssohn, Moses, 139
Merkaz Harav, 140
Messiah, xviii, xx, xxiii-xxv, xxvii-xxviii, 18, 20-21, 23, 27, 33, 36, 42, 46, 54, 61n6, 65n10, 87, 105, 120, 126, 141-142, 171, 177-179, 187-188, 191-192, 196, 200
Midbar Shur, see Kook, Abraham Isaac
Middle Ages, 86-87, 89
Middle East, 68-69
Midian, 171-172
Midrash, 78, 85n1, 116-117, 122, 155-156, 158, 167, 170-171, 175n2, 196
    Mekhilta of Rabbi Ishmael, 84
    Sifre Bamidbar, 95
    Midrash Rabbah,
        Genesis Rabbah, *also Bereshit Rabbah*, 116-117, 127n40, 137, 139, 170n61
        Exodus Rabbah, *also* Shemot Rabbah, 135-136

Leviticus Rabbah, Va-Yiqra Rabbah, 116n7, 157n23, 167n46, 170n61
Numbers Rabbah, 171n67
Deuteronomy Rabbah, 157n22, 167n48
Song Rabbah, 171n65
Ruth Rabbah, 169, 171n68
Ecclesiastes Rabbah, 170n62
Midrash Tanhuma, 141-142, 150n6, 196
Mirsky, Aharon, 87, 90
Mishnah Ta'anit, 93
Mishneh Tora, see Maimonides, Moses
mishpat, 59, 145, 147-148
Moab, 9, 120, 154, 170-171
Mordechai, 121n26, 154-155
Morgensztern, Menachem Mendel of Kotzk (Rabbi), *also* the Kotzker Rebbe, 98-99, 106, 109
Moses, 9-10, 17, 35-38, 57, 76, 85, 89, 102, 114n3, 125, 127, 149-151, 156, 162, 164, 177, 184
Moshe of Dolena (Rabbi), 188
Munich, 131
Murray, Michael, 74
Musaf prayer, 65

Nachman of Horodenka (Rabbi), 185
Nachmanides, Moses, 18, 141
National Library of Israel, 181n20
Nazis, 105, 134, 136
Nebuchadnezzar, 130
Negeb, 153
Nehemiah, 94
Nineveh, 170
Noah, 17, 57-58, 114-115, 176-177, 180, 182, 197
Nostra Aetate, 71

Oholei Yaakov, see Friedman, Yaakov
Or Hachayim, see Chaim ibn Attar
Oral Law, 87-88

Paul VI, 71
Paz, Yakir, 90
Peretz, 169
Perizzites, 161, 165-166
Philo of Alexandria, 13-14, 48, 81
Philosophical Fragments, see Kierkegaard, Soren
Piekarz, Mendel, 135-136
Pirkei Avot, 22, 140
Poland, 65, 106, 121, 133-134, 136

prayer, xix, xxi-xxii, xxvii, 13, 47-48, 65, 83-97, 110, 135, 170n63, 181-187, 190, 196
priests, *also kohanim*, xxvii, 10, 13-49, 51, 91-93, 95, 153-154, 157, 169, 176, 189, 191-193
Purim, 121n26

Quran, 196
rabbinic literature, xi-xii, xxi, xxv-xxvi, 6, 9, 15, 25, 51-54, 56, 62, 66, 68-70, 76, 78, 86, 89, 93-97, 115-116, 121, 124, 126-127, 130, 137, 139, 151, 167-169, 175n2, 177n6

Rahab, 167, 169-171
Rebecca, 4
Rishonim, 89
Rome, 156-157
Rose, Or, xxiii, 179n13, 189-191, 193
Rosenberg, Shalom, 136n6
Rosh Hashanah, 86, 170n63
Russian Empire, 121

Sabbath, 81, 136-138, 143
Sacks, Jonathan (Rabbi), 104, 111
Safed, 140
Samuel bar Nahman (Rabbi), 166-167
Sarah, 3
Sartre, Jean Paul, 106
Saul, 149, 152-155, 158-159
Schneerson, Menachem Mendel, *also* the Lubavitcher Rebbe, 30n37, 43-45, 47-48, 64
Schweid, Eliezer, xi, 192
Sefer BeShT, see Ba'al Shem Tov
Sefer Habahir, also Bahir, 175-176
Sefer Hachinuch, 74
Sefer Hasidim, see Judah ben Samuel
sefirot (emanations), 64
Seforno, Ovadiah, 18-23, 42-44, 46, 61-62
segula (essence), 22n24, 35-36, 45
Sennacherib, 159, 168, 170n60, 172
Shaharit, 84, 86
Shammai (sage), 126
Shanghai, 133
Shapiro, Pinchas of Koretz (Rabbi), 186, 188
Shavuot, 120
shekhinah (presence of God), 63, 88, 141
Shem Mishemuel, 16n7, 30n37, 45
Shema prayer, *also Shema Yisrael*, 84, 162n39
Shimon ben Lakish (Rabbi), 196-197
Shlomo Yitzhaki (Rabbi), *also* Rashi, 15-16, 18, 44-45, 54-55, 61, 127, 179

Shneur Zalman of Liadi, the Alter Rebbe, 43, 77, 140
Shoah, *see* Holocaust
Shragai, Shlomo Zalman, 129, 139-140
Shulchan Arukh, see Karo, Joseph
Sihon, 156, 162
Simeon ben Azzai (sage), 127
Sinai, 18-20, 42, 51, 60, 76, 78, 102-105, 117-118, 134-135, 137-139, 196-197
Sisera, 165, 170
socialism, 38, 136-137
Socrates, 58
Sodom, 145
Solomon, 127, 163, 166, 172
Soloveitchik, Joseph Ber (Rabbi), 101-105, 191
Spain, 59, 63, 106, 127, 133, 178n12
Spinoza, Baruch, 71
Sukkot, *also* Feast of Tabernacles, 65, 74, 127, 176
synagogue, 72-73, 88, 110-111

Tajfel, Henri, 99, 107-108
Talmud, 17, 52, 62, 65n10, 76, 78, 89, 100, 110, 116, 118, 126, 152, 155-157, 171
  Babylonian Talmud
    Zeraim
      Berakhot, 62, 110, 168n49, 184
    Moed
      Shabbat, 32n46, 34n53, 78, 117, 137, 139, 178
      Eruvin, 118, 126
      Pesachim, 26
      Yoma, 152n9, 168n51, 177
      Sukkah, 65n10
      Moed Katan, 139n11
    Nashim
      Yevamot, 101, 116, 156n19, 171n71, 183, 185
      Sotah, 169-170, 182
      Gittin, 139
      Kiddushin, 9, 151n7, 179
    Nezikin
      Bava Metzia, 139
      Sanhedrin, 137, 139n11, 156, 170n60, 176
      Makot, 76
      Shevuot, 177
      Avodah Zarah, 58, 76, 117, 157n25
Tamar, 159, 169, 171
Tannaim, 83, 85, 94n17

Ta-Shma, Israel, 89-90, 93
Temple, xxi-xxii, 20, 39, 51, 65n10, 67, 85, 88-92, 93, 96, 127-128 Second, 6, 83, 87, 94
Terah, 2-3, 5, 12
Tiferet (emanation), 63
Timnah, 156
Toldot Yaakov Yosef, see Yaakov Yosef of Pollonne
Treblinka, 133
Tree of Life, 176
Troki, Isaac, 24-25
tzadikim, 65-66, 115-116, 121n26, 124n31, 147-148, 178, 180n16, 182-184
tzedakah, 59, 145, 147

Uceda, Samuel, 140
Ukraine, 121
Ulm, 131
United Kingdom, 106n8, 108, 111
United States, xv, xxiii, 68-70, 191
Unsdorfer, Shlomo Zalman, 137-138
Ur, 2-4
Uriah, 166

Vital, Hayyim, 140

Warsaw, 107n10, 133, 135
Wasserman, Elchanan, 136-137
Wisdom of Solomon, the, 166n44, 169
Wolfsberg, Yeshayahu, 129
World War II, 42, 129
Written Law, 87-88

Yaakov Yosef of Pollonne (Rabbi), 175, 178n10, 188 *Toldot Yaakov Yosef*, 175
Yabin, 165
Yavneh, 83
Yehiel Mikhel (Rabbi), *also* the Maggid of Zlotchev, 125
Yehudah Leib of Polonne (Rabbi), *also* the Mokhiach of Polonne, 177-178
Yeivi (Rabbi), 177n6, 188
Yoder, John *When Was Is Unjust*, 172
Yom Kippur War, xi
Yoreh De'ah, see Jacob ben Asher

Ziklag, 153
Zimbardo, Philip George, 99, 107-108
Zionism, 42, 69, 129, 131, 137-138
Zohar, xxvi, 114n3, 122, 126n38, 141, 175n1, 180, 187n47, 189

www.ingramcontent.com/pod-product-compliance
Lightning Source LLC
Chambersburg PA
CBHW050106170426
43198CB00014B/2484